PRAISE FOR
KEN DYCHTWALD'S
AGE POWER

"I have been learning from Ken Dychtwald for years and am convinced that he is today's most innovative and original thinker on this important subject. This book, like all that Ken writes and says, offers a true education into the issues we all face as we age."
  —President Jimmy Carter

"Dychtwald presents a unique and entirely convincing view of life in the twenty-first century when the most powerful group in our society, the baby boomers, will be the 'new old.' This book is must reading for anyone concerned with economics, financial investment, new products, and the challenges and promises that 'age power' will pose in our daily lives."
  —Harry S. Dent, Jr., author of *The Roaring 2000s* and *The Roaring 2000s Investor*

"*Age Power* is one of the best books to read if you want to prepare for an era in which the agenda of the developed nations and the global economy will be set, in large measure, by what Dychtwald calls the 'new old.' No one understands the economic, social, and personal impact of this better than Ken Dychtwald."
  —Martin Sorrell, group chief executive, WPP Group, plc

"Ken Dychtwald offers a much-needed new paradigm of maturity as a period of health and vitality. *Age Power* provides a powerful vision of a transformed health-care system."

—Dean Ornish, M.D., author of *Dr. Dean Ornish's Program for Reversing Heart Disease* and *Love & Survival: The Scientific Basis for the Healing Power of Intimacy*

"Dr. Dychtwald has created a compelling vision of how to age with style, dignity, purpose, and love. *Age Power* gives all of us a glimpse of a bright and delightful future in which aging is vital, enjoyable, and desirable."

—Mark Victor Hansen, coauthor of the *New York Times*–best-selling series *Chicken Soup for the Soul*

"Any company doing business in the new millennium would be wise to take notice of Ken Dychtwald's unique ability to envision the age wave and its impact on a wide range of consumer needs and preferences. His insightful predictions and innovative ideas are must reading for anyone interested in understanding the twenty-first-century consumer."

—M. Douglas Ivester, former Chairman of the Board and Chief Executive Officer, The Coca-Cola Company

"There are very few people in this world who have mastered the true effects that aging will have on each and every one of us better than Ken Dychtwald. This book is a powerful look into what you need to know today to understand and protect your tomorrows."

—Suze Orman, author of *The Courage to Be Rich* and *The 9 Steps to Financial Freedom*

JEREMY P. TARCHER / PUTNAM

A MEMBER OF PENGUIN PUTNAM INC.

NEW YORK

Age Power

HOW THE 21ST CENTURY

WILL BE RULED BY THE NEW OLD

Ken Dychtwald, Ph. D.

Chart on page 205. "Generations at a Glance" from *Rocking the Ages: The Yankelovich Report on Generational Marketing* by J. Walker Smith and Ann Clurman. Copyright © 1996 by Yankelovich Partners, Inc. Reprinted by permission of HarperCollins Publishers, Inc.

Most Tarcher/Putnam books are available at special quantity discounts for bulk purchases for sales promotions, premiums, fund-raising, and educational needs. Special books or book excerpts also can be created to fit specific needs. For details, write Putnam Special Markets, 375 Hudson Street, New York, NY 10014.

Jeremy P. Tarcher/Putnam
a member of
Penguin Putnam Inc.
375 Hudson Street
New York, NY 10014
www.penguinputnam.com

First Trade Paperback Edition 2000

Copyright © 1999 by Ken Dychtwald, Ph.D.

The Library of Congress has catalogued the hardback edition as follows:

Dychtwald, Ken, date.
Age power : how the 21st century will be ruled by the
new old / Ken Dychtwald.
p. cm.
ISBN 0-87477-954-5
1. Aging—social aspects—United States.   2. Baby boom generation—
United States.   3. Social prediction—United States.   4. Twenty-first
century—Forecasts.
HQ1064.U5D926   1999   99-32738 CIP
305.26'0973—dc21

ISBN 1-58542-043-3 (paperback edition)

Printed in the United States of America
10   9

Book design by Fearn Cutler de Vicq

This book is dedicated to
Maddy, Casey, and Zak Dychtwald.
I am proud to be on this earth in this life with you.

CONTENTS

ACKNOWLEDGMENTS

I would like to thank the following very special people without whom my starship couldn't fly:

Maddy Kent Dychtwald, for being the most beautiful, radiant, energetic, insightful, and lovable person I have ever known.

Casey Dychtwald, for being so powerful and electrifyingly attractive.

Zak Dychtwald, for your deep thoughts and positive lifeforce.

Seymour, Pearl, and Alan Dychtwald, for loving, supporting, and encouraging me on every day of my life.

Sally and Ray Fusco, for nourishing me with respect and affection.

Richard, Linda, David, and Joel Kent, my terrific extended family.

Jeremy Tarcher, for being a truly Zen publisher, and Mitch Horowitz, for being the most talented book editor I have known.

Greta Mart, for providing invaluable editorial contributions and for being such an impassioned, multitalented researcher and Internet "gumshoe."

Joal Hetherington, for her masterful editing, and Rob Jacoby, for providing terrific research assistance.

Rod MacKenzie—who, when God was giving out personalities, got the big box—and for epitomizing "partnership."

Andrew Achenbaum, Steven Atlas, David Baxter, Bob Blancato, Michael Boskin, Bob Butler, Jayme Canton, Henry Fenwick, Mark Francis, Richard Haas, Tom Mackell, Stephen Moses, Cheryl Russell and Leda Sanford, for providing thoughtful editorial input.

My wonderful friends, Kenny and Sandie Dorman, Jayme and Gail Canton, Bill and Kate Burkart, Danny and Nancy Katz, Bill and Mary Lou Newman, Bruce and Emily Clark, Eric Bjerkholt and Sophie Hahn, Bart and Julie Penfold, Rod MacKenzie and Brian Boudreau, Jim Bernstein and Jean Duff, Charlie and Justine Lynch, Bob and Marilyn Kriegel, Frank and Claire Wuest, Don and Catherine Mankin, Erin Rivero, and Darren Pagtakhan—for putting up with me in spite of my ongoing battles with windmills.

And all of the members of the Age Wave Family—the absolutely most brilliant, passionate, committed, creative, playful, attractive, interesting, complex, imaginative, diverse, and righteous work team imaginable.

INTRODUCTION

My life's path made a dramatic turn in the winter of 1973. At the age of 23, I was living in Big Sur, California, conducting seminars at the Esalen Institute, the epicenter of the nascent "human potential" movement, while pursuing my doctorate in psychology and completing my first book, *Bodymind*. When I answered the telephone in my tiny redwood-surrounded cabin, I never imagined that the call would change my mind-set, my career, and my life.

The voice on the phone belonged to my friend Dr. Jean Houston, president of the Foundation for Mind Research in New York. Jean told me that psychologist, researcher, and science writer Dr. Gay Luce was assembling a research project to examine the effectiveness of newly popular mind/body disciplines, such as meditation, biofeedback, visualization, yoga, aerobic exercise, and nutrition therapy. She was looking for someone to help her craft an integrated, holistic curriculum. Because of my personal interests and studies, Jean had immediately thought of me; would I be interested?

What made the project particularly unusual was its subjects: Gay wanted them all to be over the age of 65. While caring for her own mother in her old age, Gay had noticed that despite a growing number of wellness-oriented programs for young people, no one seemed to be breaking new ground with the elderly. Her idea was to create a human potential program for senior citizens, helping them rejuvenate their minds and bodies and shattering stereotypes and misconceptions in the process.

The idea of working to create a new image of aging sparked my curiosity. At that time, I hadn't had much contact with older adults, other than occasional warm encounters with my own grandparents.

Like many other twentysomethings, I thought of elders as likely to be frail, set in their ways, and even bound toward "senility." Yet I wondered: Could you make a 70-year-old body more vital and healthy? What would it be like to teach yoga to septuagenarians? Could you rejuvenate feelings of friendship and intimacy in individuals who had been alone for years? If people could grow and improve themselves at 70 or 80, what would that say to others in their thirties and forties? And what would it be like to become close with men and women three times my own age? Intrigued, I signed on.

With funding from the National Institutes of Health, our Berkeley-based SAGE Project became the nation's first preventive health research program focusing exclusively on older adults. Our subjects, who ranged in age from 65 to 90, were divided into groups of 12 and met weekly in four-hour sessions over the course of a year. During these meetings, participants were introduced to yoga, aerobics, stress management, biofeedback, proper nutrition, and art and movement therapy, and were encouraged to share their thoughts, feelings, and progress with other group members in an open, "team-like" atmosphere.

The process produced results beyond anyone's expectations. We found that physically rigid 70- and 80-year-olds could become much more flexible by practicing techniques such as yoga and tai chi. Improving their diets enhanced their energy levels and overall health. We discovered that many participants who had seemed distant, even mentally dysfunctional, were really suffering from terrible boredom. Through the group discussions and support, they started feeling better about themselves and more confident. For others, walkers and crutches were replaced by sweatpants and sneakers. Some of our subjects were so taken by their own progress that they decided to return to school. Several widows and widowers even fell in love and formed new relationships. Many signed up to become cofacilitators as our project grew. Something special was happening: We were witnessing the metamorphosis of highly spirited, highly vigorous people who happened to be 60, 70, or 80 years old.

During my five years as codirector of the SAGE Project, I

became increasingly respectful of the depth of experience of these long-lived men and women. And I became fascinated by our similarities. Participants confided that in my friends and me they could see themselves at earlier times, and I began to catch glimpses in them of who I might be in later years. Over time, a haunting, and simple, realization came to me: The elderly are not "them"—they're "us," a few decades into the future.

In the late 1970s, as my work branched out into other aspects of gerontology, I was struck by how many of the social, economic, and physical problems of older people were preventable. I noticed that many older adults who were lonely or depressed simply had given up on making new friends or had long since resigned from social and intellectual involvement. Many who were struggling with the hardships of fixed incomes had been financially secure during their working years, but simply hadn't saved enough or managed their finances well in retirement. I repeatedly saw how a lifetime of disregard for personal health usually led to chronic disease, a kind of extended-life imprisonment.

Aging, I came to realize, is *not* something that begins on one's 65th birthday. Rather, all of the choices we make regarding how we care for ourselves, how we manage our lives, and even how we think about our futures shape who we ultimately become in our later years. It was obvious that *many of the painful, punishing challenges of old age could be prevented if informed choices were made earlier in life.*

By the early 1980s, I was a member of various scientific and social service advisory panels, a frequent lecturer at academic and business conferences, and a consultant with numerous universities and hospitals interested in developing their own programs to promote healthy aging. But the more I interacted with experts from other disciplines, the more frustrated I became by the wall of negativity toward aging that I repeatedly collided with. Businesses were focusing all of their product development and marketing efforts on the young, and there was barely an older adult to be seen in popular advertising. The entertainment media emphasized a distorted picture of the glory of youth and the decrepitude of maturity. Relatively few universities and medical schools offered courses on adult development, gerontology, or geriatrics. Since I knew that the number of older adults was rapidly multiplying, it seemed inexplicable that the *aging process* should remain so neglected.

The deeper I probed, the more dismayed I became by the way *gerontophobia* had permeated every aspect of our culture. As though Jonathan Swift had written one more chapter to *Gulliver's Travels*, I began to see that we had designed our modern world, top to bottom, to match the size, shape, and style of youth—from the height of the steps in our public buildings to the length of time it takes for traffic lights to change, from the size of the typeface in our newspapers and magazines to the auditory range in our telephones and televisions, from the age and style of the models in advertisements to our embarrassment about our birthdays. In thousands of ways, over and over, we were being influenced to like what's young and dislike what's old.

A critical piece of my puzzle fell into place in 1982, while I was serving as an adviser to the federal Office of Technology Assessment, the think tank connected with the U.S. Congress. While examining the impact of aging-related trends on the 21st century, I felt a jolt when I realized that the next population of elders would not be my grandparents' generation; they would not be my parents' generation either. Instead, tomorrow's elders would be the baby boom generation—*my* generation.

Likened by demographers to a "pig moving through a python," baby boomers have radically transformed every stage of life through which they have traveled. We have repeatedly seen that whatever the issues are for boomers at each stage, whether driven by financial, interpersonal, or even hormonal forces, these have become the dominant social, political, and marketplace themes of the time. Just as our social institutions were unprepared for the initial baby boom, I feared that our gerontophobia might blind us to the true impact of 78 million boomers barreling toward old age.

I realized that we were about to confront a demographic shift of enormous magnitude: For the first time in history, a developed society was going to contain a mass population of long-lived elderly men and women. Unlike other trends or sociopolitical forecasts, this impending transformation had its roots in simple fact. Unmistakable demographic forces—increasing longevity, declining fertility, and the aging of the baby boom—were triggering an enormous "age wave." This wave had the potential to create vibrant new stages of life—*and an equally compelling potential for social, financial, political, and personal catastrophe.*

I was also struck by the irony: The very thing we had blanked out of our societal paradigm—aging—was about to engulf us. Swiftly growing older, our young nation was on the brink of unprecedented social and political problems:

- Can our country afford to have tens of millions of us living to 80? Or 100?
- What will be the impact of four-generation families?
- Who will pay for the long-term care of tomorrow's "elder boomers"?
- Are we prepared to spend more years caring for our aging parents than for our children?
- With breakthroughs in longevity, at what age should we be considered "old" and therefore eligible to retire and receive old-age benefits?
- Will existing entitlement programs survive long enough for us to reap even part of what we have been paying in?
- Can our current healthcare system handle the onslaught of chronic degenerative diseases, such as Alzheimer's?
- Are we prepared to reengineer many of our products and services to meet the needs of maturing consumers?
- How will we come to terms with increasing "right-to-death" issues?
- Are our politicians capable of distributing limited government resources fairly among many generations, each with its own distinct needs, styles, fears, complaints, and expectations?

- How can the aging nations of the Americas, Europe, and Asia continue to be economically productive with so many dependent older citizens being supported by shrinking numbers of young workers?
- Can our political system restrain the demands that tens of millions of elder boomers will place on the social and economic infrastructure?

Consumed by the massive scale of this challenge and outraged at the absence of preparation, I decided to focus all my attention on a Paul Revere–like call that "the aging are coming, the aging are coming." There was an opportunity, I perceived, to join the tools of the nonprofit sector with those of business and media for social good. In 1986, in partnership with my wife, Maddy Kent Dychtwald, and with the counsel of successful entrepreneurs Dr. James Bernstein, and Fred Rubenstein, I founded Age Wave, Inc., as a research and consulting firm. Our initial corporate mission was to help companies and governments develop programs, products and services for the multiplying numbers of mature adults.

The very demographic changes we were proclaiming became wind in our sails. Age Wave swiftly developed a client list of Fortune 500 companies, including American Express, Baxter International, CBS Inc., Chrysler, Coca-Cola, General Motors, Johnson & Johnson, McDonald's, Merck, Prudential, RJR Nabisco, Sara Lee, Time Inc., and Warner-Lambert, as well as numerous not-for-profit organizations such as the American Hospital Association, the American Society on Aging, Blue Cross Blue Shield, the National Council on the Aging, and the White House Conference on Aging. Our standard assignment: Figure out how the age wave would impact the company or institution, and invent new ideas and solutions.

During Age Wave's first decade, we had the opportunity of managing millions of dollars' worth of proprietary studies designed to probe aspects of the mature population's needs, fears, worries, and dreams. Because we conducted our explorations and brainstorming on behalf of so many different kinds of groups, the lessons have been consistently eye-opening.

Several years ago, Age Wave transformed from a consulting firm to a venture development incubator. Age Wave, LLC, now creates, invests in, and acquires companies that serve the expanding mature market. To date, we have launched businesses in the publishing, training, marketing/advertising, retail, nutraceutical, and insurance sectors.

After nearly three decades of deep involvement in the field of aging, I am utterly convinced of two things: 1) *"Age Power" will rule the 21st century*, and 2) *In many critical ways, we are woefully unprepared*. Although I have always considered myself an optimist, I fear that our avoidance of critical aging-related issues could lead to numerous personal and social disasters down the road.

For many, life's prolonged second half will be a time to chart a new course. We'll have the time and resources to reverse past failures or build on past victories, perhaps changing careers, taking a sabbatical, or returning to school. With longer life spans and improved health, there may even be sufficient time to start another family, or to take a more active role in the lives of our children and grandchildren.

For others, however, extended longevity will be fraught with pain and discomfort. As bodies decay and minds fail, millions may well spend their final decades struggling with depressing loneliness and unrelenting pain. Large numbers of elder boomers could wind up impoverished, left stranded by dwindling old age entitlements.

Can we muster the resources, intelligence, and determination to plot the best course for our collective futures?

This book is a "wake-up call," intended to illuminate the key aging-related dangers toward which we are speeding—as individuals and as a society. After describing each challenge, I have attempted to offer preventive solutions. Deciding how to use this information and how to avoid the personal tragedies and social crises looming ahead may turn out to be the most important task we will face at the dawn of the new millennium.

CHAPTER ONE

AGE POWER

America is becoming a "gerontocracy," and four outcomes are certain:

1. More of us will live longer than in any previous generation;
2. The epicenter of economic and political power will shift from the young to the old;
3. We will need to change our current mind set about how to spend our extra years of life; and
4. How we decide to behave as elders will, in all likelihood, become the most important challenge we will face in our lives.

Living in an age when scientific and technological "miracles" are almost a matter of course, it's easy to overlook just how remarkable a thing aging is. But consider one startling fact: Throughout 99 percent of all the years that humans have walked this planet, the average life expectancy at birth was less than 18 years. In the past, most people didn't age—they died. Infectious diseases, accidents, violence, and many other hazards often brought life to an early close. Even though some people lived to 50 or 60 or even 80, they were very few and far between. During the past 1,000 years, our life expectancy has climbed from an average of 25 to 47 at the turn of the 20th century, and skyrocketed to 76 today. Until very recently, people were much more likely to die young than old.

When the first U.S. census was taken in 1790, half the population was under the age of 16 and less than 2 percent of the 4 million people who responded were 65 and older. Few adult Americans in that year could expect to live more than 35 to 45 years—about the same as in Europe. As a result, societies rarely concerned themselves with the needs of their aging citizens. The elderly were too few to matter.

Not surprisingly, our forebears didn't sit around and wonder what they were going to do in retirement, because very few were going to retire. No one contemplated lifelong learning at 75. Businesses didn't care about the "mature market" because there wasn't one. Arthritis, heart disease, and Alzheimer's weren't major health-care concerns because most people died of acute, infectious diseases before they got old enough for aging-related conditions to emerge.

Beginning in the last century, however, something volcanic has begun. Thanks to advances in sanitation, public health, food science, pharmacy, surgery, medicine, and, more recently, wellness-oriented lifestyles, *most of us will age.* In a manner unprecedented throughout human evolution, people suddenly have begun to routinely remain healthy and vigorous into their seventies and eighties, and tomorrow's elderly will, in all likelihood, live even longer.

During the 20th century, the number of Americans who are 65+ has increased elevenfold, from 3 million to 33 million. According to the U.S. Census Bureau, by 2035 some 70 million people, of whom 60 million will be elder boomers, will be age 65 and older. This is a number more than twice the current population of Canada.

This astonishing "age wave" is not unique to the United States. All the modernized nations of the world are evolving from youthful to mature societies—and the developing nations will follow suit in the 21st century. For example, in 1950 the average life expectancy for Japanese women was 61.4 years, and for men 58. Since then, it has vaulted to one of the highest in the world—83 for women and 76 for men. In one generation, the life expectancy of Japanese has increased by more than 30 percent. And the aging of Japan is destined to continue: Although Japanese seniors currently comprise 15 percent of their society, forecasts show that by 2025 that number will grow to 25 percent.[1]

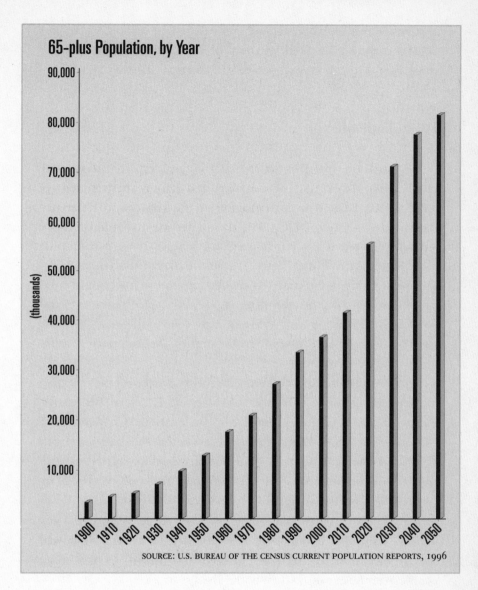

65-plus Population, by Year

(thousands)

SOURCE: U.S. BUREAU OF THE CENSUS CURRENT POPULATION REPORTS, 1996

The United Nations expects that by the year 2050, there will be nearly two billion people in the world 60 years and older—a number equal to the current combined populations of North America, Europe, and India. Today, according to the U.N.'s Population Division, 1 of every 10 persons living is age 60 or older, but by the year 2050, that ratio will double to 1 of 5. And this age shift is reconfiguring the older population segment as well. Right now, those 80 and older constitute 11 percent of the world's 60+ population; by 2050, 16 percent of the older population will be more than 80 years old.

The Birth Dearth

At the same time that we're living longer, fertility rates in the U.S., Europe, Japan, and other modernized nations are dropping. As noted by Carl Haub, a demographer at the Population Reference Bureau in Washington, DC, "Population decline due to low fertility is a new phenomenon—unlike previous declines due to catastrophic events such as the Thirty Years' War or the Black Death in medieval Europe."[2] In the United States, the fertility rate is hovering around 2.1—poised just on the edge of the minimum replacement level and down from 3.8 during the 1950s and early 1960s. If it weren't for the steady inflow of youthful immigrant families, the American population would be shrinking.[3]

Currently, there isn't a country in Europe where couples are having enough children to replace themselves. Dr. Jean Bourgeois-Pichat, chairman of the Committee for International Cooperation in National Research in Demography, observes that the European birth dearth was not anticipated: "The fertility decline started around 1965 almost simultaneously in every country and took everybody by surprise."[4] The Italian fertility rate recently plummeted to fewer than 1.2 children per woman—the lowest level ever recorded in any society. Italy also became the first country in history—followed shortly thereafter by Germany, Greece, and Spain—to have more people over the age of 60 than under the age of 20.

In China, the total fertility rate has dropped from 6.7 children per woman in 1950 to 1.8 today. At the same time, the average Chinese life expectancy has jumped 28 years since 1950. As a result, China's 60+ segment is growing seven times as fast as its total population.[5]

Demographers are chagrined to observe that the more educated and financially secure a country becomes, and the higher the numbers of women pursuing nondomestic careers, the lower fertility drops. The northern Italian city of Bologna offers a disconcerting glimpse into the future. In this city, the quality of life is good and the women are better educated than in any other region of the country. However, the fertility rate fell to .8 in 1997.[6] During the same year, the fertility rate in Japan, the nation with the world's highest longevity, dropped to 1.39, the lowest it has ever been.

Even in less-developed nations, fertility rates have dropped by 50 percent during the past several decades. "If these trends continue," says Nicholas Eberstadt, a demographer at the American Enterprise Institute for Public Policy Research, "in a generation or two there may be countries where people's only blood relatives will be their parents."[7]

Some countries are trying to reverse the trend. Worried about the future economic and workforce implications of such a low birth rate, the Japanese government has started a campaign to encourage young men and women to have more children. A few years ago in the rural town of Yamaguchi, for example, local officials began airing television commercials that portrayed a little boy playing all alone with his puppy. The caption underneath stated: "For the child's sake, one more."[8]

No country has tried harder to battle declining fertility than Sweden. Several decades ago, when officials noticed the fertility of young families dropping, the government began to provide cash payments for each child to couples in which both parents work, along with generous tax incentives and a highly flexible work-leave program that allows parents to work part-time for up to eight years after each child's birth. These programs seemed to work: Sweden's birth rate rose to 2.1 in 1990—the highest in Europe at the time.

Then the Swedish baby boom fizzled, and the birth rate fell back to 1.6. Dumbfounded, government leaders attributed the drop to the soft economy during that period. Since 1995, however, the economy has perked up but the fertility rate has not—it has fallen further, to 1.42 children per woman in 1997. "We were a model for the world," says Marten Lagergren, undersecretary in the Ministry of Social Health and Welfare. "They all came to examine us. People thought we had some secret. Unfortunately, it seems that we do not."[9]

While immigration may help shore up the birth dearth in some countries, it will not be sufficient to offset the swelling numbers of seniors. According to the Organization for Economic Cooperation and Development (OECD), Japan, Germany, and Italy would each need to import 13 to 15 million young people (and no elderly), a number equivalent to the combined current populations of Ireland, Denmark, and Norway, between now and the year 2050—something that is practically impossible.[10] Ben Wattenberg, a senior fellow at the American Enterprise Institute and author of *The Birth Dearth* is worried about the effects of declining fertility: "In my judgment, the major threat to Western values and the free world concerns the fact that, as the next century progresses, there won't be many free Westerners around to protect and promote those values."[11]

Despite the demographic changes that are gaining on us, we continue to think of our society as "youth-focused," one in which it is "in" to be young. Can we even conceive of a future in which "age power" will rule and it will be "in" to be old?

For most of history, in fact, it was maturity that was prized. Until relatively recently, the old, more than any other age group, controlled power, assumed leadership, and set the example for others. In the early centuries of American history, in nearly every aspect of community, family, and work life, old people reigned. Only during the 20th century have they temporarily been knocked to the mat, viewed largely as a social burden. But they are not down for the count: If you look around, you'll notice that during the past several decades the elderly have multiplied, growing stronger, richer, and politically tougher. They are returning to the status and control that once was theirs.

When Old Was In

Why were old people so highly valued in earlier centuries? Why did the young admire and respect them? How did they attain their position of social dominance—and how did they lose it? To comprehend the up, down, and soon-to-be-up-again saga of America's elderly, it's helpful to understand the factors that contributed to their initial stature.

THE ELDERLY AS EXEMPLARS OF MORALITY AND HEALTH

During colonial times, it was thought that those few men and women who lived to a great age were the beneficiaries of divine will. As Increase Mather, an early president of Harvard College and pastor of the famous North Church in Boston, preached in 1716, "If a man is favored with long life . . . it is God that has lengthened his days."[12]

The elderly were venerated and treated with great respect. People lived slightly longer, on average, in the American colonies than in Europe, and early Americans pointed with pride to their small but powerful elder population as living proof of an exceptional environment, a superior social system, and, most especially, God's blessing.

Because medical science had not yet formulated theories of contagious or degenerative disease, it was generally believed that the key to a long life was the practice of temperance, moderation, and religious virtue. The achievement of even modest longevity—50 or 60 years—was admired, and the elderly came to be looked upon as advisers to their less-experienced younger fellows.

Typical of this attitude is Benjamin Franklin's 1757 essay "The Way to Wealth," in which he used the telltale device of a wise elder—"Father Abraham"—to dispense worldly advice: ". . . and one of the company called to a plain, clean old man, with white locks, 'Pray father Abraham, what think you of these times? Will not those heavy taxes quite ruin the country? How shall we ever be able to pay them? What would you advise us to do?'"[13]

Commenting on the elderly's moral expertise, the Reverend Cortlandt Van Rensselaer wrote in his influential book *Old Age:*

What a blessed influence the old exert in cherishing feelings of reverence, affection and subordination in families; in warning the young against the temptations and allurements of the world; in detailing the results of experience, in exposing the fallacies of worldly maxims; in rebuking the recklessness of indiscretion and the experiments of enthusiasm; in imparting judicious counsel in church and State and private life;—in short, how much good of every kind is accomplished by the tranquilizing, wise and conservative influences of age.[14]

THE ELDERLY AS WIELDERS OF POWER

In colonial America, social control lay in the ownership of land, which was almost always retained by elder parents or grandparents. People didn't work for "money" that could be spent as they liked. Instead, they worked to complete chores, which were primarily agriculture-related and family-based. The crops and items produced were then traded for other products and services within the local community; only occasionally was an item such as a new tool or a length of silk ordered from a distant distributor or itinerant peddler and paid for with cash.

As a result, nearly all of a person's economic worth was linked to the value of the family property. In that society, most young people were totally dependent on the family for security, work, and the hope of one day owning some portion of the estate. It was common for children to be fully grown with families of their own before inheriting part of the family property. Daughters might not marry unless their parents were willing to provide a dowry; sons might not be allowed to take over the family farm unless they conformed to all the conditions set by their elders. As historian David Hackett Fischer has observed, "Land was an instrument of generational politics—a way of preserving both the power and authority of the elderly."[15]

In his book *Four Generations: Population, Land, and Family in Colonial Andover, Massachusetts*, Rutgers University historian Philip

Greven illustrates the complex generational relationships as played out in that town's Holt family:

> Nicholas Holt's second son, Henry, had eight sons. Seven of them married when they were 25. But their land did not come to them until 1717, when Henry Holt was 73 and four of his sons had been long married—from seven to 17 years. Henry's seventh son, William, never married at all. It was he who received the original homestead (at the age of 30) by a deed of gift that required him to "take ye sole care of his father Henry Holt and of his Naturall Mother Sarah Holt" for the rest of their days and to provide them with many things, all carefully spelled out in elaborate detail, even to the candles and hard cider. And if William had failed to supply "any one article aforementioned," he would have forfeited his property.[16]

"YOU'RE LOOKING VERY OLD TODAY," SAID SHE. "THANK YOU," SAID HE.

So highly valued was old age that both men and women of that time tended to exaggerate their age when asked, and the older they were, the greater was the tendency to exaggerate. Similarly, men and women of all ages actually tried to appear older than they really were. Men hid their natural hair beneath wigs, which were often powdered white to enhance the illusion of age. Men's clothing was cut in a way that emphasized the posture and build of the elderly: narrow and rounded shoulders, broad hips and waist, and coat backs designed to make the spine appear to be bent by the weight of many years.

As for women's fashions, its foremost purpose was to ensure sexual subordination and chastity; this was accomplished by head-to-toe coverage. Yet the dresses also stressed mature features. Heavy swirling skirts accentuated broad hips, and those who lacked the pear shape of advanced years were encouraged to add hoops and whalebone extenders. The popular empire-line dress, form-fitting until just under the breast, did not discriminate against a spreading torso. Formal wear called for exposed shoulders and decolletage, features that work to the mature woman's advantage. Women, too, wore powdered wigs as well as caps. A young body was not required in order to be fashionable—a far cry from our contemporary standards.

Industrialization Topples the Initial American Gerontocracy

In the world of the farmer, the experience of old people was perceived as very valuable, helping them in their work and in their role as head of the family. That arrangement, however, was shaken by the abrupt economic shift to industrialization that gained momentum in the second half of the 19th century. In 1800, approximately 80 percent of all male American workers were engaged in agriculture; by 1900, that number had shrunk to less than 30 percent.

The industrial age introduced a whole new set of priorities; youthful energy and mobility came to be prized over stability, experience, and homespun wisdom. On the farm, older men and women could continue contributing to some aspect of work or family life, but in the factory there was no sympathy for Grandpa's aging hands slowing down the assembly line. And since all of the industrial technology was new, the wisdom of the old offered no useful advantage over the enthusiasm and raw strength of the young.

The status and privilege old people had enjoyed as property owners and family heads eroded in the emerging industrial era, in which they were coming to be seen as an obstacle to progress—a social burden. Bursting with energy and unencumbered by any prejudices about how to do their work, the young were most suited to the changing times. The new city-based occupations were now considered indispensable to the nation's progress, and the young workers who filled these positions were rewarded with higher pay and higher status. The jobs also allowed young men to break free from economic dependence on their elders. For the first time in our history, knowledge of and commitment to the old ways of doing things could be seen as a distinct *disadvantage*.

This view was voiced by many prominent leaders of the time, including Dr. William Osler, one of America and Great Britain's most respected physician-philosophers. In his now infamous 1905 valedictory at Johns Hopkins University, Osler argued that men older than 40 were now useless cogs in modern society: "All the great advances have come from men under 40, so the history of the world shows that a very large proportion of the evils may be traced to the sexagenarians—nearly all of the great mistakes politically and socially, all of the worst poems, most of the bad pictures, a majority of the bad novels, not a few of the bad sermons and speeches. Take the sum of human achievement in action, in science, in art, in literature, subtract the work of men above 40, and . . . we would practically be where we are today."[17]

Britain's Anthony Trollope went even further, proposing that life should have a "fixed period" in order to abolish "the miseries, weaknesses, and imbecility of old age by the prearranged ceasing to live of those who would otherwise become old." His rationale? "Statistics have told us that the unprofitable young and the no less unprofitable old form a third of the population. . . . How are the people to thrive when so weighted? And for what good? As for the children, they are clearly necessary. They have to be nourished in order that they may do good work as their time shall come. But for whose good are the old and effete to be maintained amidst all their troubles and miseries?"[18]

Eventually, a perspective emerged arguing that older men and women should actually be *removed* from the workforce altogether. The following analysis was offered by F. Spencer Baldwin, professor of economics at Boston University, in his 1911 recommendations about the employment of aging municipal workers:

It is well understood nowadays that the practice of retaining on the payroll aged workers who can no longer render a fair equivalent for their wages is wasteful and demoralizing. The loss is twofold. In the first place, payment of full wages to workers who are no longer reasonably efficient, and in the second place, there is the direct loss entailed by the slow pace by the presence of worn-out veterans; and consequent general demoralization of the service.[19]

GERMS, NOT DIVINE INTERVENTION

With the development of the germ theory of disease in the late 19th century, medicine had a useful and compelling new hypothesis for understanding and combating the ailments that formerly had killed so many people. The new biological explanations for sickness and death cast creeping doubt on the Puritan notions that moderation and temperance led to longevity. Since it wasn't God who determined who was to live the longest, the elderly were no longer considered divinely selected experts on how to achieve a healthy old age.

Instead, the exaltation of mechanics that empowered the Industrial Revolution was extended to medicine, spurring a view of the body as a system of interdependent working parts. The diseased patient was simply the equivalent of damaged equipment, while the physician came to be viewed as nearly omnipotent in his power to "fix" what had gone wrong. As Dr. Nathan Allen commented in his paper *The Physiological Laws of Human Increase* presented at the 1870 annual meeting of the American Medical Association: "True education, all genuine civilization, and pure Christianity, in order to have a permanent basis and progress, must have their foundation and support in the laws of the physical system. . . . And who are to be the interpreters, the expounders of these laws, unless the members of the medical profession?"[20] As physician authority became entrenched, home remedies and elder wisdom were dismissed as "old wives' tales."

"New scientific theories and economic realities convinced Americans that individuals declined in old age as human existence marched on," reflects historian Andrew Achenbaum in *Old Age in the New Land*. "Because they perceived the elderly to be afflicted with pathological disorders and no longer able to keep up with the pace, it is not surprising that writers claimed old people had lost their grasp on the meaning and nature of societal development. Presuming it to be a law of nature that an individual's connection with societal progress relaxed with the coming of age, Americans gradually discounted the value of old people's insights and claimed that young people were in the best position to understand the meaning of life."[21]

Ironically, at the same time medical science was helping to create longevity for these pioneering elder citizens, it inadvertently contributed to their deterioration in status.

GERONTOPHOBIA BECOMES THE NORM

From a rural, family-based lifestyle to an urban, workplace-oriented one; from divine selection to germ theory; from veneration to a growing disregard toward the old—the tipping of the social see-saw sent the status of the elderly plummeting.

Social customs as well as social commentary reflected the changing fortunes of the elderly. No longer were the best seats in public meetings reserved for them, for instance; instead, they were simply bought by the wealthiest and most powerful community members.

In their dress also, people strove to turn back the clock where once they had nudged it forward. Instead of wigs, men donned hairpieces and toupees. The white powder that had lent the dignity of age yielded to hair dyes, tints, and preservatives. The cut of a man's coat—pulled in at the waist and puffed out at the shoulders, the back straight and broad to accentuate the power and vitality of youth—was just the inverse of earlier styles.

For women, the fashion transformation was even more remarkable. In the first two decades of the 20th century, they went from wearing hoopskirted, mature-oriented drapery to flapper dresses that emphasized an adolescent, thin-hipped build. This transition was too much for many older women, who clung to a more conservative style, with the result that for the first time there was a definite chasm between what a 20-year-old woman and a 50-year-old woman would wear in public.

Fashions in the language of the time reflect the emerging "modern" opinion of the elderly. "Gaffer" and "fogy," once terms of respect, took on negative connotations, and there were plenty of popular new words and phrases—"geezer," "codger," "old goat"—to make the same point. Young people, meanwhile, got off easily, as condescending terms such as "youngling" and "skipper" faded into obscurity.[22] Given the attitudes that these words betray, it's no wonder that census data would now show a steadily increasing trend toward distorting one's age downward, the opposite of what once held true.

POOR OLD MEN AND WOMEN

No longer valued for their experience and insight, their role as arbiters of style and behavior usurped by the young, often seen as a burden on society, the old were beset on all sides. Such unprecedented dynamics had serious consequences. By the 1920s, increasing discrimination against older men and women in employment and in the community at large exposed growing numbers of older people to the threat of poverty and loneliness. At the same time, the extended family was becoming less able to provide for their needs. In response, state and local governments stepped up their building of institutions and asylums, disproportionately populated by growing legions of impoverished elders. Most of these homes were horrible "warehouses" for the aged, the infirm, and the dying.

By 1930, approximately 30 percent of the nation's elderly were living in poverty. At that time, fewer than 15 percent of American workers were covered by any sort of pension plan. And since very few dependents were covered by these plans, less than 6 percent of the population could expect to receive any benefits if they survived to old age.[23] During this same period, medical advances continued to prolong the lives of more men and women, adding to the ranks of the poor old.

Reversal of Fortune: Elders' Growing Financial Power

The historic turning point eventually came on August 14, 1935. In the midst of the Great Depression, one in three seniors was sinking ever deeper into poverty, and their social and political status had fallen to its lowest point in American history.

Franklin D. Roosevelt and his New Deal supporters designed an ingenious plan to solve several problems at once. Roosevelt's dual goal was to create a financial safety net that would protect America's elderly from a "poverty-ridden old age" and simultaneously get young men working again. Roosevelt's "Social Security" program, passed by Congress on that summer day in 1935, initiated a bold movement toward restoring intergenerational financial security that brilliantly matched the unique needs of the era: It provided a basic level of support for America's elderly while removing them from competing for jobs with the young.

Since that day, America's elders have been rising up from being its *underdogs* to society's economic and political *bulldogs*.

Several critical economic, social, and political factors helped trigger this reversal. In addition to the immediate boost in economic stability that Social Security provided, the future financial status of the old got additional infusions from the growth in pension coverage. Throughout the 1930s, only about 4 million employees were covered by corporate pension plans. The 1940s, however, tell a different story.

Pension funds became an attractive vehicle for corporations when, in 1942, the government extended an existing ruling that both employer contributions to pensions and the earnings on these contributions were tax deductible. At the time, companies faced "excess profit" taxes approaching 100 percent, created to hinder wartime profiteering. Therefore, pension contributions allowed employers to make appealing arrangements with their employees while avoiding heavy taxation.

In addition, union officials discovered during the 1940s that while they couldn't negotiate for higher salaries because of war-related wage freezes, they could bargain for higher pensions. Union leader Walter Reuther coined the slogan "Too Old to Work—Too Young to Die," which became the rallying cry for workers demanding retirement benefits.[24] These new pensions were tax deductible and, as future obligations, didn't show up on a company's books. Attractive to both workers and companies, pensions proliferated. At that time, union membership represented 22 percent of labor force participants. As a result, by 1950 pension coverage had expanded to approximately 10 million employees, representing some 25 percent of the private sector labor force.[25]

Another great boost to the future status of this generation was set in motion at the end of World War II by the GI Bill. This new law gave veterans the opportunity to have their college education or vocational training heavily subsidized by the government. Between 1944 and 1956, more than half of the returning veterans (nearly 8 million people) took advantage of it, receiving some $14.5 billion in educational support. In 1947, fully half of all college students were veterans.[26]

As I will discuss in greater detail in Chapter 5, in the 1960s the elderly also became the recipients of a windfall of support from Medicare. In 1965, the average senior struggling against an impoverished old age received $1 per year in healthcare-related government support. Thanks to Medicare, that number has vaulted to $7,000 today.

The average 65+ couple today receives approximately $22,000 each year from Social Security and another $12,000 of yearly value from Medicare—for life. Urban Institute senior fellow C. Eugene Steuerle calculates that, using today's prices, an average-income couple retiring in 1960 could expect at that time to receive about $100,000 in lifetime Social Security benefits. A typical couple retiring in 1999 would receive nearly $500,000 in Social Security and Medicare benefits (about equal amounts of each).[27]

Today's 50+ men and women now control 80 percent of all the money in U.S. savings-and-loan institutions and represent $66 of every $100 invested in the stock market. A critical part of the growing economic clout of today's older adults comes from the compounding of the investments they made with dollars earned years ago. Many have benefited dramatically from the stock market updraft that they've ridden in their lives: Remember that the Dow has multiplied from 200 in 1950 to 10,000+ today. Because they had their children early, hit their peak earning years after their kids were grown, and were careful with their money, the majority have been able to save and invest far more than any generation before or since.

In addition, a remarkable 70 to 75 percent of all older men and women own the homes in which they live, about three-quarters of which are completely paid off. Many older homeowners were initially able to buy at a low cost, aided by extremely low interest rates—usually 4 to 5 percent on GI loans. Under the 1944 GI Bill and its successors, some one-fifth of postwar mortgages for single-family homes were subsidized by the Veterans Administration. In the 1950s or '60s, these homes might have cost $10,000 to $15,000. Property values rose steadily during the next decade or so, then went "through the roof" (as can be seen in the chart on the following page) when these couples' children—the boomers—entered the housing market, pushing property values up 500 percent from 1970 to 1995.[28]

That lift in real estate values, caused by the combination of increasing mobility and a demographic fluke, has given a valuable benefit to today's elder population that boomer elders won't experience. To illustrate these points, I recently asked the audience in one of my presentations if anyone was over 65 and living in a home they'd

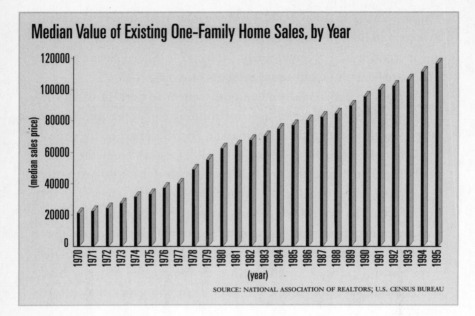

Median Value of Existing One-Family Home Sales, by Year

(median sales price)

(year)

SOURCE: NATIONAL ASSOCIATION OF REALTORS; U.S. CENSUS BUREAU

bought more than 25 years ago. Of the several people who raised their hands, I called on an elderly couple who, I learned, had bought their home 27 years before. They had qualified for a 4 percent GI mortgage loan on their house, which at that time cost $31,000. Their mortgage payments, which they were still paying, were $87 per month. I then asked the audience if anyone had purchased a house in the same neighborhood within the past three years. Several baby-boomer couples raised their hands. The couple I called on said that their home had cost $385,000 and, with the 7.06 percent loan they were able to secure, their payments were about $2,600 per month. Think about that: $1,000 per year versus $31,000 per year to live in the same kind of house in the same neighborhood.

Robust government entitlements; home ownership; a lifetime of savings and investment; and recent attractive discounts on airfares, hotel stays, rental cars, movies, financial services, and dining have all contributed to drive the official poverty rate for those age 65 and over from about 35 percent early in the 1960s to an all-time low of 10.5 percent today.[29]

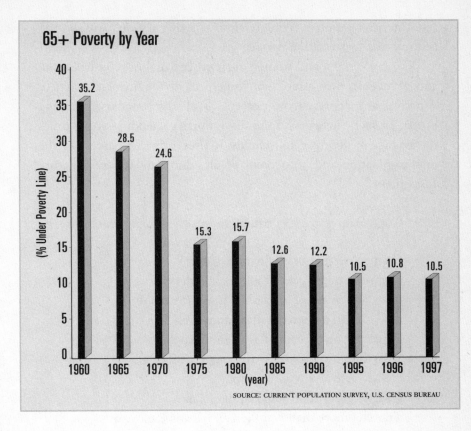

65+ Poverty by Year

(% Under Poverty Line)

35.2 — 1960
28.5 — 1965
24.6 — 1970
15.3 — 1975
15.7 — 1980
12.6 — 1985
12.2 — 1990
10.5 — 1995
10.8 — 1996
10.5 — 1997

(year)

SOURCE: CURRENT POPULATION SURVEY, U.S. CENSUS BUREAU

AGE POWER IS CREATING A NEW "MATURE MARKET"

Until recently, corporations, marketers, and entrepreneurs paid little attention to 50+ men and women. There was, after all, little to spark their interest in a group whose members tended to be financially disadvantaged, frugal, and perceived as set in their ways and uninterested in new products and technologies.

Though still entranced by young consumers, marketers are slowly coming to realize that they can no longer afford to ignore mature adults. Although they still represent only 5 percent of all advertising targets, a startling statistic surfaces if we examine the size of this segment. In the year 2000, approximately 76 million Americans will be past the age of 50: This is exactly the number of Americans that there were—*in total*—in the year 1900. It's as though the American nation is giving birth to a "senior nation" and the 20th century was the gestation period.

These 50+ men and women currently earn almost $2 trillion in annual income, own more than 70 percent of the financial assets in America, and represent 50 percent of all discretionary spending power. In fact, their per capita discretionary spending is 2.5 times the average of younger households. Representing 27 percent of the total population and 36 percent of all adults, today's *new* mature consumers:[30]

- Control more than $7 trillion in wealth—70 percent of the total
- Own 77 percent of all financial assets
- Comprise 66 percent of all stockholders
- Own 40 percent of all mutual funds ($1 trillion)
- Own almost 60 percent of all annuities
- Represent 50 percent of IRA and Keogh holders
- Own their own homes—over 79 percent of all 50+, by far the highest rate of any age group[31]
- Own 46 percent of home equity loans
- Transact more than 5 million auto loans each year
- Purchase 42 percent of all homeowner's insurance (50 million policyholders)
- Own 38 percent of all life insurance—a $90 billion industry[32]
- Purchase more than 90 percent of long-term care insurance, representing $800 million in annual premiums—a figure that's growing at 23 percent per year[33]
- Comprise 35 percent of the auto insurance market (50 million consumers)
- Represent 40 million credit card users, owning almost half of the credit cards in the U.S.[34]
- Purchase 41 percent of all new cars (they're much less likely than their younger counterparts to buy used cars) and 48 percent of all luxury cars, totaling more than $60 billion

- Represent more than $610 billion per year in direct healthcare spending[35]
- Account for 51 percent of all over-the-counter drug purchases
- Consume 74 percent of all prescription drugs, a $103 billion market
- Represent 65 percent of all hospital bed days, 42 percent of all physician's office visits, 1.5 million residents in nursing homes, and 1.5 million residents in continuing-care retirement and assisted-living residences.[36]

Just in case you had any lingering doubt about which demographic segment now has the greatest net worth, consider the following chart:

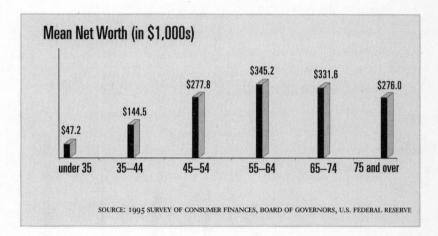

Mean Net Worth (in $1,000s)

under 35	35–44	45–54	55–64	65–74	75 and over
$47.2	$144.5	$277.8	$345.2	$331.6	$276.0

SOURCE: 1995 SURVEY OF CONSUMER FINANCES, BOARD OF GOVERNORS, U.S. FEDERAL RESERVE

In addition, while youthful consumer segments are struggling to make ends meet, the percentage of mature men and women who are financially well-off has multiplied phenomenally during the past decade, as the following charts illustrate:

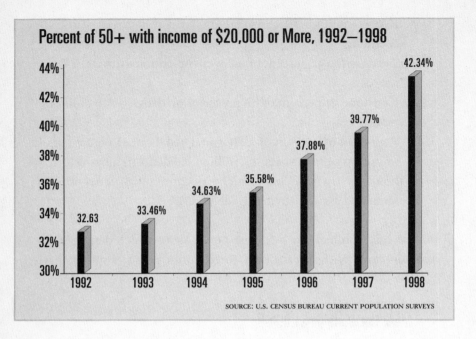

Percent of 50+ with income of $20,000 or More, 1992–1998

- 1992: 32.63
- 1993: 33.46%
- 1994: 34.63%
- 1995: 35.58%
- 1996: 37.88%
- 1997: 39.77%
- 1998: 42.34%

SOURCE: U.S. CENSUS BUREAU CURRENT POPULATION SURVEYS

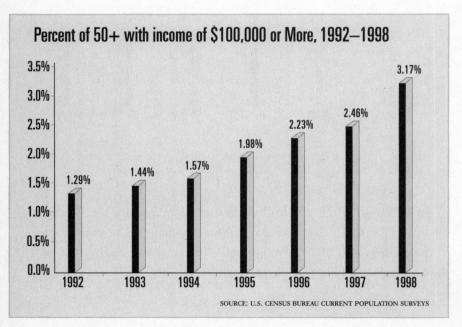

Percent of 50+ with income of $100,000 or More, 1992–1998

- 1992: 1.29%
- 1993: 1.44%
- 1994: 1.57%
- 1995: 1.98%
- 1996: 2.23%
- 1997: 2.46%
- 1998: 3.17%

SOURCE: U.S. CENSUS BUREAU CURRENT POPULATION SURVEYS

Jump! How High? The Elderly Take Control of the Polls

Concurrent with their growing economic power, older adults have for years been growing in political influence. As reflected in the following chart, nearly 70 percent of Americans 65 and over voted in 1996, compared with only 33 percent of those between the ages of 18 and 24. Although the elderly have recently tended to divide their votes 60/40 between Democrats and Republicans, they quickly become a unified power block whenever their interests are threatened.

In the 1996 presidential primaries, it became a virtual prerequisite even among the most conservative candidates to declare their

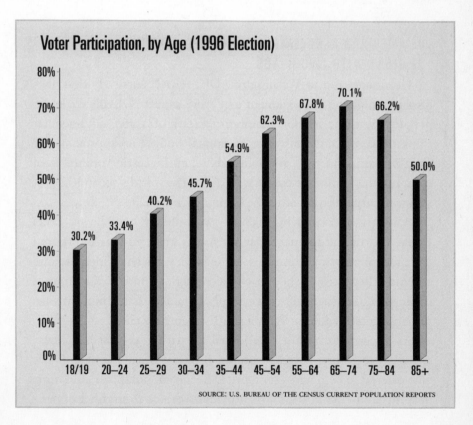

Voter Participation, by Age (1996 Election)

Age	Percent
18/19	30.2%
20–24	33.4%
25–29	40.2%
30–34	45.7%
35–44	54.9%
45–54	62.3%
55–64	67.8%
65–74	70.1%
75–84	66.2%
85+	50.0%

SOURCE: U.S. BUREAU OF THE CENSUS CURRENT POPULATION REPORTS

support for Medicare and vow not to cut it. Even when "cutting" meant nothing more than slowing the program's growth, Democratic candidates in the 1998 congressional elections found a potent and feared weapon to use against their challengers. Representative Peter DeFazio of Oregon certainly was looking to fan these fires when he declared, "Mr. Speaker . . . the Republicans would actually take oxygen from the lungs of senior citizens and disabled around this country to finance tax cuts for the wealthy. And I am not making this up. The measure before us today cuts the payments for oxygen and oxygen equipment by 20 percent and freezes payments through 2002 to save $1.6 billion. . . . Is this fair? I do not think so."[37]

The elderly have become so powerful that very few politicians have the nerve to tangle with them.

THE AMERICAN ASSOCIATION OF RETIRED PERSONS: THE GIANT WITH TWO HEADS

Headquartered in Washington, DC, AARP currently describes its mission as the improvement of "every aspect of living for older people." With 32 million members, a staff of 1,700, a 32-scholar think tank, 19 staff lobbyists, an annual budget of approximately $550 million, and tens of thousands of enthusiastic volunteers in communities across the country, AARP is the world's second-largest nonprofit organization after the Catholic Church.[38]

AARP was created in 1958 by two unlikely bedfellows: Ethel Percy Andrus and Leonard Davis. Andrus was a 72-year-old retired high school principal from Los Angeles who was chagrined because she and other retired schoolteachers could not find health insurance because of their age. She was deeply troubled that senior citizens were being treated unfairly by a youth-oriented society.

As fate would have it, she joined up with a 32-year-old, hard-driving, New York–based insurance broker named Leonard Davis who offered to help her—for a price. Seeing an untapped gold mine in Andrus and her peers, Davis provided $50,000 to start her organization—initially called the National Retired Teachers Association (NRTA)—in exchange for the exclusive right to sell insurance to its membership. At first, Davis did his insurance deals through Continental Casualty of Chicago, but as the group's membership grew to 750,000 in 1963, he founded his own insurance company, Colonial Penn, to maximize his profits through this NRTA-AARP connection. By the early 1970s, Andrus's dream had attracted 10 million members, while Davis had netted himself more than $160 million.

As AARP has grown, this giant's two heads—target marketer and altruistic social crusader—have never reconciled, a dual nature that has some disturbing elements.

AARP's Right Head: Moneymaker Extraordinaire

Since the initial Continental Casualty of Chicago/Colonial Penn deals, AARP has taken its complicated formula of advocating for members' social policy enhancements with one hand while extracting their money with the other even further, branching out into a myriad of deals and arrangements. By using its aura as a concerned charitable organization, AARP has built a wide array of marketing and sales programs that rival for-profit competitors like American Express, Citibank, Time-Warner, Merck-Medco, Fidelity, and Microsoft.

By any standards, the association's business performance is impressive. In 1997, AARP collected $139 million from membership dues. According to executive director Horace Deets's annual report, the association earned approximately $107 million dollars in "commissions" (and interest on premiums before they are turned over)—which AARP euphemistically refers to as "administrative allowance"—from the Group Health Insurance Program, renamed AARP Health Care Options (AHCO) in January 1997. In addition, from its exclusive deals with auto, home, and life insurance providers and its credit card and mail-order pharmacy ventures, AARP's "programs" generated another $77 million.

AARP also has an impressive track record as a national publisher. *Modern Maturity* charges advertisers the highest page rate of any publication in the country, $248,800, and regularly turns down ads from companies other than its vendor partners. Competitor magazines *New Choices* and *Mature Outlook* brought in $18 million and $9 million respectively in ad sales in 1998—but bimonthly *Modern Maturity* (and the *AARP Bulletin* newsmagazine) together generated a whopping $63 million in revenue.

With so much money in its coffers, AARP in 1997 earned more than $66 million in investment income alone. And last, but certainly not least, this hub-and-spokes marketer requested and received more than $80 million from federal and other grant programs.

Many marketers observe with awe the ways in which AARP and its merchant partners work their wonders on current and prospective members: The group brilliantly blends social welfare and commercialism to build trust and loyalty among members. It amasses detailed files on members' purchasing history, which AARP uses to hone its own and its vendor partners' marketing messages. AARP benefits from nonprofit postage rates—its mailings are so large and so frequent that it even has its own zip code, 20049. *Modern Maturity* and the *AARP Bulletin* reach 32 million members with AARP's selected promotional messages while allowing few editorial counterpoints and no competitors' ads. AARP's nonprofit status allows it to reap numerous rewards without paying *any taxes*. And, the icing on the cake, it operates with no real competition.

AARP's Left Head: Power Broker Extraordinaire

While one side of AARP's split personality is wheeling and dealing, the other side is proclaiming altruistic intentions. In 1998, *Fortune* magazine surveyed opinion leaders to determine the 25 most powerful lobbying organizations in the country, and AARP ranked number one.[39] Consider AARP's strength in comparison to other well-known, powerful associations:

- League of Women Voters: 110,000 members
- NAACP: 400,000 members

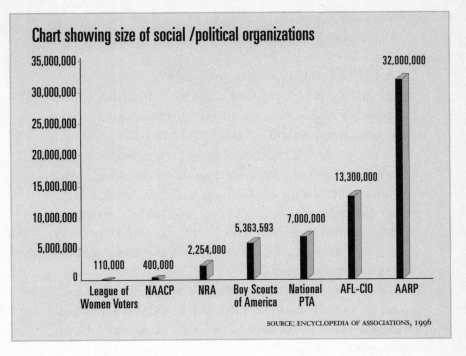

Chart showing size of social /political organizations

SOURCE: ENCYCLOPEDIA OF ASSOCIATIONS, 1996

- National Rifle Association: 2.5 million members
- Boy Scouts of America: 5.5 million members
- National PTA: 7 million members
- AFL-CIO: 15 million members

With its *33 million members*, AARP has more heft than all of these other associations combined! It's as though AARP has become the self-anointed "party of the old." Ethel Percy Andrus would be amazed to see what her dream has become.

Like a thousand–armed octopus, AARP reaches out to wield its power in countless ways: lobbying on Capitol Hill, hosting or cohosting hundreds of conferences and meetings, sponsoring thousands of workshops and programs, conducting research into dozens of aging-related subjects, advising employers, serving as an ongoing "source" for the media, and mobilizing grassroots activism that can put an instant stranglehold on its opponents' efforts. An excellent example of this last capability is recounted by Charles Morris in his book *The AARP:*

> AARP counts the defeat of the Balanced Budget Amendment in 1995, which doomed a key part of the Republican "Contract with America," as a major legislative success, and it is a classic demonstration of the AARP lobbying technique.
>
> In the last days of the debate, as the preliminary vote count hovered right at the required two-thirds majority, AARP focused its efforts on the two senators from North Dakota, Kent Conrad and Byron Dorgan—look-alike conservative Democrats, both business school graduates and former state tax commissioners, and among the last remaining senators not to have taken a position. . . .
>
> "Telephone trees" were activated throughout the state. When a "tree" is turned on, each AARP volunteer starts making phone calls to a list of people who are asked to call the target's office, and to call other friends to make similar calls. Within hours, the two senators' switchboards were flooded with thousands of calls. Mass mailings went to every AARP member in the state asking them to call or write in favor of a "no" vote. Rallies were held in the state capital. AARP spokespeople were logged onto local radio and television talk shows. A full-time AARP staffer was dispatched to Bismarck to be sure the campaign went smoothly. "We mobilized all over the landscape," says [Jim] Butler. [Washington AARP/Vote Director] When Dorgan and Conrad eventually voted the right way—they admitted to being almost overwhelmed by the "no" vote partisans—the same process was repeated to "give them a big round of thank-yous and support to show our appreciation."[40]

Politicians at every level who are looking for votes pay great respect to AARP's clout. When informed that both the Reagan and

Bush administrations had neglected to invite AARP legislative counsel to the White House, President Clinton exclaimed, "What, couldn't they count?" The Clinton administration *could* count: Records of Hillary Rodham Clinton's healthcare task force obtained from the National Archives show that John Rother, AARP's legislative and public policy director, personally guided the administration in drafting a healthcare reform bill to AARP's liking.

Age Power Rising

Rebounding from a temporary period of poverty, powerlessness, and social isolation, today's elders have grown in numbers, have become powerful and influential, and have managed to become more financially secure than any group in our nation's history. They are extraordinarily well connected, vote in higher concentrations than any other age group, and have AARP—the country's largest special interest group—to lobby for their interests.

America is becoming a gerontocracy.

CHAPTER TWO

THE NEW WILD, WILD WEST OF HUMAN ENHANCEMENT AND LIFE EXTENSION

In 1899, Charles Duell, director of the U.S. Patent Office, reflected the sentiments of the nation when he declared, "Everything that can be invented has been invented." He obviously couldn't envision the hundreds of thousands of scientific breakthroughs and inventions that were waiting around the corner. Today, we stand similarly poised at the beginning of a new century that will overflow with breakthroughs, particularly in the areas of human enhancement and life extension.

Although all of our intergenerational entitlements and policies assume only modest changes in life expectancy during the next 50 years or so, we are on the brink of developments that have the potential to dramatically alter both the quality and length of our lives. While we might not find the "Fountain of Youth," we will definitely tap long, cool drinks of extended life. As this occurs, nearly all of our priorities and policies regarding lifestyle-related responsibilities and rewards will fall by the wayside.[1]

The Longevity Revolution: A Long Time Coming

For as long as humans have sought to control their environment and their lives, they have searched for ways to postpone death. The quest for magical cures for aging, born of that ancient craving, has inspired many of the major advances in human exploration, as well as some of the most embarrassing episodes in the annals of science and medicine. Before exploring the bio-wonders tomorrow will bring, let's consider some of those past attempts to stop the biological clock.

TAOIST PRACTICES FOR LONG LIFE

Among the pioneers in the ancient quest for immortality were the Chinese Taoists. The classical writings in Taoism, by Lao-tzu, Chuang-tzu, and Lieh-tzu, date primarily from about 600 to 250 BC. The ultimate goal of the Taoists' studies was to prolong life and achieve immortality. According to their tradition, there existed a class of immortals, or *hsien*, who had mastered the techniques of life extension.

Taoist practitioners ate "longevity-inducing" foods, usually derived from animals and plants recognized as having longer life spans than man. In addition, they developed special gymnastic techniques, such as kung fu, to facilitate proper use of the breath and harness the body's subtle energies.

The ancient Chinese were among the earliest to enunciate the recurrent theme that associates longevity with the husbanding of sexual energy. Taoist practice included a technique for preventing ejaculation, theoretically causing the semen to return and revitalize the system. A similar technique was practiced in the Tantric yoga of India. With the emergence of a more metaphysical emphasis in both Taoism and Hinduism, these sexual practices waned, although they were never entirely suppressed.

ALCHEMY'S MAGIC FORMULAS

The 13th-century English monk Roger Bacon was the leading early popularizer of alchemy in Europe, and also a strong proponent of the search for life extension. The theme of transformation that runs through medieval alchemical writings centers on the legendary "philosopher's stone," believed to be capable of freeing metals of their "impurities." Likewise, the stone was considered able to cleanse the human organism of the impurities that accumulated with aging. Bacon sought to create an "elixir of immortality" that would transform people into deathless beings. As it turned out, such elixirs often contained poisonous compounds of sulfur, mercury, arsenic, and gold, and were probably responsible for the demise of more than a few longevity seekers.

Bridging the transition from medieval alchemy to modern science was the 16th-century figure Paracelsus, whose experiments with chemical compounds are often credited with forming the cornerstone of modern chemistry. Like his forebears, he believed that man had the potential for extended longevity.

In his writings, Paracelsus related recipes for various life-preserving elixirs, along with some rather disturbing instructions for their use. After describing the various ingredients of one of his potions, he recommended that it be put into a good wine, and then:

> Some of the wine must be drunk every day, about dawn, until first all of the nails fall off from the fingers, afterwards from the feet, then the hair and teeth, and lastly the skin be dried up and a new skin produced. When all of this is done, that medicament or potion must be discontinued. And again, new nails, hair and fresh teeth are produced, as well as the new skin and all diseases of the body and mind pass away.[2]

THE PROMOTION OF HYGIENE

In his late thirties, Italian nobleman Luigi Cornaro became desperately run-down and ill because of decadent habits. Warned by doctors that he would survive only a few more months, he converted to a temperate and orderly life. He swiftly recovered, and went on to live to a very old age, dying in 1565 at the age of 98. In his later years, beginning at 83, Cornaro composed a series of discourses spelling out his plan for temperance.

Wisely enough, he wrote that the keys to healthy aging were simple: control of diet, reducing the amount of food eaten, avoiding food that is hard on digestion, and clean living. His goals were modest; he didn't think it was possible to achieve rejuvenation or radical life extension, and rather sought mainly to avoid disease.

SEMEN AS THE "ELIXIR OF YOUTH"

The battle against aging turned to the sex organs in earnest toward the end of the 19th century. At that time, new discoveries were being made about the functioning of the endocrine glands, and many researchers believed that these glands and the hormonal substances they secreted might be the sources of youthful vigor and, possibly, long life.

The respected French neurologist Charles-Édouard Brown-Séquard maintained that if semen was injected into the blood of old men, they would regain their previous mental and physical powers. In 1889, at the age of 72, Brown-Séquard commenced a series of rejuvenation experiments, injecting himself with a mixture of blood, water, and semen from dog and guinea pig testicles. He claimed that this procedure made him feel 30 years younger, and that he was able to endure long hours of work that had previously exhausted him.

The Russian physician Serge Voronoff went even further. During a stint at the turn of the century as personal physician to the Khedive 'Abbās II of Egypt, Voronoff closely observed the eunuchs, castrated in youth, who guarded the harems. These unfortunate individuals exhibited not only feminine characteristics and muscular weakness but also a tendency toward obesity, premature aging, and a whole spectrum of health problems.

Voronoff theorized that not only were the hormones secreted by the testicles responsible for the development of secondary sex characteristics such as beard growth, but the "internal secretion of the testicle is more vital to the preservation of the physical energy of the body and the lucidity of the mind than to the maintenance of the vigor of the sexual organs."[3] Hypothesizing that decrepit old men were effectively eunuchs "emasculated . . . by the wear and tear of old age," Voronoff began to test his theories on animals. Among his first subjects was a group of feeble old rams. After grafting the testicles of young animals onto these rams, Voronoff observed: "My old rams became young in their gait, bellicose and aggressive. . . . The miserable old beasts became full of vitality and energy."[4] To rule out the possibility that the improvements were merely a matter of improved diet in the hands of their new caregiver, Voronoff removed the grafted testicles. Three to five months later, he reported, the animals once again became feeble, spiritless, and timid.

Buoyed by such results, Voronoff proceeded to do transplants on humans. Unable to locate willing human donors, he began implanting sex glands from monkeys into his human patients. Between 1920 and 1927, Voronoff performed such operations on more than 1,000 elderly men, each of whom paid at least $5,000 for the procedure.

Typical of Voronoff's claims is the story of one of his elderly patients: "He had lost half his obesity, his manner was jovial, his movements active, his eyes clear and twinkling with amusement at our astonishment. . . . He bent his head and revealed to our astonished eyes a growth of white down, where formerly there had been a bald expanse. . . . The grafting had transformed a senile, impotent, pitiful old being into a vigorous man, in full possession of all his faculties."[5]

Despite the apparent initial satisfaction of his clients, Voronoff ultimately died in obscurity in 1951. By that time, many of the monkey-testicle grafts were being rejected by their recipients. Even worse, most of these unfortunate patients had become infected with syphilis, which apparently had run rampant among Voronoff's simian donors.

MODERN APPROACHES TO HUMAN ENHANCEMENT AND LIFE EXTENSION

In spite of all these ambitious efforts, the dream of extending human life largely remained just that—a dream—until the 20th century. Thanks to dramatic improvements in sanitation, public health, nutrition, fitness, pharmacy, and modern medicine, the average life expectancy has risen more in the past 100 years than in the previous 1,000. In the late 20th century, we began to realize the dream of history: creating long-lived humans.

Leading the assault on aging-related conditions, the pharmaceutical industry is on the verge of producing dozens of new drugs. The fact that Viagra accounted for 94 percent of all new prescriptions written in the United States three weeks after it was introduced was not lost on pharmaceutical movers and shakers.[6] As of this writing, the industry is actively pursuing 178 new compounds aimed at various symptoms of aging.

Other drugs have already been deployed in the battle against aging, including Lipitor to lower cholesterol, Aricept to boost memory, Celebrex to eliminate the pain of arthritis without creating gastrointestinal problems, Ambien for restful sleep, Evista to control bone loss and prevent osteoporosis, Detrol to halt urinary incontinence, Rogaine and Propecia to foster hair growth, Meridia to promote weight loss, Renova to banish wrinkles, and hundreds more.[7]

What if we wake up a decade from now—or even a month from now—and find that there's a new medicine with which we can prevent cancer or Alzheimer's? What if a new nanotechnology is able to rid the vascular system of atherosclerotic buildup, thereby eliminating heart disease? What if a new generation of nutraceuticals provides the specific micronutrients that will fortify our aging immune systems? What if we use our knowledge of how to clone individual organs to farm and harvest as many "spare parts" as we might ever need? And what if scientists discover a way to slow cellular aging and elevate life expectancy as high as 200 years for those who can afford to buy the treatment? Which raises other questions: If breakthroughs do occur, who will get them? Would a world in which some people lived to 200 and others died at 50 be dominated by a new politics of longevity?

Based on 25 years of study and analysis, I am convinced that dramatic anti-aging breakthroughs are going to surface within the next decade, with the "human enhancement" floodgates opening wide in the years to follow. I am also convinced that our social, medical, and political institutions are totally unprepared for the consequences.

Tomorrow's Anti-aging Sciences and How They Will Affect Your Life

New life-science technologies are emerging that may well become the bio-tools with which human enhancement and life extension are brought about. Let's take a peek into the near future and explore the strongest candidates.

1. Super-Nutrition
2. Hormone Replacement
3. Gene Therapy and the Manipulation of Cellular Aging
4. Bionics: Toward Cyborg Humans
5. Organ Cloning and Other Novel Approaches to "Spare Parts"

Anti-aging Breakthrough #1: Super-Nutrition

To date, only one technique has consistently extended the life span of animals. By providing a diet rich in nutrients, but very low in calories—just half the usual level—scientists have repeatedly been able to nearly double the longevity of mice.

Examples of humans who live on nutritious yet calorie-restricted diets are difficult to find. On the Japanese island of Okinawa, however, people eat about 30 percent fewer calories than their compatriots elsewhere in Japan. Okinawa has almost 40 times as many centenarians per capita as the rest of the country.

According to Dr. Richard Sprott, head of the National Institute on Aging's biology of aging program, "If we could understand how caloric restriction produces its effects, then we'd understand a great deal more about the basic biological mechanism of aging. And that would give us a way to intervene. It could provide that magic bullet we talk about."[8]

NUTRACEUTICALS

Other new connections are currently being made between nutrition and longevity. Dr. Stephen DeFelice is widely viewed as one of the pioneers in the modern super-nutrition movement. As a young endocrinologist in 1965, he noticed that when women suffering from hyperthyroidism were given carnitine (produced in the liver when two amino acids combine), their conditions reversed within a week. The next year, he tried the same supplement with prison inmates suffering from angina pectoris and noticed that it helped them, too. For more than 30 years, DeFelice has been campaigning to get carnitine and other natural substances accepted as nutrition-based therapeutics. It was DeFelice who coined the term "nutraceuticals," which he defined as "any substance that may be considered a food or part of a food and provides medical or health benefits, including the prevention and treatment of disease." It was also DeFelice who noted early on that because such natural substances couldn't be patented, few nutrition or drug companies would take any interest in spending the hundreds of millions of dollars necessary to prove their efficacy.

In recent years, however, scientific research has begun to draw encouraging correlations between specific food ingredients and disease prevention. Although we don't yet know whether antioxidants, the microsubstances that fight damaging free-radical molecules, can actually extend human life, there is a growing mountain of evidence that some—especially vitamins C and E, beta-carotene, and selenium—can fortify the immune system and help ward off heart disease and possibly cancer. One group of antioxidants, called nitrones, has been showing particular promise. Experiments at the Okayama

Medical School in Japan have shown that a nitrone called PBN (phenyl-butylnitrone) significantly extends the lives of aging mice. And research at the University of Kentucky in Lexington suggests that in lab animals PBN can help protect the aging brain against free-radical damage.

PHYTOCHEMICALS AND MICRONUTRIENTS

Before the 20th century, many young men and women suffered from a myriad of malnutrition-related conditions, from scurvy to rickets. During this past century, refinements in food production, manufacturing, and distribution have eliminated nearly all of these conditions in modern societies. There is a downside, though: As our food undergoes layers of processing, many key nutrients are lost.

Spurred by consumer demand and emerging life-science technologies, scientists are now finding that beyond the basic vitamins and minerals, plants contain thousands of naturally occurring compounds, called phytochemicals, that may provide important health benefits, including the prevention of conditions like heart disease and cancer. For example, the phytochemical indole-3-carbinol, found in cauliflower, seems to reduce the risk of breast cancer by triggering an enzyme that causes the emergence of a harmless form of estrogen instead of the type linked to breast cancer. Among the thousands of phytochemicals that exist in tomatoes, p-coumaric acid and chlorogenic acid are believed to suppress the formation of cancer-causing substances. Similarly, sulforaphane, a phytochemical found in broccoli, has been shown to keep laboratory animals from getting cancer by boosting synthesis of anticancer enzymes.[9]

Now that the floodgates have been opened, hundreds of plant hormones are being analyzed for their youth-extending or disease-battling properties. Devra Lee Davis, senior science adviser at the U.S. Public Health Services, reports: "There is growing evidence that these natural products can take tumors and diffuse them. . . . They can turn off the proliferative process of cancer."[10]

In response to the tireless efforts of campaigners like DeFelice, in 1994 Congress passed the Dietary Supplement Health and Education Act (DSHEA), which allows makers of vitamins and herbal cures to make mild health claims. With the passage of DSHEA, it is believed that the nutraceutical industry could soon grow to $250 billion—half the size of the entire American food market. Food and beverage manufacturers are jumping on the bandwagon, including everyone from Kellogg's, which recently launched a nutraceutical division, to McNeil Consumer Products Company, which in 1999 introduced a unique margarine named Benecol containing a fat-soluble plant derivative that actually lowers cholesterol, to Age Wave's own LifeSource Nutrition Solutions, which will prepare and home-deliver meals, soups, smoothies, and snacks that have been custom-fortified with macro- and micronutrients. With the converging trends of aging demographics, evolving nutrition science, and an emphasis on preventive medicine, a whole new generation of super-nutritional foods will soon emerge.

Anti-aging Breakthrough #2:
Hormone Replacement

Hormones are the body's chemical conductors that orchestrate gene functioning and regulate how tissues and organs grow and repair themselves. When we're young, our hormones engage in a symphony of activity spurring us through various rites of passage, growth, and sexual awakenings. As we age, however, our production and regulation of hormones falters. Many gerontologists and medical researchers believe that as our hormonal symphony degenerates, our bodies decline and lose ground to the forces of aging. In his recent book *The Superhormone Promise,* Dr. William Regelson of the Medical College of Virginia expresses his belief that by replenishing the aging body with hormones, "it is possible to slow and even reverse the aging process."[11] In recent years, many hormone-related targets have emerged in the millennia-old battle against decline.

ESTROGEN

Prior to menopause, women have much lower levels of athero-sclerosis and much lower rates of heart attack than men. As a woman passes through menopause, however, her ovaries produce less and less estrogen. According to the *Harvard Heart Letter,* "This decline in estrogen can produce bothersome symptoms, such as hot flashes, and is believed to cause a rise in LDL cholesterol—the form of cho-lesterol most strongly associated with risk of heart attack. After menstruation ceases, a woman's chances of developing heart disease increase dramatically—so that heart attack is the leading cause of death among elderly women."[12]

On the other hand, tampering with Mother Nature's hormones is not without its risks. Numerous studies have shown that the longer a woman is exposed to high levels of estrogen, the greater her chances of eventually getting breast cancer.

Studies are emerging worldwide, however, that demonstrate that women who use carefully monitored hormone replacement therapy tend to have a lower risk of dying from heart disease. For example, a study published in the *Journal of the American Medical Association* in April 1997 showed that taking estrogen after menopause increased the life expectancy of most women (even those at risk of breast can-cer) up to 41 months. There is also compelling evidence that estro-gen replacement therapy can dramatically slow the postmenopausal bone thinning that develops into osteoporosis. In recent years, anec-dotal evidence has also begun to suggest that estrogen may serve to delay the onset of Alzheimer's disease, which is now believed to be influenced in part by the body's hormonal activities.[13]

TESTOSERONE

Testosterone is responsible both for igniting the male sexual drive and for secondary gender-linked characteristics—including muscle and bone thickness, skin quality, and overall energy. Just as women experience a decline in production of estrogen as they approach and pass 50, most maturing men produce lower and lower amounts of testosterone.

Recent research has attempted to demonstrate that testosterone therapy can bolster the vitality of these bodily dynamics. In 1992, Dr. Joyce Tenover of the Emory University Medical School placed 13 elderly men on a six-month regimen that included three months of testosterone and three months of placebo. While taking the hormone, the men gained muscle mass, their bones grew stronger, their cholesterol levels fell, and their energy and libidos rose compared to the control group's outcomes.

Testosterone replacement therapy is a pretty simple matter, thanks to the Testoderm skin patch approved by the FDA in 1993. The original playing card–sized patch was designed to be attached to the scrotum and released a steady flow of the hormone into the bloodstream. The arrival of Androderm in 1998 simplified matters: A smaller, circular patch, it can be worn on the back, upper arm, thigh, or abdomen.

These patches are designed to elevate testosterone levels to normal values. "No question, men feel 100 percent better," says medical researcher Dr. Richard Spark of Harvard. "They have a greater libido, they're more competitive, and they're more effective in their business dealings."[14]

But there are also good reasons to be wary. At high doses, testosterone can cause a wide range of undesirable side effects including breast development, sterility, and the proliferation of prostate tumors. Since testosterone enhances the production of red cells, it could also thicken the blood, raising the risk of stroke.

MELATONIN AND DHEA

Melatonin, a naturally occurring hormone produced by the brain's pineal gland, apparently plays an important role in regulating various biorhythms, such as distinguishing between night and day, and in triggering various hormonal activities. Russell Reiter, Ph.D., co-author of *Melatonin: Your Body's Natural Wonder Drug,* has discovered that in the laboratory, "high doses of melatonin kill free radicals, which can promote cancer and other immunological diseases." In the body, Reiter has found, melatonin is a good antioxidant and protects against damage to DNA. But so far, its anti-aging claims have been based on studies in mice, whose bodies don't even produce melatonin naturally.[15]

Both men and women produce DHEA (dehydroepiandrosterone) in their adrenal glands. Similar to testosterone, DHEA proliferates during early adulthood but nearly disappears as we age. The growing number of proponents proclaim that recreating youthful DHEA levels can trigger a wide range of rejuvenating effects, from preserving lean body mass and elevating mood to improving memory and boosting energy and libido.

The problem with both melatonin and DHEA is that while these substances may be potent anti-aging hormones packed with benefits, they could also turn out to be horrible mutagens. We simply don't know enough yet about the long-term effects.

HUMAN GROWTH HORMONE

Human growth hormone (HGH) was originally used in the 1960s as a novel treatment for children with developmental problems such as dwarfism, with the substance extracted from the pituitary glands of cadavers. The anti-aging crossover occurred in 1990 when Dr. Daniel Rudman of the Medical College of Wisconsin began injecting human growth hormone into elderly men whose levels were extremely low. The short-term results were powerful. According to Rudman, it was as though these men had shed 10 to 20 years in age. Within months, their fat had shrunk by 14 percent, their lean body mass had grown by 9 percent, and their skin had increased in thickness by 7 percent.[16] Rudman's results have since been confirmed by other researchers.

Notwithstanding the fact that HGH has not been approved by

the FDA as an anti-aging treatment, thousands of doctors are now prescribing the expensive therapy ($15,000 to $20,000 per year) to growing numbers of their affluent patients. These youth-seeking guinea pigs are drawn by the hope of enhanced memory, sex drive, and cardiovascular capacity and improved mood. Rudman believes that, down the road, it will be common for patients to visit anti-aging doctors to have their hormone levels checked and get prescriptions for "custom-tailored cocktails" that will help them stay fit and youthful.

Even with the public's growing fascination with HGH, most studies published after Rudman's initial work in Wisconsin have showed that subjects derived little or no *long-term* anti-aging benefit from this hormone. "It's not yet proven to have anything to do with longevity," says Dr. Mary Lee Vance, an endocrinologist and professor of medicine at the University of Virginia Medical Center in Charlottesville.[17]

The real problem with hormone treatments, however, isn't their expense, making them readily available only to the rich; it's their potentially problematic side effects. Scientists fear that use of growth hormone may ultimately cause conditions ranging from carpal tunnel syndrome and other kinds of joint inflammation to severe fluid retention, possibly causing heart failure, to dangerous enlargement of the organs and bones.

According to Dr. Bruce J. Nadler, a Manhattan plastic surgeon who became fascinated with HGH therapy a few years ago, "Have you seen the covers of those bodybuilding magazines? Do you notice how the bodybuilders have spaces between their front teeth? That's because they're taking too much HGH and their skulls have grown, causing their teeth to spread apart."[18] Dr. Robert Butler, esteemed professor of geriatrics at Mount Sinai School of Medicine and director of the International Longevity Center, warns, "We could be deeply regretful if HGH causes things to grow, and may contribute to certain cancers . . . and there's no legitimate appropriate use."[19]

"I tell everyone who calls, 'Don't take it!'" says Dr. Stanley

Slater, associate director of geriatrics at the National Institute on Aging.[20]

Anti-aging Breakthrough #3:
Gene Therapy and the Manipulation of Cellular Aging

Although average life expectancy has been swiftly rising, the maximum human life span still hovers around 120 years. What if we could reprogram our cells to extend that to 150, 175, even 200 years? Some scientists think they have a start on that possibility, beginning with the extension of maximum life span in two species: the nematode worm and the fruit fly. Dr. Siegfried Hekimi at Montreal's McGill University has multiplied the roundworm's life span from 9 days to 50 by selectively breeding for longevity. Similarly, at the University of California, Irvine, biologist Michael Rose has successfully doubled the maximum life span of a species of fruit fly.

Since 1953, when biologists Francis Crick and James Watson first discovered the double-helix nature of DNA and its role in controlling all biologic processes, genetic research has grown by leaps and bounds. Like the speed of computer chip development, predicted by Moore's Law,[21] the scientific rate of genome development is also doubling every year or so. It is now believed that humans may have more than 100,000 genes and approximately 3 billion base pairs. In the mid-1970s, the research cost of deciphering one gene was approximately $2.5 million. Today, genes can be quickly sequenced for around $100. Scientists now anticipate that, by 2003, all human genes will have been mapped.[22]

As we decode each unit of genetic information, we will eventually reveal the biologic map of human life—and unleash the ability to make corrections. For example, by studying long-lived people, researchers have discovered that a gene known as APOE4 is far more prevalent in the very elderly than in the rest of the population. Other aging or anti-aging genes are being discovered on a weekly basis. As the body's genetic puzzle is decoded, scientists are learning that the long-sought-after "Fountain of Youth" may reside deep within our cells.

As was shown by Dr. Leonard Hayflick in his classic experiments in the late 1950s and early 1960s, most human cells can duplicate and replace themselves only a finite number of times before they lose this capacity and die. Not unlike the metaphorical nine lives of a cat, each of our cells is governed by a preprogrammed mechanism that permits approximately 50 duplications before the cell automatically shuts down.

Scientists have recently learned that this process is controlled by cellular clocks, called "telomeres," situated at the tips of chromosomes. In a 1973 paper, Alexey Olovnikov, a senior researcher at the Russian Academy of Sciences in Moscow, proposed that "the telomere shortening could serve as a counting mechanism, which, like a molecular bookkeeper, counts the number of cell doublings already performed."[23] These speculations were validated in the early 1990s as researchers noted that individuals with Down's syndrome, Hutchinston-Gilford syndrome (rapid aging disorder), and Werner syndrome (an adult-onset rapid aging disorder) have particularly *short* telomeres.

From analysis of these dynamics, researchers surmised that as cells age and divide, the telomere strands on the tips of the chromosomes shorten. As a result, the clocks run down and eventually stop. In the January 1998 issue of *Science,* researchers from the Geron Corporation in Menlo Park, California, reported the effects of adding the enzyme telomerase to normal human cells in culture. The results were incredible: The cells "rejuvenated" and ignored their usual limit. According to Geron's senior scientist Calvin Harley, "For the first time, we showed that if you specifically modulate telomere dynamics, you can see the predicted effects on life span. It proves the causal relationship between telomere length and aging."[24] New understanding of telomerase function could pave the way to the production of muscle stem cells for treating muscular dystrophy, insulin-producing cells for patients with insulin-dependent diabetes, skin cells for burn patients, and cartilage cells for those with osteo- and rheumatoid arthritis, as well as more sensitive cancer diagnostics and even treatment of AIDS.

Researchers at Geron also hypothesize that aging could actually be reversed by adding telomerase so that the telomeres relengthen. By splicing telomere "caps" made of telomerase onto the chromosomes, biologists have apparently been able to make the cells divide up to 90 times, almost double the normal limit of 50.

While genetically enhancing our longevity potential hints at an almost unimaginable future, there are many worries. The risks of altering genetic traits in humans are as yet completely unknown. We don't know if adding or manipulating genes could trigger cancers or other mutant diseases. But as gene mapping advances and scientists locate more and more genetically coded disease risks, or if they can successfully manipulate the "biologic clock" itself, we will have entered a new stage of human evolution, and no process will be affected more dramatically than human aging. When this happens, "age power" will become turbo-charged.

Anti-aging Breakthrough #4:
Bionics: Toward Cyborg Humans

On October 8, 1958, Arne Larsson of Sweden became the first human recipient of an implanted biomedical device. Succumbing to Stokes-Adams syndrome, which decreases blood flow to the brain, Larsson agreed to have an experimental, hockey puck–sized pacemaker implanted in his abdomen. Two weeks later, he was discharged from the hospital with a regular heartbeat and a smile on his face.[25]

NASA scientists Manfred Clynes and Nathan Kline coined the term "cyborg"—short for "cybernetic organism"—in the 1960s while investigating novel ways to enhance the survivability of humans in space. Clynes and Kline believed that if people could be "improved" with implanted technology, they'd be more suited for the rigors of extended space travel. Today, many of these technologies are being applied to human enhancement and life extension on earth.

There are currently more than 2 million men and women being kept alive with the help of a cardiac pacemaker, and it's estimated that more than 500,000 of the devices will be implanted each year. Similarly, in 1998 approximately 250,000 synthetic hips and 200,000 synthetic knees were transplanted into needy men and women.[26] The "bionic man," once the stuff of TV fantasy, is becoming a reality as doctors replace failed or injured limbs with mechanized substitutes as a matter of course. In fact, the number of cyborg men and women today already outnumbers the entire population of Singapore.

FROM DUMB TO SMART BIONICS

Until recently, most of the widely used artificial replacements have been functional but "dumb"—a Teflon hip socket, for example. However, bionics is about to enter a new era. As computing technology swiftly evolves—becoming both more powerful and smaller—smart chips, neural stimulation, and wireless communication are helping to break down the barriers between man and machine. Biomedical engineers can now envision a day when tiny yet enormously powerful computers with a wide range of monitoring and control responsibilities will be inserted directly into the human body to make it function better for longer.

CYBORG LIMBS

Thanks to advancing technology, we've come a long way from the peg leg as a solution to amputation. In 1995 a British company, Blatchfords, produced the first "intelligent knee." According to Ben Blease, a research prosthetist with the company, "Previous prosthetic knees were free-swinging or used a hydraulic system, which meant amputees had to put a lot of effort into making the leg move faster because it couldn't detect speed changes, but this is controlled by a microprocessor and is therefore able to detect when you want to speed up, and to respond accordingly."[27] The NovaCare Sabolich Prosthetic and Research Center in Oklahoma City offers a $28,000 artificial leg that has fully working joints and processor chips in the knee to measure pressure and adjust the leg's gait.

In August 1998, Campbell Aird, an English inkeeper who had lost his arm to cancer 16 years earlier, was equipped with the world's first fully electronic prosthesis. Known as the Edinburgh Modular Arm System (EMAS), the GBP 100,000 is a carbon fiber construction enveloping a symphony of electronics and covered with a synthetic silicone skin complete with nails, pores, cuticles, wrinkles, and fingerprints. It is powered by rechargeable battery packs concealed within the upper arm.

When Aird thinks about a movement, electrical pulses travel from his brain to sensors in the arm and the relevant commands are executed by electronic motors distributed between the shoulder, elbow, and fingers. As Aird exclaims, "It can't quite manage fiddly tasks, but practical things like tying my shoelaces, hammering in nails, and pouring a glass of beer I can do for the first time in 16 years. . . . Nobody who's never lost a limb could understand what it means to have a tool like this."[28]

At the University of Delaware, researchers are developing the next-generation prosthesis: a system of sensors that, when attached to a robotic limb, allows the wearer to "feel" objects. Named the Freehand System, this bionic technology may help tens of thousands of patients with spinal cord injuries. And at California-based Advanced Bionics, the research team is creating a digital spine system, consisting of a chip implanted in the backbone that will process information sent by sensors in robotic limbs, then send signals to the brain via the central nervous system. Although not slated to be on the market for another decade or so, these advances will, scientists hope, grant users of robotic prosthetics the same control and flexibility as they would have over a natural limb.

Besides bionic limbs, we may soon have a replacement for muscles. The Artificial Muscle Project at the MIT Artificial Intelligence Laboratory is creating faux muscles from polymer hydrogel. Just like human muscle, the plastic-liquid composite can be expanded and contracted by electrical stimuli. One of the immediate medical applications of this work is the development of an artificial sphincter, which would be a godsend to the millions of older adults who suffer with urinary or fecal incontinence.

BIONIC HEARTS, LUNGS, AND OTHER ORGANS

Although heart and vascular failure account for more adult deaths than all other causes combined, only about 250 heart transplants are performed annually because of the shortage of donor organs. Even then, one in five recipients dies within a year and only a handful survive more than a decade, mostly because the foreign tissue is rejected.

The National Heart, Lung, and Blood Institute of the National Institutes of Health has recently financed new artificial heart projects at both Penn State University and the Texas Heart Institute at St. Luke's Episcopal Hospital in Dallas. The team at Penn State has already implanted an artificial heart in Ferdinand, a Holstein calf who is reportedly doing well. Meanwhile, Robert Jarvik, the American engineer who invented the first generation of artificial hearts, has crafted a thumb-size synthetic heart, the Jarvik 2000. Jarvik is convinced that his new titanium hearts are immune to rejection and far superior to his earlier models. At Tokyo's Waseda University, researchers have recently developed an artificial lung that is performing well in animal tests. Similarly, mechanical livers, pancreases, and other vital organs are expected to appear in future years that may extend the lives of ailing older adults.

CYBORG SIGHT AND SOUND

Those with limited sight may one day be able to turn to Elvis—the nickname for LVES, Low Vision Enhancement System. Developed by NASA and Johns Hopkins University, Elvis consists of a video display worn on the head like a crash helmet covering the eyes, with three cameras and a zoom system attached. Large and awkward as the equipment is now, as technology grows smaller and more powerful, the apparatus will eventually be hidden either within a standard pair of eyeglasses or implanted directly in the skull.

In time, bionics may also eliminate deafness—a condition that prevails among older adults. Although modern hearing aids amplify sounds reaching the sensory receptors of the inner ear, if those receptors are damaged or destroyed, no amount of amplification will allow that person to hear. However, French scientists in the 1950s reported success with electrical stimulation of hearing nerves by inserting an electrode directly into a deaf person's inner ear. The patient could then hear rhythms of speech. This encouraged the development of the cochlear implant, a microprocessor inserted directly into the mastoid bone behind the ear. While the first devices used a single electrode, able to produce a perception of sound that the patient likened to crickets chirping, newer models contain as many as eight electrodes that can process 91,000 bits of auditory information per second.

A British study found that totally deaf adults using the implant could identify common environmental sounds, 95 percent identified more words correctly when using the implant in conjunction with lipreading than they did when relying on lipreading alone, and 35 percent showed some understanding of questions posed over the telephone.[29] Currently, the contraption is relatively large, but Advanced Bionics hopes to eventually miniaturize the whole system to a chip the size of the head of a pin.

BIO-ORCHESTRATORS

Remember the '60s science-fiction film *Fantastic Voyage,* in which a miniaturized submarine and crew performed microsurgery within the body of a defecting Cold War scientist? If so, you won't be surprised by Maryland-based S4MS Inc.'s latest project. The company is developing a tiny, implantable health monitor, the size of a button, that detects irregularities in the blood and transmits readouts to a watchlike device worn on the arm. It is intended to monitor the glucose level of diabetics. Down the road, we might imagine a nanocomputer that would monitor all of the body's functions— blood pressure, glucose level, heart rate, brain wave activity—and make adjustments to optimize health and vitality when things fell out of sync. If an individual wanted relief from a period of high stress, he or she could simply direct the bio-orchestrator to instigate the "relaxation response." During sleep, such a device could also switch certain hormonal and nervous system functions to a hibernation mode so that rest and repair could occur more effectively.

STEVE AUSTIN OR JOHN GLENN?

Usually when we envision bionically enhanced men and women, we picture them as strapping thirtysomethings like *The Six Million Dollar Man*'s Steve Austin. This is a mistake. In the years ahead, the recipients of these new technologies are likely to be the growing ranks of elderly men and women whose body parts and processes have begun to fail. We would do better to envision tomorrow's cyborgs as looking more like eightysomething John Glenn.

Anti-aging Breakthrough #5:
Organ Cloning and Other Novel Approaches to Spare Parts

While we have become increasingly comfortable grafting mechanical valves onto our hearts and transplanting blood, kidneys, and other organs from one person to another, the problem with replacement organs is twofold. First, there aren't that many of them around. Each year thousands of desperate patients die in the U.S. alone because of a critical shortage of replacement organs. And second, the human body often rejects alien tissue. But what if spare body parts and tissues were readily available?

CHIMERA PARTS

To create a supply of spare parts for aging bodies, researchers have already begun to breed pigs that have been genetically engineered to grow certain organs whose tissue is nearly identical to humans'. These transgenic pigs have been raised in solitary confinement in ultra-clean rooms from birth so that they'll be as disease free as possible. According to John J. Fung, transplantation director at the University of Pittsburgh Medical Center, "Pig organs could help save 200,000 lives a year in America."[30]

Some of the early results from animal to human transplantation are extraordinary. In Boston, for example, 12 advanced Parkinson's disease patients have had pig cells inserted into their brains. The transplanted animal cells survived and grew, replacing those destroyed by the disease. Several of the patients have astounded the researchers by beginning to walk again.[31]

Of course, these breakthroughs are not without problems. Recently, researchers at London's Institute of Cancer Research reported that a virus found in pig cells has crossed over and infected human cells. Some scientists worry that cell transplants could unleash an unimaginable spectrum of new viral epidemics.[32]

HUMAN ORGAN CLONING

In Bath, England, better known for its healing waters than for biotech breakthroughs, Dr. Jonathan Slack announced in October 1997 that he had determined how to manipulate the genes of frogs in such a way as to have particular parts either present or absent in their offspring. In the laboratories at Bath University, Slack and his colleagues have devised a method that makes it possible to create and essentially "farm" specific organs in a laboratory by the manipulation and suppression of certain genes. Slack believes that this technology, applied to humans, could solve the shortage of transplantable organs. With this progress, "when your vital organs develop any defect, the doctor may just clone a partial embryo from any one of your cells of that organ, grow it in a Kuwabara [hydroponic-type] tank, and get a healthy rejection-proof organ from it."[33]

While dramatic process is being made on organ cloning, another approach has recently caught the attention of scientists. Just as you might jump-start a yogurt culture with a sample from a thriving culture, two Harvard researchers, Dr. Anthony Atala and Dario Fauza, have figured out a way to grow new organs from tissue samples.

So far, the Harvard Medical School team has successfully replaced dogs' diseased bladders with new, healthy ones grown in moldlike scaffolding shaped to perfectly match the original bladders' size. "In every case in which the dogs received a new bladder, the organ began working successfully within four to six weeks of implantation," reports Dr. Atala.[34] He predicts that this remarkable procedure could have relevance for many different organs and could be available for use in humans within a few short years.

Organ cloning and fabrication would be a lifesaver for aging patients with brain diseases such as Parkinson's or Alzheimer's because it could provide them with healthy neural tissues identical to their own. Or patients dying from certain forms of leukemia could receive an unlimited supply of healthy bone marrow culled from their body's own DNA.

Enhanced Humans

Today there are more than 100,000 anti-aging related research projects under way in numerous disciplines in all corners of the world: More progress has been made in the battle against aging in the past decade than in the previous 10,000 years. Within a few years, these efforts will, in all likelihood, begin to bear fruit. As new discoveries become available—either legally or through an emerging anti-aging black market—millions of men and women will be turning themselves into human guinea pigs. Whether we are transformed into a Shangri-La society of youthful longevity pioneers or a Gerassic Park of cyborgs remains to be seen. One thing is for sure, aging is about to get a radical face-lift . . . and a hip replacement, a hormone injection, and an organ transplant.[35]

As the boomers age, their lifelong obsession with youth will drive large numbers toward these new technologies. In fact, I anticipate that by the year 2020, more than 90 percent of all surviving boomer elders will have had their life expectancies impacted by one or more of the technologies discussed in this chapter (or, possibly, even more advanced capabilities to come). Given these scientific enhancements, all bets would be off regarding how long we might live in the 21st century. As we will explore in subsequent chapters, even at the level of current progress and growth in longevity, all aging-related laws, policies, programs, and entitlements will have to undergo radical transformations.

CHAPTER THREE

THE AGE WAVE IS COMING: IS THE WORLD READY FOR ELDER BOOMERS?

On April 1, 1946, an earthquake occurred in the depths of the ocean surrounding the Aleutian Islands of Alaska. The quake's enormous shock wave immediately began traveling outward from the source. As it sped through cold Pacific waters, many fisherman didn't even notice the foot or two of swell under their boats because it was traveling so deep within the ocean. Moving at jet speed, 550 miles per hour, in less than five hours the wave struck the Hawaiian Islands—thousands of miles away.

For a few moments, the wave caused the Hawaiian coastal waters to rush out, leaving boats and fish stranded on the bare sand. Then the waters reformulated into a massive, towering tsunami that came crashing onto the islands' shores, destroying everything in its path.

During that same year, a demographic quake began that would last nearly two decades. After dropping for centuries, from nearly 7 births per woman in the late 1700s to 2.1 in the 1930s, the birth rate rose to 3.8 in a postwar fertility boom that produced 76 million children— nearly one-third of the U.S. population—between 1946 and 1964.[1] Similar baby booms occurred in Canada, Europe, Asia, Australia, and New Zealand, although some were a few years shorter in duration.

The force of this demographic quake has been reverberating through society's institutions ever since. Although it began as a baby boom, it now rising up into an *age wave,* destined to crash upon society's shores, transforming everything in its path.

We saw in Chapter One how the "new old" are already reconfiguring politics, markets, and social institutions worldwide. In Chapter Two, we opened a window on the future and glimpsed some of the ways in which boomers will benefit from new life-extension technologies. Now let's look backward to see how the wave of boomers has transformed society during each of their previous lifestages, then turn to the future to envision how they will soon revolutionize the social institutions and marketplace dynamics pertaining to life's second half.

Boom Times

With the end of the Depression and World War II, a hopeful new social era had begun. In this period of newfound prosperity, the reuniting of America's victorious soldiers and the young women who were waiting for them led to a fantastic boom in births.

When the leading edge of the baby boom arrived, however, America and its institutions were totally unprepared. Waiting lists and long lines developed at hospitals across the country; facilities and staff were inadequate, and in some hospitals, hallways were used as labor rooms. Similarly, apartments and homes didn't have enough bedrooms for boomer kids, there was a shortage of baby food and diapers, and department stores couldn't keep enough toys in stock to meet the multiplying demand.

The boomers were born into a radically different world than that of their parents and grandparents, whose lives had been traumatized by World War I, the Depression, and then World War II. Struggling through decades of social and political uncertainty, often shadowed by the threat of poverty, most were forced to make peace with modest means and delayed gratification. As noted by researchers J. Walker Smith and Ann Clurman in the Yankelovich report *Rocking the Ages*, the boomers' parents "believed that a lifetime of commitment was required to accomplish their goals. Duty came before pleasure."[2]

In response, the parents of this postwar generation hoped to give their own children a new level of stability and comfort—even luxury. "Gone, for the first time in history," declared *Time* in 1955, "is the worry over whether a society can produce enough goods to take care of its people."[3] Notwithstanding their attempt to teach their children their own values and sense of discipline, these parents hoped to shower them with abundance.

Suddenly, a new range of products and "parenting philosophies" came into vogue. Dr. Benjamin Spock became one of America's best-selling authors by dispensing sensitive child-rearing advice to young parents with his 1946 book, *The Common Sense Book of Baby and Child Care.* The diaper business prospered, growing from a $32 million industry in 1947 to $50 million in 1957.[4] When boomers took their first steps, the shoe, photo, and Band-Aid industries skyrocketed. Similarly, sales of tricycles, Slinkies, and hula hoops exploded as the marketplace was flooded with products for kids.

Born as it was at almost the same time as the boomer generation, the emerging television industry embraced it with shows for and about kids like *The Mickey Mouse Club, The Little Rascals, Howdy Doody, Captain Kangaroo,* and *The Shari Lewis Show.* Boomers, who began watching TV at the age of 2, gave rise to the term "the media generation." Between 1948 and 1952, the number of television sets in U.S. households vaulted from several thousand to 15 million. By the time the first boomers were 6, each of them had watched roughly 5,000 hours of television—more than their parents had watched in their entire lifetimes. According to Landon Jones, the author, magazine editor, and social commentator who coined the term "baby boomer," "By the time the average child of the baby boom reached the age of 18, he or she would have been under television's hypnotic influence an average of 4 hours a day for 16 years. The total of roughly 24,000 hours—one-quarter of a person's waking life—is more than children spent in classrooms or with their parents."[5]

Commercials began to make aggressive pitches for children's hearts and minds, giving new power to products like Ovaltine,

Wheaties, Wonder Bread, Frosted Flakes, Barbie, and M&M's. In 1950, just 3 percent of companies' media spending went to television. However, when they realized how effective a medium it was for influencing boomers and their parents, they responded quickly. By 1955, television was getting 80 percent of Madison Avenue's media budget.[6]

But television did far more than sell breakfast cereal: It shaped the consciousness of a new generation. For the first time, children could observe different lifestyles and hear different regional accents, from the southern drawl of Amos and Andy to the New York squawk of Jerry Lewis, without leaving home. Serving as a potent homogenizing medium, TV allowed children from all walks of life to share so many shows, characters, and historical moments.

NEW NEIGHBORHOODS, NEW SCHOOLS

While many parents of boomers were raised in the crowded confines of urban apartments or row houses, they envisioned a different environment for their children. By the early 1950s, hundreds of thousands of new homes were built, in some cases resulting in the creation of new communities, such as Long Island's Levittown—America's first "suburb." By the late 1950s, more than 45 million Americans would call suburbia home. Backyards and front lawns became as common to the American scene as tenements were a generation earlier.

Just like the hospitals a few years before, the public school system was totally unprepared for the boomers' arrival. There weren't enough school buildings, classrooms, playgrounds, or teachers, and there certainly weren't enough tax funds readily available to meet the onrushing demand. By the 1960s, class size ballooned and many schools were forced to go into multiple sessions, while the boards of education professed surprise at the situation—yet they'd had 13 years to see the boomers coming. As social and public planners belatedly realized that the boom posed a serious demographic challenge, the game of catch-up began in earnest.

Commenting on the unpreparedness of public institutions, social analyst and author Charles Morris reflected, "The boomers were forced to endure grossly overcrowded classrooms, double and triple school sessions, long bus rides to regional schools, and a host of other daily indignities. Spending on education rose very sharply in the 1950s and 1960s, of course, but it did not rise nearly fast enough to provide the individualized, activity-rich, educational programming that boomer parents hoped for."[7]

While public institutions' timing was way off, businesses once again pounced on the boomers' changing needs. As teenagers in middle-class households, boomers substantially fueled the surge in the economy. In 1963, American adolescents accounted for an estimated $22 billion in sales. They drank 55 percent of all soft drinks and consumed vast quantities of fast food, kicking proliferating franchise chains like McDonald's, Jack in the Box, and Kentucky Fried Chicken through year after year of 20 percent annual growth. The number of Kentucky Fried Chicken franchises increased from 400 in 1964 to more than nearly 3,000 in 1969. In his book *Great Expectations: America and the Baby Boom Generation,* Landon Jones provides a good example of how boomers and business intertwined:

Take blue jeans. The company founded in 1853 by a penniless Bavarian immigrant named Levi Strauss had been a modest success in its first century selling its model 501 Double X denim jeans to farmers and cowboys. Then, in the mid-1950s, James Dean wore jeans in *Rebel Without a Cause* and Marlon Brando wore them in *The Wild One* just as the first baby boomers were growing up. Suddenly, jeans were more than clothes: they were a symbol of a way of life that was anti-Establishment, anti-adult, anti-elitist, earthy, proletariat, democratic, and more than anything, youthful. That mystique made blue jeans the worldwide uniform of the baby boom generation. They were banned in American schoolrooms, bid up to extortionate prices in Paris, and smuggled behind the

Iron Curtain. But Levi Strauss had caught a wave. Between
1962 and 1970, its sales and net profits grew fivefold, and
between 1970 and 1977, its sales again quintupled while profits almost septupled. It became the largest clothing manufacturer in the world.[8]

Yet Jones offers a word of caution to companies targeting the
boomers, who forget that they were followed by a baby bust: "Every
marketer in the country should be required to inscribe in his or her
soul by law: Those Who Live by the Baby Boom Shall Die by the
Baby Boom."[9] In 1999, the Levi Strauss company, whose marketing
has continued to target youth, was forced to close 11 North American plants and lay off 40 percent of its employees—approximately
6,000 workers—in response to declining sales.

Teen boomers nearly reinvented the entertainment industry. In
1968 alone, the under-25 crowd bought 53 percent of all movie tickets
purchased and spent $1.2 billion on records, 43 percent of total sales.
Social commentator, author, and music fan Sidney Zion wrote a compelling article for *The New York Times Magazine* in which he reflected
on how the boomers' demographic mass not only boosted record sales,
but transformed the entire music industry to suit their tastes:

> Radio was in a panic in the early 1950s over the threat of
> television and began to zero in on the teen-agers with a hard
> sell that carried a hot message to kids: Rhythm and blues,
> rock-and-roll, is "your music."
>
> The timing, as it turned out, could not have been better.
> Kids had more money than ever before, the move to suburbia
> was in overdrive, and family life was in a major state of flux. If
> parents didn't like it, so much the better. As Mick Jagger said,
> "The whole rebellion in rock-and-roll was about not being
> able to make noise at night and not being able to play that
> rock-and-roll so loud and boogie-woogie and not being able to
> use the car and all that."

Nearly all of the major record companies resisted, leaving the field to the small, independent labels. By the late 1950s, the majors began to come around to "all that." . . . The older artists and their songs had largely disappeared from the record stores and the airwaves. It was a world for the children, by the children, and of the children. . . .

On Dec. 30, 1963, [Capitol Records] . . . released its first Beatles single, "I Want to Hold Your Hand," and sold a million copies in less than three weeks. Two months later, the Beatles came to New York amidst fabulous hoopla, appeared on *The Ed Sullivan Show*, and their career skyrocketed. . . . By April 1964, the Beatles had the five top singles and two top albums in the country. According to *The Book of Golden Discs*, the Beatles had 15 titles in the top 100 at one time in 1964, and "60 percent of all discs on the U.S.A. airwaves were by the Beatles—the most amazing avalanche in disc history.". . .

By the late 1960s, when "Never trust anybody over 30" became the slogan of a generation, the popular-music business had decided that nobody over 30 existed. Whether grassroots or hype, it was a revolution for certain. In its wake, the great pre-rock treasury of American song was left for dead.[10]

THE TIMES THEY WERE A-CHANGING

The assumption that the boomers would migrate through life's stages in exactly the same way as the smaller and more traditional generations before them proved to be way off base. Much more indulged, boomers were also more inclined to question the status quo and more willing to speak out and challenge authority than any previous generation. They believed themselves to be young, free, and in charge.

This youthful exuberance was tempered and twisted by the assassinations of John and Robert Kennedy and Martin Luther King. As the media exposed the boomers to the injustices of racial prejudice and the war in Vietnam, many blamed their parents' generation for prevailing social problems; hence the "generation gap," as the sociopolitical views of the young and the old diverged. Reflecting this unexpected zeitgeist, the corny yet popular cult movie *Wild in the Streets* showed the youth generation transforming all the laws of the land: With 30 the mandatory retirement age and 14 the minimum age for voting and holding public office, the young in *Wild in the Streets* took charge of everything and rendered their elders obsolete.

As part of their path toward fulfilling rising expectations, more boomers continued their education after high school than in any previous generation. When they entered college, their demographic heft was, once again, an almost unmanageable strain on the institutions they were passing through: The number of college students *tripled* between 1965 and 1975.

Alumni groups praised college administrators for the wonderful job they were doing in attracting students during these years. Yet, in reality, the growth had little to do with savvy marketing—it was simply a matter of this massive generation migrating from one stage of education to the next. Because of the huge demand, it was especially difficult for the average college applicant to get into the school of his or her choice, as seen by the substantially lowered rates of acceptance from the late 1960s through the 1980s. Whereas the acceptance rate at Stanford University had been a confidence-boosting 85 percent in 1952, the enormous increase in the number of applicants sent it plummeting to a frustrating 30 percent by 1972. After floundering for a few years, the higher education boom got going and 743 new colleges were opened in the 1970s to help absorb the glut of students."[11]

The creation of a $100 billion market for higher education wasn't the only effect of the boomers going off to school: After living their first 18 years under the control of straight-arrow parents, millions of hormonally and intellectually stimulated middle-class young men and women were getting their first taste of lifestyle freedom. Previous generations had had to limit their "acting out" to afternoons with rowdy friends or an evening in the backseat of a car on lovers' lane; for the boomers, the sky was the limit in their parent-free dorms and apartments. No matter how much James Dean's character in *Rebel Without a Cause* fretted over his parents not understanding him, he nevertheless went to bed every night in their home and ate breakfast across from his mom and dad. In comparison, life on campus in the late '60s and '70s was wildly free.

During the 1970s, as more boomers entered young adulthood, they found themselves grappling with the uncertainties of establishing their own personal values and a new, mature sense of identity, distinct from their parents'. Not surprisingly, issues of self discovery, self-esteem, and lifestyle experimentation became the compelling social and marketplace themes of that era.

Many boomers began to realize that what they couldn't change in the world, they could change in themselves. In response, introspective books such as *I'm OK, You're OK, How to Be Your Own Best Friend, Your Erroneous Zones,* and *What Color Is Your Parachute?* became mega-sellers. Self-improvement became a growth industry, as boomers sorted out the goals, philosophies, and skills of young adult life en masse. New business franchises such as EST, Lifespring, encounter groups, and Transcendental Meditation sprang up to help boomers make sense of their inner uncertainties.

TRADING LOVE BEADS FOR STOCK OPTIONS

When the first wave of boomers began buying cars of their own, the auto industry quickly shifted into high gear, producing new cars at a rate of growth twice that of the U.S. population. Not surprisingly, the housing market—like hospitals and schools before—was overwhelmed by boomer needs. This was good news for homeowners and homebuilders, as an unprecedented demand for a limited supply of homes raised the roof on housing prices.

By the 1980s, the "tune in, turn on, drop out" philosophies of earlier years had vanished. As is common in the third decade of life, boomers ratcheted up the economic ladder (albeit with some help from Visa, MasterCard, and American Express), and began to pursue increasingly materialistic goals. Just as the image of the "hippie" had come to stand for much of what made the '60s unique, the "yuppie," yet another version of the continually evolving, maturing boomer, came to stand for the '80s.

As the leading-edge boomers focused intensively on careers and families, publications such as *The Wall Street Journal, Esquire, GQ, Money, Forbes,* and *Fortune* entered periods of record growth, while sales of *Psychology Today, Rolling Stone,* and *New Age Journal* declined. Not surprisingly, books about business and financial success, such as *In Search of Excellence, Megatrends, Iacocca,* and *Swim with the Sharks Without Being Eaten Alive* climbed the best-seller charts.

As many boomers became parents, fantasies of singles parties were replaced by worries about childcare; *Saturday Night Fever* transitioned into *Parenthood* and *Kramer vs. Kramer.* New crises arose: There weren't enough daycare providers to meet the needs of this generation, and the onslaught of demands for more flexible hours and benefits from boomer parents—and especially working moms—took employers by surprise.

Is There Life After Youth?

During the '90s, millions of boomers began migrating into the early stages of maturity, their lives characterized by growing responsibilities as parents and increasingly powerful roles at work. In addition, as we will explore more deeply in Chapter 6, boomers faced the growing realization that they are likely to wind up as long-term caregivers to their parents.

FAMILY LIFE: FRONT AND CENTER

Today, three-quarters of the boomer generation are married (many for the second time), three-quarters have had children, and two-thirds are homeowners.[12] Naturally, family and home life are front and center with the prominence that hasn't been seen since the 1950s. As we might have expected from this rule-breaking generation, however, they are reconfiguring many of the traditional roles of marriage and parenthood. Currently, 75 percent say they believe that an equal marriage is preferable to the traditional model. According to a 1998 national survey, 84 percent of today's fathers say they spend more time with their kids than their fathers spent with them. Middle-aged boomers are more likely to share domestic chores as well. In 1949, only 40 percent of couples reported that husbands helped with cooking and 62 percent helped with housework; according to Gallup polls, those percentages had jumped to 73 and 85 percent by 1997.[13]

SEEKING WELLNESS AND LIFE BALANCE

Fully 85 percent of all baby boomers hold jobs—the highest percentage of any generation of Americans thus far.[14] Perhaps the single biggest change compared with earlier generations is the percentage of women who work outside the home. While these new roles and rules are in many ways liberating, they have also turned out to be confusing and often stress-producing. A typical boomer complaint is the feeling of being continually pushed and pulled by a myriad of conflicting responsibilities.

With tens of millions of moms and dads both working long, hard hours, causing stress-related mental and physical health problems to rise, some families are choosing new work/life arrangements. One company that stands out as a good match for such individuals is Melaleuca, Inc., a global manufacturer and direct-to-consumer marketer of wellness-oriented products. According to Founding President Frank VanderSloot, "We believe that Melaleuca is unique—both in its offering of superior natural products and in the company's commitment to advocating wellness in all its forms—physical, family, inner, social, intellectual and financial."

For thousands of Melaleuca's marketing executives, this philosophy is having a positive impact. Take Jeff and Holly LaChappell of California. Before beginning their new careers with Melaleuca, Jeff toiled 70 hours per week in his flower shop while Holly spent 60+ hours teaching her elementary school classes and preparing her lessons. According to Holly, they were working to exhaustion and their lives were totally out of balance. "I felt I was giving to 40 other children all day, then my own three children just got what was left over. And every time a holiday came around, Jeff was working extra long hours and had no quality time with our family."

Through the flexible work arrangement that Melaleuca offers, the LaChappells have completely reorganized their lives around physical, personal, family, and financial wellness. Holly now teaches school only three days per week and has renewed time for family, friends, fitness, and volunteering. Jeff works their Melaleuca business full-time but has made sure that he has plenty of time for fun with Holly and their kids and never misses holidays or important events like he used to. And they haven't sacrificed earning power with their new lifestyle. In fact, their income has vaulted to nearly $300,000 per year, and they have recently purchased their first home in California's Sierra Mountains.

Boomers like Jeff and Holly LaChappel are pioneering an important new trend—pursuing a wellness-oriented lifestyle *and* work-style and putting their lives back in balance in the process.

LIKE A PIG MOVING THROUGH A PYTHON

As we've seen, the boomers have dominated American culture for five decades. Every time they've taken a step, the spotlight of the media has swiveled to illuminate them. The massive numbers of their generation have amplified and intensified the importance of whatever experiences they've had at each new moment in their lives. Just as surely as they learned to use a baby bottle, they learned to read, to play records, to buy cars, to vote, to rent condos, and to invest in the stock market.

When they reach any stage of life, the issues that concern them—whether financial, interpersonal, or even hormonal—become the dominant social, political, and marketplace themes of the time. Boomers don't just populate existing lifestages or consumer trends, they *transform* them. According to Smith and Clurman in *Rocking the Ages*, "The most important thing to remember about boomers is that they are rule breakers. Individuality over conformity is a consistent boomer pattern. They always have done it differently than the way it was done before."[19] Some examples:

- Boomers didn't just eat food—they transformed the snack, restaurant, and supermarket industries.
- Boomers didn't just wear clothes—they transformed the fashion industry.
- Boomers didn't just buy cars—they transformed the auto industry.
- They didn't just date—they transformed sex roles and practices.
- They didn't just go to work—they transformed the workplace.
- They didn't just get married—they transformed relationships and the institution of the family.
- They didn't just borrow money—they transformed the debt market.
- They didn't just go to the doctor—they transformed healthcare.
- They didn't just use computers—they transformed technology.
- They didn't just invest in stocks—they transformed the investment marketplace.

Yet the boomers' demographic weight has not always made things easier for them. While the group's large size consistently *benefits* others who sell them products and services, it is a distinct *disadvantage* to individual boomers. Their vast numbers have created fierce competition for everything they've wanted throughout their lives: for school space as children, for team and club memberships as teenagers, for college entrance, for homes and good careers as young adults. At every stage, they've had to fight their way through the demographic bottleneck that their own numbers have caused. They may have received more attention as a *group* than any other, but as *individuals,* the odds of receiving satisfying benefits have always been—*and always will be*—against them.

The Emerging "Silver" Market

Inevitably, the steady aging of the boomers will continue to produce many demographically motivated revolutions in the consumer marketplace. As the boomers pass through their middle years and on to maturity, five key factors will reshape supply and demand:

1. Their concern about the onset of chronic disease and their desire to do whatever is possible to *postpone physical aging.*
2. *Increasing amounts of discretionary dollars* (for some—but not all) as a result of escalating earning power, inheritances, and return on investments.
3. Entry into *new adult lifestages* including empty-nesting, caregiving, grandparenthood, retirement, widowhood, and rehirement—each with its own challenges and opportunities.
4. A psychological shift from acquiring material possessions toward a *desire to purchase enjoyable and satisfying experiences.*
5. The continued *absence of "disposable time"* due to complex lifestyles.

A wide range of opportunities await companies and individuals who anticipate the emerging needs and interests of the new silver market. To prime the pump, consider the following 50 major areas of marketplace change and product/service/business ideas brought on by the swell of new 50+ consumers.

HEALTHCARE

- A new science of "human biomarkers" utilizing "genomics" that become the key indicators of an individual's health, immunologic fortitude, mental vitality, and potential for longevity.
- Specialty diagnosis and treatment centers for particular body parts, such as the eyes, ears, muscles, bones, or nervous system. Each center would have the capability of re-engineering any defects or problems within its area of specialty. The activities of these specialty centers would be orchestrated by an integrated human/computer Internet-based medical system.
- Cloned kidneys, livers, lungs, hearts, skin, blood, and bones for "tune-up" and replacement purposes.
- Body fabrication clinics where new tissue, organs, and muscles can be created and transplanted.
- Eldercare coordination firms that support older adults and their families as they navigate the services necessary to maintain health and independence at home.
- Adult daycare offering nonresidential care and support for elders while providing respite for their family members.
- Homecare nurses and aides (both human and robotic) who would assist individuals with chronic health problems to maintain their independence at home.

ANTI-AGING/HUMAN ENHANCEMENT

- Nutraceuticals—appetizing drinks, meals, snacks, and supplements engineered with macro- and micronutrients to fight aging and safely promote energy, relaxation, sexuality, mental alertness, endurance, recuperation, wellness, and other desirable physical and mental states.
- "Cosmeceutical" rejuvenation therapies for men and women made from pharmaceuticals, herbs, botanicals, minerals, and vitamins that will keep the skin and hair youthful longer.

- Customized youth-extending hormone therapeutics that will retard the aging process.
- Brain enhancement herbs, vitamins, drugs, acupuncture, visual stimulation, software downloads, and mind exercises to prevent dementia, promote better memory, and stimulate higher intelligence.
- Bio-implants that will continually monitor biomarkers and deliver anti-aging nutrients and hormones on an as-needed basis.
- Anti-aging spas that offer intensive revitalization programs, ranging from stress reduction, toxin purging, and metabolic adjustments to muscle toning and nervous system tune-ups.

TECHNOLOGY

- Inernet-based, personal "intelligent agents" that would build in-depth profiles of their elder "clients" in order to anticipate what they want, need, or like and make recommendations as to what to buy, when, and at what cost.
- Adult Furby-like androids that would be programmed to talk, remember and react to their owner's thoughts and concerns, even play bridge or discuss current events. They could take any shape—dog, robot, angel, butler—or could be "virtual" companions existing in the owner's PC or portable handheld computer.
- Microsensory maximizers to replace eyeglasses, and hearing aids that boost neurosensory functioning.
- At-home, biomarker diagnostics that would screen an individual's daily aging-related status and make nutrient, pharmaceutical, and exercise recommendations. The sensors and micro-laboratories could be situated within the bathroom toilet plumbing.
- High-tech exercise gear and equipment programmed to precisely "train" users to build stronger, healthier, and more

youthful bodies. These devices could also be used to expedite the rehabilitation of recovering stroke and trauma patients.

- Smart clothes that sense and adjust temperature in different body zones depending on the circulatory needs of the older wearer—particularly useful for diabetics and individuals with circulation problems.
- Smart acoustic systems in telephones, radios, and TVs that customize signals to accommodate the auditory range of each user's ears.

FINANCIAL SERVICES

- Long-term care insurance financing to provide security against the possibility of late-life chronic health problems, targeting both elders and middle-aged workers.
- Bill-paying services—human as well as Internet-based—for older adults who prefer to have these chores handled by a responsible professional.
- Longevity insurance that, rather than paying an individual's family in case of early death, provides financial support for people who live very long.
- Retirement planning and investment management services to help tens of millions of aging boomers prepare for late-life financial security.
- Investment insurance that people can purchase to provide additional security for their retirement funds.
- Estate management and trust services to help families manage the $10 trillion inheritance cascade that is about to occur, without sacrificing too much in taxes and family duress.
- Reverse mortgages to help older adults who find themselves cash-poor but "brick-rich" draw cash out of their homes.

WORK/LEISURE

- Silver Seals—"for-hire" teams of elders with various problem-solving talents who are deployed to "fix" difficult community or business issues. Unlike the Gray Panthers, whose focus was rebellion, the Seals' talent would be sorting out and remediating social problems.
- Elderhostel-style "lifelong learning" programs at colleges, universities, churches, and community centers and on cable TV and the Internet that include both vocational retraining for older adults and avocational instruction on the arts, music, cooking, public speaking, and so on.
- Retirement Zone stores and websites featuring products and technologies appealing to older adults with free time, including golf clubs, skis, musical instruments, computers, software, speedboats, and RV's.
- Adventure travel services that send older adults to off-the-beaten-trail locations via special programs for groups of singles, empty-nesters, and grandparents/their grandchildren.
- Apprenticeships whereby retirees master a new skill, craft, or field of knowledge by becoming private students of talented individuals.
- Mature employment and career transition coordinators who would assist maturing adults in career and lifestyle transitions by navigating through a network of job opportunities with minimum hassle.

LIFESTYLE SUPPORT

- Lifestyle managers who will take responsibility for a comprehensive range of time-consuming functions such as laundry, dry cleaning, lawn mowing, snow clearing, transportation shoe repair, shopping, and waiting in line for tickets.
- Autovideography production services that create documentary-like videoportraits of ordinary individuals,

telling the story of their long lives and capturing the essence of their views, philosophies, and lifestyles.

- Adult and elder-focused psychiatrists who will help people sort out their inner worlds toward the end of their lives.
- Experience agents—similar to travel agents—who can be commissioned to orchestrate any type of function a client requests, whether it's a party, learning program, psychotherapy, sabbatical, travel adventure, spiritual retreat, introduction to new friends, date, or business partnership. They could also help retirees find useful and satisfying hobbies, volunteer involvements, and housing options.
- Mature escorts and companions for older men and women who need or want a companion to accompany them to the movies, the doctor, or on a vacation.
- Transportation services to take older adults who are unable to drive to the doctor, the airport, the beauty salon, or the bank.
- Mature dating services to help the tens of millions of single mature women and men find new relationships.

HOUSING/TRANSPORTATION

- Re-engineered home elements that are ergonomically appropriate for older bodies—door levers instead of doorknobs; easy-open drawers, windows, and cabinets; slip-resistant flooring, stairs, and driveways.
- Smart home-security systems that will monitor all entry points as well as all internal activity for high-risk pattern changes, helping older residents feel less vulnerable in their homes.
- Smart windows for homes and cars that sense the amount of glare or low light levels based on the programmed requirements of each older resident or driver and continually adjust the tint of the glass to minimize distortion and maximize visibility.

- Home management services that deploy professionals to fix plumbing, replace a broken window, shingle the roof, or sweep the floor for older adults who are unable or unwilling to tackle these chores.
- Senior roommate finders to link older adults with housemates who meet their needs.
- New varieties of retirement housing catering to the needs and fancies of new mature adults: longevity communities for health-minded elders, intergenerational communes, high-tech complexes for "wired" older adults, Club Med residences for those who enjoy active social programming, urban arts retirement complexes that focus on cultural pursuits, university-based retirement communities for elders who desire lifelong learning, hedonism complexes for elder swingers, multinational time-shares for those who aren't interested in settling down in one location.

DEATH AND DYING

- Hospice-like caregivers specially trained to care for the dying and help them pass away with dignity and comfort.
- Custom cremation services to replace traditional burial plots, accommodating elder boomers' mobility and the absence of available land.
- High-tech funeral enterprises that will create a video-documentary of the deceased and build and maintain an Internet-based gravesite—complete with the deceased's photos and favorite poems, books, music, and television shows—so that future generations can "visit" the lives of their ancestors.
- Theme-oriented dying retreats, where people can select the mood and atmosphere they prefer for their final days. Spiritual, nostalgic, romantic, science fiction, or party-oriented themes can be arranged to support each individual's customized death experience.

The Baby Boom Was Born to Become an Age Wave

On January 1, 1996, the first baby boomer turned 50. By the second decade of the 21st century, boomers will evolve into the largest elderly generation in history. Once their oldest members start turning 65 in 2011, the numbers will skyrocket, from approximately 40 million to 70+ million by 2030. As they age, the look, meaning, experience, and purpose of maturity will be transformed.

It's obvious that in the commercial marketplace, known for quick innovation, boomer demands have consistently led to successful new product launches. In the public arena, which is all too often shackled by political expedience and near-term thinking, the evolution of the boomers has consistently led to delayed reactions and inadequate solutions.

Just as society's institutions have been grossly unprepared for the baby boom, the teen boom, and the yuppie boom, we have as yet done far too little to prepare for the coming elder boom. Ten million new nursing-home beds will not appear overnight. Teacher shortages were patched over in the 1950s by occasionally pressing bright high school graduates into service, but it takes far longer to produce a neurosurgeon or oncologist. And, of course, so many boomers making demands on retirement benefits could easily break the back of the Social Security Trust Fund in the early decades of the 21st century.

When the boomers were young, their economic demands on society were relatively small, and the contributions that government programs made to their lives were considered wise investments in the future. The better educated and better prepared they were, the more they'd be able to return during their working years. Now, in their peak earning and tax-paying years, boomers are putting in far more than they're taking out. Today's seniors often claim that the entitlements they're receiving are funded by the taxes they themselves paid in. As we will see in Chapter 7, this idea is vastly removed from reality. Instead, it is the record taxes that the large boomer generation is *currently* paying that are funding the robust social and financial security of our present-day elders.

When boomers become elders, however, their demands will be large and their political might daunting, yet the economic payback that society will derive from investing in them is questionable. To make matters worse, the younger generations behind them won't be nearly large enough to support their needs in old age.

In the 1950s, our society was caught off-guard and lacked the necessary services and institutions to meet the needs of the baby boom. The outcome was sometimes chaotic, but entirely fixable. Should we find ourselves off-guard and lacking in the necessary services and institutions to meet the needs of the coming elder boom, however, the outcome could be catastrophic.

The Five Social Train Wrecks We Need to Prevent

Although a few years remain before this age wave crashes upon society's shores, it is not too soon to begin considering strategies both to reap the benefits of maturity and to avert the catastrophes that it will create. Of all the possible obstacles and opportunities awaiting us, I believe that there are *five key aging-related train wrecks* toward which we are heading—all of which are preventable if we take corrective action now.

Train Wreck #1:
Using 65 as a marker of old age—and the onset of old-age entitlements—is meaningless, unfair, and even dangerous.

Forget 65. In preparation for Germany's first pension plan, Chancellor Otto von Bismarck selected 65 as the marker of old age in the 1880s. At that time, the average life expectancy was only 45. On the day that Social Security began, the average American lived 63 years and there were 40 workers per recipient. Today, life expectancy has risen to 76 and the dependency ratio is only 3.3 to 1, and declining steadily.

As a result of impending breakthroughs in life extension, nearly every intergenerational financing program, including Social Security and Medicare, will ultimately collapse if we continue to plan our lives according to this outdated number. Yet these programs could be made secure for decades to come, if we transition entitlements to align with reality.

If, however, the threshold of eligibility for "old-age" entitlement programs remains unchanged while life expectancy continues to rise, in a few decades our economy will be crushed by the weight of long-lived elder boomers' demands.

Train Wreck #2:
Without a dramatic shift in healthcare skills and priorities,
our society will face epidemics of chronic disease.

Currently, 47 percent of people over age 85—the world's fastest-growing demographic segment—suffer from some form of dementia. Alzheimer's ultimately destroys its victims' brains and exhausts loving family members along the way as they care for each ailing spouse or parent an average of 8 to 10 years. Unless a cure or treatment is found in our lifetimes, 14 million Americans will be stricken with dementia by the middle of the next century, and tens of millions of adult children will be shackled by the bills and countless hours of care.[20]

While we have eliminated many of the childhood diseases that took our ancestors' lives, our healthcare system is woefully inept at treating or preventing the health problems that arise in life's later years. In addition to Alzheimer's age-related chronic conditions such as arthritis, osteoporosis, diabetes, prostate and breast cancer, and heart disease have already reached pandemic proportions. If we continue to elevate life expectancy without fostering "healthy aging," too many of us will live on for decades riddled with decay and pain.

Train Wreck #3:
A caregiving crunch could become the social
and economic sinkhole of the 21ˢᵗ century.

Throughout the 1980s, childcare was one of the main issues of concern to working families. Just as the children of that generation are leaving the nest, however, a new concern is about to develop: eldercare. The average 21ˢᵗ-century American will actually spend *more years caring for parents than for children.* Already on any given day, an estimated 22 million American households are involved in eldercare, and within the next two decades the number is expected to double. These responsibilities will drain not just the savings of caregivers but precious years from their lives as well.[21]

Although today's business leaders and government policymakers avoid this issue, caring for elders and lovingly supporting them as they slowly die could become the social and economic "sinkhole" of the 21ˢᵗ century.

Train Wreck #4:
Tens of millions of boomers are heading
toward a poverty-stricken old age.

A perilously high percentage of boomers have accumulated high levels of debt; to make matters worse, they will not be the beneficiaries of mature discounts, demographically driven home equity growth, or entitlement boosts. At the same time, pensions are becoming less certain as employers replace guaranteed benefits with defined-contribution programs.

Even though some boomers are now preparing for financial security, many more are caught in a dangerous state of "financial paralysis" with no established pattern of saving, investing, or planning. From the average of 11.7 percent in the 1950s, the U.S. household savings rate dipped to 10.8 percent in the 1970s and has plummeted to 4.9 percent in the 1990s. Excluding pensions, the personal savings rate is 1 to 2 percent—compared to 25 percent in South Korea, 12 to 15 percent in Japan and 10 percent in Europe.[22] If tens of millions of boomers reach maturity with insufficient preparation, a new era of mass elder poverty will emerge, placing enormous burdens on the global economy and on the children forced to support them.

Train Wreck #5:
Without envisioning a new purpose for old age,
we are creating an "elder wasteland."

Although medical science has focused on how to prolong life, social scientists and community leaders haven't yet created a compelling vision for what tens of millions of long-lived men and women might *do* with those additional years. Currently, 40 million retirees spend an average of 43 hours a week watching television.[23] Decades from now, if elder boomers are takers rather than givers, "age wars" could erupt in which the young lash out in anger and frustration at the weighty demands placed on their increasingly strained resources. Ultimately, if the new old give little back to society and govern merely to enlarge their own interests and benefits, they will surely devastate the retirement programs, healthcare systems, economies, and, ultimately, the social order of the developed world.

To avert this catastrophe, a new, more productive role for life's later years—including social contribution, productivity and intergenerational leadership—needs to be established and integrated into all aspects of our culture. Otherwise, an elder wasteland will emerge in which more than 70 million couch-potato retirees drift through their mature years watching TV, surfing the Net, wandering through malls, and playing various games while siphoning off society's resources.

BACK TO THE FUTURE

In a twist on a popular science fiction story, a group of scientists belonging to a futuristic human civilization have created a powerful time machine. This timeship allows them to travel back through millennia to view the distant past. Before they close the door on their great ship and prepare for their maiden journey to prehistoric times, they take a loving look at their advanced civilization. As the engines fire up, however, there is one important caveat: When they land, they must keep to a very confined space around the ship. They must be careful not to touch or impact anything in the surrounding area in any way. The master chrono-scientists are concerned that any influence they might have on the distant past could reverberate back to the future.

After traveling backward more than 100 million years, they land in a wondrous world of dinosaurs and prehistoric plant life. They step out of the ship and conduct careful observations of their surroundings. As their brief visit nears its end, one of the scientists spots a particularly beautiful flower and steps toward it for a better view. While doing so, he inadvertently squashes a rainbow-colored butterfly resting on the ground. He looks around to make sure that none of his fellow time-travelers have noticed, and then returns to the timeship for the journey home.

They return safely to their present; a quick scan of the computer screen reveals that all seems well. When the door opens and the crew steps out, they're shocked to discover that their modern world is exactly the same as when they left it—but without *color* of any sort. By killing a rainbow butterfly in the past, the future has been transformed to a bleak and colorless one.[24]

Using a similar framework—that a small action can ripple forward to transform the future for better *or* worse—imagine that we are living about 25 years from now. Further imagine that all of our medical, social, and political institutions pertaining to aging and intergenerational dynamics have remained status quo. If that were the case, I am convinced that our future society would be filled with pandemic levels of chronic disease while our social and economic systems would have been devastated under the weight of the age wave. The U.S. would fall into an aging sinkhole, and much of the rest of the world would be sucked in with us.

The way to avert such a troubled future, of course, is to return to the present and begin to make the changes and corrections necessary to create a different and far superior future. After seeing how unpre-pared we've been for this "pig moving through the python," again and again for 50 years, can we muster the courage and longer-term vision to lay new foundations for a better tomorrow?

In the following chapters, I will explore all of the five key aging-related train wrecks I've described and offer solutions showing how they can be averted and transformed.

CHAPTER FOUR

THE CHANGING MARKERS OF AGING

In 1997, former President George Bush celebrated his 72nd birthday by commemorating his last parachute jump, when he'd escaped from a crippled airplane in World War II, by jumping again half a century later. U.S. Senator John Glenn, who in 1962 became the first American to orbit the earth, recently returned to space at 77 as a silver-haired "payload specialist." At 82, Lena Horne remains talented and beautiful, and 69-year-old Sean Connery is still considered one of the world's sexiest men.

Beverly Sills, 70, who became the first woman general director of the New York City Opera, is now its president. Rather than retire as Federal Reserve chairman, Alan Greenspan at 73 doesn't appear too old to oversee the nation's economy. Similarly, turning 81 has not slowed down *60 Minutes* correspondent Mike Wallace.

No one thinks of these individuals as the "believe it or not" miracle that Grandma Moses seemed just half a century ago when, in her seventies, she took up the art of painting. Today, Bush, Glenn, Horne, Connery, Sills, Greenspan, and Wallace are just a few of the most prominent examples in an emerging wave of healthy, productive elders.

When I first met my literary agent, he told me that he remembered attending his grandfather's funeral. Although he was just a young boy, he distinctly recalled people commenting that his grandfather, who'd died at the age of 62, had lived a long life and died an "old man." As fate would have it, his father died at the exact same age, 62. At this funeral, everyone lamented that his father had lived such a short life and died so young.

Old simply isn't what it used to be.

How Old Is Old?

Historically, social scientists have charted all of the stages of life to fit within the boundaries of a much shorter life span than we enjoy today. Until now, psychologists have defined the period of "youth"—including infancy, childhood, and adolescence—as running from birth to approximately age 18; then "young adulthood" occupies the years from 18 to 35. "Middle age" is considered to begin in the late thirties, ending around age 50. "Late adulthood" picks up from there and runs right into "old age," which is usually defined as starting at 65 and continuing until death.

Longer life spans are reshuffling this deck. Greater longevity doesn't mean that we'll charge through our lives as people always have, only to be *old* for additional decades. Instead, it means that we'll be *young* and *middle-aged* longer, and that we'll be getting *old* later. During this century, we have added 100 days of longevity for each year that has passed—approximately 2 days per week. Because of this success, it no longer makes sense to retain 65 as the gateway to old age—or old-age entitlements. My own studies at Age Wave indicate that due to the "liberated" lifespace that is being created by sliding old age back a decade or so, all of the earlier lifestages are extending as well.

A GENERATION OF PETER PANS

The delay and reconfiguration of traditional lifestages is nothing new to the youth-oriented boomer generation. As a group, they stayed in school longer than previous generations, put off the start of their careers, got married later, and waited longer to have children and buy homes. In *The Postponed Generation*, author Susan Littwin argues that one outgrowth of the social changes of the 1960s and '70s is that it now takes about 10 more years to "grow up." Twenty-five years ago, the Gallup organization asked the American public to define "young adulthood." Most respondents said it was ages 18 to 24. When the same question was asked 15 years later, the response was 18 to 40.[1] Some social observers have commented on this phenomenon as if it is a failure of character among boomers, rather than a change precipitated by both greater longevity and greater public acceptance of extended youth.

Just as the boomers have already redefined the start and end points of every lifestage they've experienced, they're about to delay and then extend the next stages of their lives. Of all the lifestages boomers have successfully postponed, those pertaining to maturity will likely be the ones they put off the longest. Moreover, as boomers barrel along the lifeline, they will actually carve out *new* lifestages in the process.

AT THE MIDPOINT OF LIFE

As they reluctantly migrate out of youth, boomers have already begun to engineer a new and vastly extended middle period of life: *middlescence.* If the idea of inserting a modified and expanded lifestage into the accepted pattern seems peculiar, consider that it has happened before: The lifestage we call "adolescence" didn't really emerge until just after the turn of the 20th century. It was established when teenage peer groups formed, usually in high school, giving rise to behaviors and mores characteristic of a new group of people who were no longer children but were not yet shouldering adult responsibilities.

This new group generally became known as "adolescents" when, in 1904, American psychologist and educator G. Stanley Hall published his massive, two-volume study, *Adolescence.* Hall proposed that just as geologic shifts can induce land masses to rise up, the pressures of modern industrial society were giving rise to a new stage of life. Prior to that time, a person was considered either a child or an adult; there was no in-between stage. Most cultures maintained some kind of ritual event, be it a week of hunting, a bar mitzvah, or even a wedding, to symbolize the abrupt transition from youth to adulthood. Hall felt that this new adolescence was, however, a very unpleasant stage of life, fraught with "emotional instability, antisocial conduct, and identity crises."[2]

Half a century later, in his seminal book *Childhood and Society*, psychologist Erik Erikson promoted another pre-adulthood stage, *young adulthood*. Observing the growth of formalized training programs and colleges in the 1940s, he anticipated that the mind-set and responsibilities of adulthood would likely be delayed a few more years. Into this new lifespace, young adulthood bloomed with its own styles, concerns, and social dynamics. Erikson believed that the key psychosocial challenges of young adulthood were the clarification of personal identity, which had begun in adolescence, and the development of the capacity for intimacy.[3]

Today, with the postponement of old age that is being caused by extended longevity, we are witnessing a new lifestage—*middlescence*—rising up between 40 and 60. Like adolescence, it is emerging because a sizable group is not quite ready for life's next stages—in this case, late adulthood and old age. Also like adolescence, this new middlescence will likely turn out to be a period of high-spirited growth and ascension, not retreat and decline.

Ernest Hemingway said, "Every young man believes he will live forever"—yet in middle age, mortality rears its head, as people experience the decline or deaths of parents or perhaps friends. Many middlescent men and women begin to see their lives in terms of "time left," rather than "time since birth." Once an individual realizes that he or she may have only 20 or 25 summers left, a sense of urgency emerges, posing difficult questions: "What's the point of it all?" "What have I accomplished?" "What can I do in the years I have left?" In these newly elongated middle years, according to Roger Gould, author of *Transformations*, "the desire for stability and continuity which characterized our thirties is replaced by a relentless inner demand for action. Whatever we must do, we must do now."[4]

These perceptions drive many to consider dramatic change: Should I start a new business, buy a new car, or change my lifestyle—before it is too late?

REDEFINING SUCCESS FROM THE INSIDE OUT

Many boomers assumed that their superior education would breed superior results in corporate and professional life. In fact, the number of top jobs in established venues has not grown to match their numbers. And because there are only so many executive positions to go around, middlescent boomers will soon accept that some of their youthful aspirations of being in charge and changing the world may be unattainable. Many will eventually decide to make dramatic career changes when faced with what seem like dead ends in their current jobs. Others will choose to remain at their lifelong careers but on more flexible terms than their early work life offered, and in response, companies will be forced to expand programs such as flextime, job sharing, and flexplace.

It's also likely that a new, scaled-down version of the American dream will evolve. In a recent national poll conducted by Roper/Age Wave, a representative sample of boomers asked to vote on the key elements of their own American dream surprised the pollsters by putting "power, influence, and wealth" at the bottom of the list. Their top priorities: "being true to myself, not selling out, and achieving inner satisfaction." In contrast to earlier generations who tended to define success from the *outside in*—title, status, power, and so on—middlescent boomers seem to be redefining success from the *inside out,* with a heightened emphasis on self-esteem, the quality of personal relationships, and personal freedom.[5]

A NEW SECOND HALF OF LIFE

In our youth-oriented society, many people reaching midlife still fear that they have arrived at the "beginning of the end"—that all of the best parts of life, all of the action, romance, and friendship, all of the adventure and growth, have already occurred within the first 35 years or so. This outdated view was captured on the October 1991 cover of *Life* magazine, an issue devoted to "The Journey of Our Lives." The cover line "Most Important Moments of Every Life-time" topped an oddly truncated list: "Birth, Adolescence, Marriage, Death."[6] Yet today's adults are experiencing quite a lot that's positive in life *beyond* marriage and *before* death.

In February 1999, a report by the MacArthur Foundation painted an extremely positive picture of life's new middle years, and should help to set the stage for a revised image of maturity as well. The 10-year study, "Successful Midlife Development," posed 1,200 questions to 8,000 Americans on nearly every facet of midlife, from whether they take vitamins to how often they attend religious services and how frequently they have sex. Researchers found that rather than being a time of despair and crisis, for most people the midlife years have become a time of self-confidence, good health, productivity, and satisfying community involvement.

In fact, the MacArthur study found that a relatively small percentage of men and women were encountering the once widely discussed "midlife crisis": Only 23 percent of the respondents reported having one. Of that group, only a third attributed their angst to aging-related issues. Instead, the study's subjects reported feeling 10 to 15 years younger than their actual age and were optimistic about "their health and the prospects for it in the future." Men and women in midlife also reported great satisfaction with their marriages and pride in their children; 72 percent of the spouses aged 35 to 64 described their marriages as "excellent" or "very good."

For women, the myth of the midlife crisis is often associated with the effects of menopause. One of the study's more intriguing findings was that more than half of all the women polled reported having no hot flashes and that the general distresses of menopause had been substantially overstated. Similar conclusions about the overdramatization of menopause are also being reached in Japan.[7]

In the new middlescent years, boomers are going to have the health, time, and self-awareness to rethink many of life's early choices. While their grandparents may have done some such ruminating when they passed 35 or 40, there's a critical difference between their generation and the boomers. When life expectancies were short, there was time only to regret and mourn the less-than-happy outcomes of earlier decisions. The new long-lived generations, however, will have the energy to plant new seeds and the time to harvest the new outcomes as well. In today's more longevous world, middlescent adults are realizing that another whole life remains before them.

According to Dr. Orville Gilbert Brim, director of the MacArthur Foundation Research Network, "On balance, the sense we all have is that midlife is the best place to be."[8]

Old Age Is a Moving Target

As noted earlier, our contemporary marker of old age—65—was selected over a century ago by Germany's Otto von Bismarck. In 1881, Bismarck shocked Europe when he proposed that the German parliament create the world's first retirement program. He asserted that German workers should be granted retirement pensions as well as other benefits, such as national health insurance. At a time when no other government provided these services, Bismarck argued that the state should give the poor "a helping hand in distress. . . . Not as alms, but as a right."[9]

Bismarck's proposal was not motivated by humanitarianism: He was afraid that the growing class of impoverished, underclass, urban workers would swing votes toward the Socialist Party. While admitting that a welfare state would be expensive, Bismarck was convinced that it would avert a revolution. After careful review, his government recommended 65 as the "modern" demarcation point of old age and retirement.

In the United States, when Franklin Roosevelt created Social Security in 1935, the average American could expect to live 63 years. Government actuaries understood that life expectancy had risen considerably since Bismarck's time, but 65 still seemed old and, with 40 workers per each 65+ retiree, they felt confident that there was plenty of room at the margin. However thoughtful New Deal planners were, they never anticipated the scientific and medical breakthroughs that have steadily lengthened life. In fact, so unmindful were politicians of rising life expectancy that they actually worried that the system would be overwhelmed with resources that could never be fully used. Senator Arthur Vandenberg of Michigan, an influential leader in 1937, said, "The reserves that finance the system could eventually be so big that they will inundate the federal government."[10]

Reflecting the lack of concern about increasing life expectancies, nearly every modernized nation in the world—including Australia, Austria, Belgium, Canada, Finland, Germany, Greece, Mexico, the Netherlands, Poland, Portugal, Spain, Sweden, Switzerland, and the United Kingdom—has followed Bismarck's lead and set 65 as the standard threshold of old age and eligibility for old-age entitlements. Several countries, among them France, Hungary, Japan, Korea, and Turkey, still use 60 as their old-age boundary.

THE DOUBLE-EDGED SWORD OF LONGEVITY

Two years ago I was invited to speak before 500 retirees at a conference in Cincinnati. They were an energetic and attractive group, so I asked them to tell me at what age they believed that people were becoming old today. By a show of hands, they indicated that they felt people don't really become old until around 75. So I said, "Do I understand you correctly? You believe that your generation is growing old more youthfully than older people have at any previous time in history?" And they gave themselves a huge round of applause in reaction. I then said, "So you believe that because of things like medical science and better self-care, you're getting old later than you imagined you would." This assertion was also met with resounding applause. Then I said, "So then, I guess you wouldn't mind not getting your old-age entitlements until you're 75?" They responded with stony silence.

I have repeated this exercise with more than 100,000 people since that day, and I always get exactly the same results—regardless of whether my audience is old, middle-aged, or young.

Just as was the case hundreds of years ago, there are still 60 seconds in each minute, seven days in each week, and 52 weeks in a year. Yet the point along the life span at which old age is encountered has retreated considerably—while the point at which eligibility for old-age entitlements begins has not.

We'll cover this issue further in Chapter 7, but it is worth noting one troubling phenomenon here: In recent years, many men and women have actually been retiring and receiving old-age entitlements *earlier* than 65. The National Commission on Retirement Policy noted that in 1965, 57 percent of Americans over age 55 were in the workforce. That figure today is only 38 percent, and more than 70 percent of Social Security recipients now opt for early-retirement benefits before they turn 65.

Yet as further breakthroughs occur in medicine, nutrition, pharmacology, biotechnology, and fitness, old age will continue to be postponed. As a result, if current early-retirement trends continue, millions of people are slated to receive old-age entitlements at—relatively speaking—earlier and earlier ages, at the expense of younger tax-paying generations. The problems caused by this increasingly premature distribution of "old-age" benefits are destined to grow in the years ahead.

And so, the elevation of life expectancy is a double-edged sword. On the one hand, boomers will live much longer than previous generations and enjoy new lifestages. On the other, they're going to have to accept the idea that they should be receiving their benefits 5 to 10 years later than today's elders. Unless you reset your retirement plans to include several extra years of work, the odds are you will come up very short in the final decades of your life.

Let's turn now to a variety of solutions to these and other problems created by the extension of youth, the appearance of middlescence, and the postponement of old age.

Adjusting to the Changing Markers of Aging

The conflicts that will arise when yesterday's markers of aging meet tomorrow's life spans are brand new to the world. As such, they will require new solutions. Some of these have already emerged and are working their bugs out; others have yet to be created. In considering the new markers of aging, we must:

1. Unhinge old age from the obsolete marker of 65 and index entitlements to rising longevity.
2. Let people choose to retire when they are ready and when they can afford to, instead of holding everyone to uniform standards.
3. Smash the "silver ceiling" and make it easier for people to pursue meaningful employment in maturity.
4. Replace the "linear" life paradigm with a new "cyclic" one that takes maturity into account as a time of new life pursuits and passions.

Solution #1:
Unhinge Old Age from the Obsolete Marker of 65 and Index Entitlements to Rising Longevity

Programs like Social Security and Medicare were established as old-age entitlements, not middle-age ones. Sixty-five must be eliminated as the marker of old age and the onset of entitlements. We can no longer afford it, and it's dangerously out of touch with reality. If tomorrow's mature men and women will be getting "old" 5, 10, or even 15 years later than people used to, why are we planning on raising the eligibility for old-age entitlements only two years to 67 by the year 2027? Considering the longevity revolution that is occurring, this shift will be far too little, far too late.

While politicians are characterizing this challenge as an *economic* one—with the solution being for workers to contribute an even greater portion of their compensation toward taxes—the problem is really a *demographic* one, driven by shifts in life expectancy, and should be solved with a demographic adjustment. However, our policy leaders would prefer to push this issue way into the future and address it only modestly, letting future politicians and elder boomers take the heat for the intense catching up that will inevitably be required later on.

I can tell you who we'll damage with this denial and avoidance: Ourselves, our children, and their children.

Part of the problem is that today's seniors are terrified that entitlement cuts will leave them out in the cold. Gray lobbying organizations like AARP are so worried that today's elders will be negatively impacted that they're obscuring the key elements of this issue. I can't say that I entirely blame them: I'd be worried too if I were already 68 and living on a fixed income. Of course, a fair transition program would be necessary with any raising of the entitlement age so that today's elders won't bear the brunt. With continually elevating life expectancies and the migration of the boomers into maturity, however, we ultimately *must* recast old age and its entitlements. The longer we wait, the less time we'll have to cope.

In fact, if old age is going to become a steadily moving target, we may have to *continually* reset old-age markers in the years ahead. Most sensible would be to determine at what relative percentage point along the lifeline old age should be *indexed*. For example, when the average life expectancy was 72, perhaps the right retirement age should have been 65, which turns out to be 90 percent of 72. With this model, we might assume that it's reasonable and fair for subsidized retirement to constitute 10 percent of a life span (of course, we could decide instead that it should be 7 percent, 12 percent, or whatever other percentage makes social and economic sense). According to this model, when the average life expectancy at birth rose to 75, the retirement age should have shifted to 67.5 (90 percent of 75). Similarly, if we are fortunate enough to have the average life expectancy at birth rise to 80, the age of eligibility for old-age entitlements would rise to 72.

Nearly every intergenerational financing program, including Social Security and Medicare, could be made secure for decades to come if we *indexed* old-age entitlements to align with the real beginning of old age. If we transitioned eligibility for Medicare benefits to 70 instead of 65, for example, we would save approximately $600 billion over the next 10 years—an enormous windfall that could be used to fund critical research into aging-related diseases, provide healthcare to uninsured children, or support other such initiatives.

Can the markers of aging be changed? It's already been done with nearly every other stage of life, from adolescence to middlescence. Can countries successfully raise the age of eligibility for old-age entitlements? They are already doing so.

When Japan enacted a major reduction in future pension benefits in 1986, the Ministry of Health and Welfare evaluated the current and future needs of citizens of varying age groups and issued a concise justification that called for "equity between the generations." Japan's average life expectancy had risen from 61.27 in 1950 to 78.9 in 1986. At the same time, the average Japanese fertility rate dropped from 3.65 in 1950 to a below-replacement level 1.54 in 1986.[12] Japan's former prime minister, Ryutaro Hashimoto, noted that these changes in life expectancy and fertility required an immediate increase in the outdated eligibility age of 55 for old-age benefits. Stressing the importance of this change, Hashimoto offered a speech on "equity between the generations" on his very first day in office. Few objections were voiced from either the public or policymakers as his proposal to raise the retirement age to 60 was swiftly adopted.

Several years ago, I was invited to Tokyo to attend a brainstorming session with members of the Japanese government on their national policy toward old-age pensions and entitlements. Their longevity is one of the highest and the fastest-rising in the world—77.19 for men and 83.82 for women—and the fertility rate has sunk to 1.43. As a result, they have correctly concluded that even 60 has become obsolete as a marker of old age and are considering changing the pension age again, from 60 to 65. Some members of government even advocate moving it to 70. Although this readjustment has not yet occurred, the Japanese have concluded that, regardless of previous commitments, greater longevity and changing dependency ratios between the generations warrant continued upward shifts in the age of entitlement.

Japan is not alone in these considerations. Denmark, Iceland, and Norway have already elevated their entitlement ages to 67, and France, Sweden, Italy, and the United Kingdom are considering increases in their retirement age. Although some of these shifts have provoked strong debate, the disagreement has almost always been over how best to allocate public resources, rather than whether the government has the right to alter the age of entitlement based on current and future demographic and economic factors.

Solution #2:
Let People Choose to Retire When They Are Ready and Can Afford to, Instead of Holding Everyone to Uniform Standards

Prior to this century, retirement didn't exist. In general, it had always been believed that there was great value in the continued contribution of the community's elders, and they were relied on for their wisdom and insight. The average person tended to keep right on working until he or she passed away.

Compared to the turn of the 20th century, when nearly 90 percent of older men who were capable of working continued to do so, less than 20 percent of elderly men work today. Retirement has been promoted as such a desirable goal in maturity that fully 70 percent of working-age Americans believe that a comfortable retirement is a fundamental part of the American dream.

Even though life expectancy is getting higher and higher, during the past decade workers have been retiring younger and younger. The Social Security system and outmoded employer practices collude to give employees an incentive to retire before their 65th birthdays. More than 50 percent of newly retired workers currently receive benefits at age 62, and more than two-thirds retire before age 65. By retiring at 62, a worker can collect monthly benefits equal to 80 percent of what he or she would have received by waiting until 65. While 62 percent of U.S. corporations currently offer early retirement plans, only 4 percent offer inducements for older workers to extend their working years.[13] With deals like these, most people have come to think of early retirement as the sensible way to go.

This approach makes no sense for the future. Let's not lose sight of the fact that retirement is a relatively new and "experimental" lifestage that was initially envisioned to last 3 to 5 years, not 20. Assuming that life expectancy continues to rise, only a tiny fraction of aging boomers will have the *means* to retire as young as their parents did. And in the years ahead, many men and women will continue working longer because they'd prefer to spend these years productively engaged. When the National Institute on Aging recently conducted a health and retirement survey, three-fourths of workers aged 51 to 61 said they would like to continue working beyond the traditional retirement age.[14]

In addition to simply shifting the boundary of retirement back a few years, another idea worthy of serious consideration is "phased retirement." Long practiced in Europe, phased retirement is the gradual tapering off of working hours and responsibilities, building to a final break from the company.

A variation on phased retirement is the so-called "boomerang job," in which an employee retires for a few months or even a few years, then bounces back to the company—usually with limited hours and lighter responsibilities. For example, Monsanto's Retiree Resource Corps was launched in 1991 with 60 retirees at the company's St. Louis headquarters. It has now grown to 800 people in a wide range of positions at 24 locations. Participants have no set schedule but are called as needed, with a central database tracking their skills and hours.

Monsanto figures boomerangers cost 12 to 15 percent less than temp workers because of the savings on training costs and agency fees. "They know what needs to be done," says the program's founding director, John Brugger. Since they receive only the regular pension and health insurance coverage they are entitled to anyway as retirees, there are no added benefits costs.[15]

Since each person ages and migrates through maturity at his or her own pace, what if we abandoned a "fixed marker" of old age altogether? One of the earliest modern proponents of the elimination of a fixed retirement age was Claude Pepper, the former congressman, who argued, "Age-based retirement arbitrarily severs productive persons from their livelihood, squanders their talents, scars their health, strains an already overburdened Social Security system, and drives many elderly people into poverty and despair. Ageism is as odious as racism and sexism."[16]

The flourishing pension system in Chile, which I will examine in greater detail in Chapter 7, is a fascinating experiment in unhinging retirement from a specific age. When he became Chile's minister of labor and social security in 1978 at the age of 30, Harvard-educated José Piñera was eager to construct a new model of work and retirement in which "every worker can determine his desired pension and retirement age in the same way one can order a tailor-made suit."

In Chile, there is no particular emphasis on age 65. Each individual can decide at what age to retire and how much his or her pension will be, based on how much the person has contributed—and accumulated—over the years. According to Piñera, "As should be expected, individual preferences about old age differ as much as any other preferences. Some people want to work forever; others cannot wait to cease working so as to indulge in their true vocations or hobbies, like writing or fishing. The old pay-as-you-go system did not permit the satisfaction of such preferences."[17]

Some enterprising seniors, such as 75-year-old Vera Pember, have decided not to wait for the government or the Fortune 500 to break free of their ageist practices. In the spring of 1991, after her husband had passed away, Vera found herself worrying about how she would possibly live out her remaining years with a sense of self-respect and financial security. Certainly not on the modest $300 per month that she was receiving from Social Security.

As fate would have it, one of Vera's sons, Merrill, had recently become involved as a part-time marketing executive with Melaleuca Inc., the wellness-oriented consumer products company. When Vera observed how much Merrill liked his new work and how much additional money he was beginning to earn, she thought, "I like the products and I like the people . . . maybe I could do this too." And so, instead of letting her age slow her down, or ratcheting down her expectations in order to make do with her monthly government checks, Vera got to work.

Now at the age of 85, not only is Vera having fun and inspiring others, but she's also become quite the financial success story. She's currently earning more than $70,000 per year as a part-time Melaleuca marketing executive. In 1994, Vera bought a new dream home and, although the local bank provided her with a 30-year loan, Vera recently opted to pay off the entire mortgage. "I was really thrilled that I could actually afford to make one payment and pay it all off! I love this wonderful new home, and it feels really great to know it's mine." Now instead of paying her mortgage, Vera plans to double what she donates to children's charities.

Vera points out that part of her motivation can be attributed to the fact that Melaleuca actively encourages its marketing executives to manage their finances wisely and get out of debt. In fact, the Melaleuca management team even travels to the homes of marketing executives who have recently paid off their mortgages to celebrate with them in a mortgage burning ceremony.

During the company's recent annual convention, Melaleuca President Frank VanderSloot invited Vera and her family to the stage for a special mortgage burning ceremony. As her mortgage papers were reduced to ashes, the crowd of more than 5,000 attendees rose to their feet to provide a standing ovation in tribute to an 85-year-old woman's journey from financial dependency to personal financial freedom.

Solution #3:
Smash the "Silver Ceiling" and Make It Easier for People to Pursue Meaningful Employment in Maturity

Another outcome of extended longevity will be that aging boomers will find themselves working longer than their parents. Yet they may also find that as older workers, they are discriminated against—and they won't like it.

Two industries that shape many of our popular views about life are entertainment and advertising; two of the most neurotically *ageist* sectors of our society. In the television industry, for example, writers past the age of 50 are routinely shut out of prime-time shows because network executives in their thirties believe they're out of touch. According to Larry Gelbart, the 71-year-old creator of the *M*A*S*H* television series, "I know writers who have taken *M*A*S*H* off their resumes because it makes them too old. . . . Like there were 'Red Channels' in the '50s, now there are gray channels."[18] In the 1950s, blacklisted writers sometimes submitted scripts under their friends' names. These days, some older writers team up with younger colleagues just to get a chance to pitch show ideas to the networks.

Sixty-eight-year-old writer Saul Turteltaub rebels against this prejudice: "I wrote for *Sanford and Son,* and I wasn't black, I wrote for Shari Lewis, and I wasn't a puppet," he says. "You don't have to be the age, sex, race of the thing you're writing about. You have to be a talented writer."[19] And Goldie Hawn, who among other roles played youth-obsessed characters in both *Death Becomes Her* and *The First Wives Club,* voices frustration over the fact that there is so limited a range of potent roles for aging actresses: "There are only three ages in Hollywood—Babe, District Attorney, and Driving Miss Daisy."[20]

Madison Avenue image-shapers are caught in a similar youth trance. Several years ago, High Yield Marketing of St. Paul, Minnesota, conducted a study on ageism in advertising. It found that while 50+ households control more than 70 percent of the total U.S. consumer net worth, most "advertising agency professionals are most comfortable advertising to younger consumers like themselves."[21]

This bias is strikingly reflected in the fact that although less than one-fifth of 1 percent of all employed Americans work in advertising, age-discrimination lawsuits from this industry comprise about 20 percent of the claims filed with the Equal Employment Opportunity Commission. Ad industry guru Jerry Della Femina calls ageist attitudes in his industry a "dirty big secret." According to Della Femina, "I've told people, 'Dye your hair; get contact lenses. If shooting collagen in your face before an important meeting keeps you from having lines in your face, shoot collagen.'"[22]

AGE DISCRIMINATION: ILLEGAL YET PERVASIVE

Some progress has been made toward eliminating practices and policies that discriminate based on age. The landmark Age Discrimination in Employment Act (ADEA) of 1967 prohibits age discrimination in hiring, firing, and compensation of persons over 40. Initially, the coverage of ADEA ended at age 65. In 1978, it was extended to 70, then in 1986 the upper limit was removed altogether, virtually eliminating mandatory retirement in all but a few select professions.

Nevertheless, age discrimination continues to flourish in almost every workplace in the country. More than 15,000 claims of age discrimination have been filed in the past five years—a number that is expected to multiply by the year 2005, when half of all U.S. workers will be over 40 years of age. Although most complaints are from older individuals who believe they are terminated unfairly, the problem is just as significant when it comes to the discrimination that older adults encounter when they're seeking employment.

According to Exec-U-Net, a Connecticut-based executive job information organization, unemployed older adults have a very difficult time finding new employment. Exec-U-Net's research found that it takes 18 percent longer for a 41- to 45-year-old executive to secure a job, compared to a 35- to 40-year-old. For someone 46 to 50 it takes 24 percent longer, 44 percent longer for a 51- to 55-year-old job seeker, and 66 percent longer for those aged 56 to 60. According to Exec-U-Net, it can take nine months to a year for an older worker to find a new management-level job.[23]

In a recent study, AARP dispatched pairs of individuals with equal credentials to apply for 102 entry-level sales or management positions. One member of each pair was 32 and the other was 57. Even though their skills and abilities were equivalent, the younger applicants received more favorable responses in 41 percent of the situations. Three-quarters of the rejections occurred before the older applicants were even granted an interview.[24]

There are three strong reasons to smash this silver ceiling and promote elder employment. First, due to the baby bust in the 1960s and 1970s, we are currently experiencing a shortage of skilled workers. As noted by Secretary of Labor Alexis M. Herman: "At a time of notable skills shortages, older workers are a resource that America cannot afford to squander. . . . Global competition and job growth will put pressure on us to fully utilize our experienced older workers in the 21st century. They have too much to offer American business."[25]

Second, people are much healthier in their fifties, sixties, and even seventies than ever before, and there are more nonstrenuous jobs from which to choose. In the Information Age, youthful strength is far less important than a worker's knowledge, dedication, and experience—qualities that strengthen with maturity. The Commonwealth Fund, a New York–based philanthropic group, recently sponsored research to determine whether worker performance declines with age. While productivity did fall off slightly when manual labor was involved, researchers found no correlation between age and work quality among supervisors and professionals.[26]

Dr. Eileen Crimmins of the University of Southern California has been analyzing data from a representative sample of about 12,000 older Americans for the past 15 years. Participants in the ongoing study are asked a variety of questions designed to probe their ability to work. She has found that "fewer and fewer people said their ability to work was impaired. For example, in 1982 about 27 percent of men aged 67 to 69 said they were unable to work. But in 1992, just 20 percent of men in that age group could not work." Dr. Crimmins noted that the declines in work-related disability she observed applied equally to all races and economic classes.[27]

Third, the proportion of people's lives that is spent working has plummeted over the centuries and the balance may need to be adjusted. A typical male born in the United States or Europe 150 years ago, with a life expectancy of just over 40 years, would have started work in his early teens and would, in all likelihood, have worked around 60 hours per week for all but one or two weeks of the year. If we assume that he slept 8 hours per night, he would have spent approximately 40 percent of his waking life working. A boy born 100 years later could expect to start working at around 17, live approximately 64 years, and work around 50 hours per week. Some 30 percent of his waking life would have been spent at work.

Today, the average young man doesn't start working until his 20th birthday, can expect to live 75 years, and retires around 61. In addition, the average workweek has dropped to 40 hours and the number of weeks off annually has grown to six. The result: Today's men are spending a mere 16 percent of their waking lives working.

If the average individual worked the equivalent of five more years, either through full- or part-time employment, it would add only two or three percentage points to this equation—hardly enough to ruin a person's life—yet it would dramatically improve every aspect of our intergenerational economics.

About 25 percent of today's retirees say they plan on going back to work, and I anticipate that many boomers will extend their work lives—either because they'd like to or because they'll need to. A recent poll of 2,000 baby boomers conducted for the AARP by Roper Starch Worldwide found that 80 percent of 33- to 52-year-olds expect they will continue to work during retirement. Of these, 35 percent say they plan to work part-time for pleasure, while 23 percent say they'll do so mostly for money. Only 16 percent don't plan to work at all.[28]

IT WILL BECOME "IN" TO WORK IN MATURITY AND "OUT" TO RETIRE

Psychologist and adult development expert Erik Erikson argued that retirement was not necessarily a positive experience and that older workers should be encouraged to stay involved as long as they wished. During my career I have met many retirees who are perfectly satisfied to live their lives completely removed from the world of work, but I have met just as many who find retirement boring and unchallenging. However, among those who wish they were still employed, nearly all are seeking the stimulation and social interaction that accompanies work, not the stress and pressure.

Of those workers currently in their forties and fifties who intend to keep working after 65, most comment that they would prefer to secure part-time employment that's less stressful than the jobs they had during their normal worklife. In their book *Successful Aging,* Drs. John Rowe and Robert Kahn highlighted the fact that while many older workers would prefer greater flexibility in work content and a healthier balance between work and leisure, the overwhelming majority of employers will not accommodate them.[29] In the years ahead, employers will be increasingly pressured to come up with more flexible approaches for a growing class of older workers.

A good example of a company that has learned the value of

employing older workers is the Vita Needle Company, based in Needham, Massachusetts. The sign on the factory door states: "Help wanted. Light machine operators. Part-time. Employees set own hours/days. Predominantly senior citizens. NO retirement age."

Why does Vita Needle hire seniors? In the 1980s, the company was pressured to expand its line of medical products due to the spread of AIDS. Initially it began recruiting older workers because they were reliable and inexpensive. In addition, management appreciated that 65+ workers were very careful and tended to have half as many work-related accidents as younger workers. Management also came to regard them as harder-working, more loyal, and less prone to personal problems than many younger workers. Vita Needle's annual sales have grown by 20 percent every year for the past five years. Average age of Vita Needle employees: 73.

Similarly, Travelers Insurance has taken a leadership role in using older workers by creating a job bank of temporary employees from a pool of retirees. The higher productivity of these workers has saved Travelers $1.5 million a year. General Electric has discovered that it is more economical to retrain veteran engineers in emerging technologies than to hire new ones. The Boeing Corporation regularly brings back capable retirees to help with new aircraft production. Likewise, Bonne Bell, the cosmetics manufacturer in Westlake, Ohio, created a "Seniorsonly" production group—the brainchild of chairman and CEO Jess A. Bell, himself 74.

This trend toward *rehirement*, not retirement, will accelerate as more aging trendsetters such as Jimmy Carter, Warren Buffett, Lee Iacocca, Beverly Sills, Barbara Walters, John Glenn, Sean Connery, and Helen Thomas make it "in" to remain productive in maturity.

Solution #4:
Replace the "Linear" Life Paradigm
with a New "Cyclic" One

When people lived an average of 50 or 60 years, life was "linear"—you grew up, went to school, worked hard while marrying and rearing a family, then died. Everything had its place and life was too short for second chances.

Increased longevity totally transforms this paradigm. All around us, the traditional "linear life plan" is being replaced by a more flexible *"cyclic life plan."* We will cycle in and out of several different careers throughout adulthood, each interspersed with periods of rest, retraining, and personal reflection. In addition, rather than saving all of our leisure and retirement for the end of our lives, regular breaks throughout adulthood for *re-creation* will become commonplace.

LIFELONG LEARNING

If we're going to be working more years than previous generations, we'll also be returning to school again and again. In the past, education was geared to preparing the young for their lifetime careers. Yet the speed of technological innovation guarantees that you can't be alive for eight or nine decades without needing to retrain multiple times throughout your worklife. A recent National Research Council study asserted that a worker's "occupational half life"—the span of time it takes for half of a worker's skills to become obsolete—has declined from 7 to 14 years to 3 to 5 years. And it is anticipated that the average worker will hold seven jobs during his or her working life.[30]

Because of these factors, a thriving adult education industry has begun to grow exponentially, including magazines, books, audio, video, Internet-based learning programs, and adult-education seminars, workshops, and courses. Currently about 40 million adults participate in one or more educational activities each year.[31] As the need to continuously upgrade skills becomes a requirement, lifelong learning will become commonplace.

A quiet revolution has occurred in higher-education enrollments—the escalation of the "non-traditional student," a euphemism educators now use to label older students. The percentage of 35+ students was just 5.5 percent of total higher-education enrollment in 1970; today 22 percent of all college students in the U.S. are now aged 35 and older.[33] Whether the vehicle is a formal program of study at a college or university, employer-provided training, or distance learning through correspondence programs and the Internet, adults of all ages are returning to school as never before.

In response, colleges and universities across the nation have begun to aggressively pursue adult students. As recounted in *USA Today*, "Admission officers and financial-aid directors from campuses across the USA echo the message: Older students are as desirable—often more so—than the traditional 18-to-24 college crowd. And they're just as eligible for grants and loans as their younger brethren. Adults, they say, are better motivated, usually have educational goals in focus, and have experiences to share with younger students."[32]

To further accommodate this trend, the majority of the nation's higher education institutions are now awarding credit for life experiences acquired in noncollegiate settings. In lieu of SAT scores and high school transcripts, many returning students are now asked instead to provide a personal portfolio, including a presentation of work-related experiences and skills. The American College Testing Association has recently developed a formal evaluation-of-life experience test that schools are using to award dozens of credits for useful experiences.

RECREATION BREAKS ALONG THE WAY

If we're going to be working longer and getting retrained again and again, we're probably going to want to take time off along the way to renew and refresh ourselves. With extended work lives, most people won't want to wait until they're 65 or 70 to get a break from the attendant stress and pressure. As a result, formal *sabbaticals* and informal work-leaves should become increasingly popular. The notion of the sabbatical is borrowed from the Mosaic method of agriculture, whereby fields are left fallow every seventh year to ensure soil revitalization. This approach has been extended from agriculture to the university and is just beginning to catch on in corporate settings.

Some employers are recognizing that marathon hours and the frenzied pace of change quickly produces burned-out employees, and it makes good sense to allow them to recharge their batteries without losing them altogether.

Currently only 10 percent of all U.S. companies offer paid sabbaticals and 20 percent allow unpaid work-leaves as part of their perquisite packages, the average length being five weeks after five years of service.[34] Sabbatical beneficiaries report that the time off was incredibly valuable and rewarding, permitting them to spend quality time with their families, take an extended vacation, or pursue a learning program. In response to the initial positive results, increasing numbers of employers are beginning to see that sabbaticals could be important core employment benefits rather than superfluous perks.

The New Old

We are growing old younger and later than ever before. All around us we see vibrant examples of a "new" style of aging. This long-sought-after revolution is welcome relief to the tens of millions of maturing men and women who dread each passing birthday because of their fear of being considered "old." In the years ahead, advances in science and lifestyle management will push the onset of old age even further down the lifeline. The luxury of being able to choose how we arrange our various life tasks and pursuits, long the prerogative of the upper class, will become more commonplace. Unhinged from the negative expectations of the linear life plan, we will be more free than any previous generation to grow more expansive as we grow older.

In contrast to the 20th century, when most of the interesting innovations in human lifestages occurred within the youthful periods, the expanded middlescent lifestage and the new years of vital maturity will provide new opportunities for comebacks, late blooming, and second chances. In the 21st century, adulthood will explode with lifestyle experimentation and personal transformation.

Tips for Age-Proofing Your Life

- Plan to live a very long life—80 or 90 years—and take steps now to guarantee the intellectual and social stimulation you'll want in your later years.
- Don't get trapped in yesterday's "linear" model of aging: Adjust your psychological, social, and financial expectations to support a "cyclic" life plan.
- Envision new career goals and challenges. Intellectual flexibility and the ability to learn new skills and technologies will be key assets in a more longevous era.
- Be prepared to reinvent yourself several times in adulthood— you may discover aspects of your potential you never knew existed.

CHAPTER FIVE

TITHONUS' REVENGE OR HEALTHY AGING?

In an ancient Greek fable, Eos, the beautiful goddess of the dawn, falls deeply in love with the warrior Tithonus. Distraught over his mortality, she goes to Zeus's chamber to request a special favor: She wants to love Tithonus until the end of time and begs Zeus to grant her lover immortality. "Are you certain that is what you want for him?" Zeus challenges. "Yes," Eos responds.

As Eos leaves Zeus's chamber, she realizes in shock that she forgot to ask that Tithonus also remain eternally young and healthy. With each passing year, she looks on with horror as he grows older and sicker. His skin withers and becomes cancerous. His organs rot, and his brain grows feeble. As the decades pass, Tithonus' aging body becomes increasingly frail, yet he cannot die. Ultimately, the once-proud warrior is reduced to a collection of pained, foul, and broken bones,—but he continues to live forever.

Tithonus' story is a fitting allegory for what is occurring in our healthcare system today. Until recently, most people died relatively young of infectious diseases, accidents, or in childbirth. During the past century, however, healthcare breakthroughs have eliminated many of those threats. Smallpox and cholera are almost nonexistent. The death rate from tuberculosis, one of the leading causes of premature death a century ago, has been reduced by more than 99 percent. Measles and streptococcal infections have been transformed from killers into childhood annoyances. Pneumonia and influenza are no longer fatal by themselves. Whooping cough and syphilis, once major epidemic diseases, now kill fewer than 1 in 200,000 people. Typhoid and diphtheria no longer kill Americans at all.[1]

111

At the beginning of the 20th century, the overwhelming majority of deaths were due to infectious diseases; by the end, these caused fewer than 4 percent. As a result of these advances, we are creating— for the first time in history—a mass population of long-lived men and women. But what kind of long life have we created?

Although we've managed to prolong life, we have done far too little to promote *healthy* aging. One century ago, the average adult spent only 1 percent of his or her life in a morbid or ill state; today's average adult will spend more than 10 percent of his or her life sick. While in this century we have added 29 years to the average life expectancy, for many older adults the later years are a time of illness, pain, disability, and suffering.

HEALTH AND LONGEVITY: B-

According to the U.S. Census Bureau's International Data Base, 35 countries can boast a higher life expectancy than the U.S., ranging from Andorra to Japan, New Zealand to Kuwait. (see chart below)[2]

Our relatively mediocre rating is not because of inadequate funding. Each year, the U.S. devotes an increasing percentage of its resources to healthcare. In 1960, healthcare expenditures were 5.2

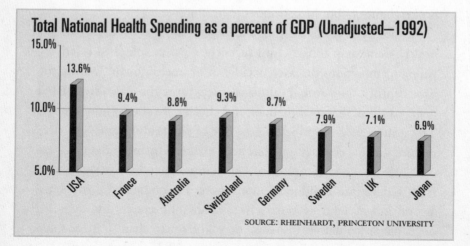

Total National Health Spending as a percent of GDP (Unadjusted—1992)

USA	13.6%
France	9.4%
Australia	8.8%
Switzerland	9.3%
Germany	8.7%
Sweden	7.9%
UK	7.1%
Japan	6.9%

SOURCE: RHEINHARDT, PRINCETON UNIVERSITY

percent of the gross national product (GNP); by 1990, they had more than doubled to 12.2 percent of the GNP. At 13.6 percent of the GNP in 1996 (more than twice that of Japan), healthcare spending in the United States passed the trillion-dollar mark for the first time. If current trends continue, the Health Care Financing Administration projects that healthcare could consume an unmanageable 31.5 percent of the GNP by the year 2020. Tithonus' revenge threatens not only our personal happiness, but our national economy as well.

As we might expect, a disproportionate share of these resources is spent on trying to treat the diseases of the elderly population. The 13 percent of our population over 65 now accounts for 24.1 percent of all doctor's office visits and 44 percent of all hospital-bed days. On the eve of the New Deal, all levels of government spent roughly $1 a year on healthcare for the average older American. By 1965, when Medicare was launched, the figure had risen to roughly $100 per year ($484 in 1995 dollars). In 1995 (the latest year for which figures are available), funding had multiplied 70 times, to roughly $7,000 per senior adult.[3] However, as we will see, *these expenditures are wildly misdirected*.

The true costs of aging-related healthcare go far beyond government entitlements. Medicare covers less than 50 percent of a typical elder's healthcare costs and does not reimburse for many of the expenses associated with disease prevention and long-term care. Medicare will cover the cost of a quadruple bypass, but will not reimburse for services to help prevent heart disease through proper nutrition and other changes in lifestyle. In addition to public funding, older people themselves pay premiums, copayments, and deductibles, and for such items as prescription drugs, all of which costs $2,750 a year on average. And even though more than 60 percent of elders will need long-term care at some point, with the average extended nursing-home stay of 2.5 years costing more than $100,000, Medicare pays for only 25 percent of such services.[4]

Part of the problem lies in the fact that we now have the *wrong*

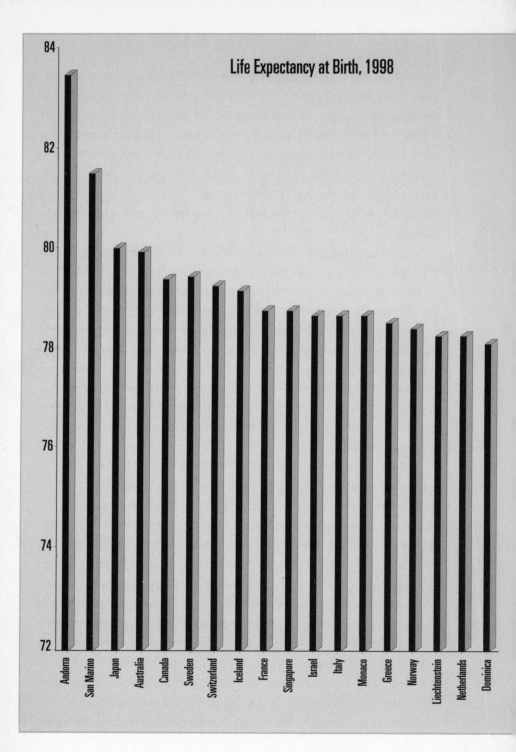

Life Expectancy at Birth, 1998

Malta
Spain
Luxembourg
New Zealand
Austria
Belgium
Finland
United Kingdom
Germany
Bermuda
Cyprus
Kuwait
Taiwan
Denmark
French Guiana
Ireland
Montenegro
United States

SOURCE: U.S. CENSUS BUREAU INTERNATIONAL DATA BASE

healthcare system for our new aging-related needs. Over the past century, we have built an approach to healthcare that is excellent at diagnosing, treating, and reimbursing the kinds of acute illnesses that beset infants, children, and young adults. Advances in medical diagnostics, pharmaceuticals, surgical techniques, and nutrition have eliminated many of the problems that once caused people to die prematurely, enabling millions to live longer lives with chronic conditions. The irony of our successes is that we have produced legions of long-lived elders who struggle with exactly those chronic problems—heart disease, cancer, arthritis, osteoporosis, Alzheimer's—that our system is ill-prepared to handle.

HEALTHCARE MISMATCH

Many aspects of our current healthcare system are out of sync with our emerging problems: Our scientific research priorities are misaligned with the diseases of aging; healthcare professionals are not skilled in geriatric medicine; our financing mechanisms do not emphasize the prevention or cost-effective treatment of age-related illnesses; and, as we will explore in Chapter 6, our long-term care services are undeveloped and fragmented. Even Medicare is based on an acute-care model most appropriate for the young. We are spending enormous sums of money on the wrong things and, not surprisingly, the results are mediocre at best.

As we saw in Chapter 2, we are about to tap a wellspring of life-extension and human-enhancement technologies that promise to revitalize some aspects of the body's hormone system, repair "broken" parts or replace failing organs, perhaps even slow the aging process so that we can extend average life expectancy by 10 years or more. Yet we're still years away from scientific validation, and even further from widespread public use of such new methods. Even if they occur in our lifetimes, unless we also find ways to wipe out diseases of the aging brain such as Alzheimer's, or failings of the musculoskeletal system like arthritis and osteoporosis, or cardiovascular and respiratory system debilities such as atherosclerosis and emphysema, we will simply be creating a population of long-lived Tithonuses.

There's a Healthcare Train Wreck in Our Future

Why am I so concerned—even frightened—about how our healthcare system handles the very old? Because I have seen the future, and you can see it, too. Don't go to the NASA exhibit in Washington, DC, to Epcot in Orlando, or to the Media Lab at MIT. To see the future, visit your local nursing home. Take a walk around. Look at the residents.

While who we will be at 60 or 70 can sometimes be seen on tennis courts or golf courses or in friendly McDonald's ads, the 80- and 90-year-old versions of ourselves lie suffering in long-term care establishments. After you've witnessed the enfeeblement and dementia of the elder residents, take a close look at the personal photographs that sit on their night tables. You'll notice that when they were your age, they looked a lot like you do now. They were handsome, loving adults surrounded by family members and friends—just like in the pictures you might have taken last summer. Somewhere in the later years of their extended lives, however, they succumbed to diseases that nobody cared enough about to prevent or cure.

According to the Health Care Financing Administration, 80 percent of the 65+ population have one or more chronic diseases, 50 percent have two or more, and 24 percent have problems so severe as to limit their ability to perform one or more activities of daily living.[5] The more troublesome challenges ahead, however, are largely due to the rising incidence of often untreatable diseases among the *oldest old*. Although some of today's 85+ population are fit and independent, 62.5 percent are so disabled that they are no longer able to manage the basic activities of daily living without help. These men and women have become the lepers of the late 20th century. There are millions of

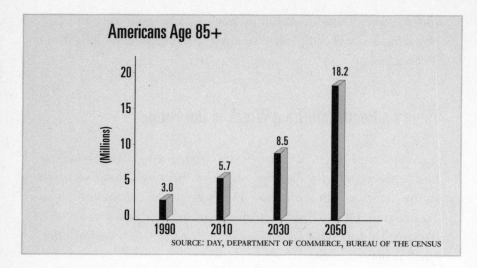

Americans Age 85+

SOURCE: DAY, DEPARTMENT OF COMMERCE, BUREAU OF THE CENSUS

them, and the colony is growing. Those aged 85 and older are multi-plying faster than any other segment of our population.[6]

In 1900, there were only 122,000 people aged 85+ in the United States. In 1999, there were 4.1 million (as many as there were total Americans in 1800), representing an increase of 3,280 percent. The 85+ population will continue to grow, quadrupling in size to approx-imately 16 million—including more than a million centenarians—by the year 2040.

The cost of our unpreparedness is already staggering:[7]

- Heart disease, which accounts for more adult deaths than all other causes combined, costs our nation $183 billion in direct and indirect costs annually. One in three men and one in five women suffer from different forms of cardiovascular disease such as angina, arteriosclerosis, congestive heart failure, and stroke.[8]
- Cancer, in all its forms, afflicts 8.2 million older Americans and drains $107 billion annually, accounting for 10 percent of the total cost of healthcare spending in the United States. While the overall risk increases dramatically with age, some types, such as breast and prostate cancer, are particularly predatory among older adults.[9]

- Strokes among older people are the third leading cause of death, and those who survive are usually left disabled. Strokes alone result in healthcare costs of almost $45 billion annually.[10]
- More than half of all elder Americans have some type of musculoskeletal disorder such as arthritis, which afflicts 15 to 20 million seniors, or osteoporosis, which affects 20 million women and 5 million men and leads to more than 250,000 hip fractures each year. The direct and indirect costs of arthritis and osteoporosis are already $80 billion annually and rising.[11]
- Today, an estimated 4 million older Americans suffer from Alzheimer's disease. For 1998, the combined direct and indirect annual costs of Alzheimer's were estimated to be more than $100 billion.[12]

ALZHEIMER'S: ELDERLY AIDS

In old-age homes and retirement communities, I have often heard Alzheimer's referred to as "elderly AIDS." This disease, one of the most prevalent among the very old, could become the *scourge of the 21st century*. Although noninfectious, Alzheimer's is a degenerative disorder that steadily robs its victims of memory and judgment, leaves patients unable to carry out the most basic functions on their own, and ultimately destroys the brain. Alzheimer's seldom occurs before middle age, but after age 60 its likelihood doubles about every five years. Currently, less than 2 percent of people aged 60 suffer from Alzheimer's; 3 to 4 percent have it by age 65, and 6 to 8 percent by 70. At age 75, 15 percent have it, and 25 to 30 percent are afflicted by age 80; a frightening 47 percent of people over 85 have this devastating disease. Without advances in the battle against Alzheimer's, breakthroughs that postpone or eliminate heart disease, cancer, strokes, diabetes, or other terminal illnesses will inadvertently be creating longer-lived but *demented* men and women. Unless a cure or treatment is found in our lifetimes, it is estimated that 14 million boomers and generation Xers will be stricken with "elderly AIDS" by the middle of the next century—up from 4 million today. And where the average duration of Alzheimer's before death is currently 8 to 10 years, improvements in other areas of medicine could wind up extending this to 15 to 20 years.[13]

If we care about our own futures and the futures of our families, it is imperative that we commit the talent, energy, and financial resources needed to treat and, if possible, eliminate the debilitating diseases of late life. Unless we intervene, and soon, Alzheimer's, heart disease, cancer, osteoporosis, and arthritis, with all their pain, suffering, and expense, will be our inheritance.

The Five-Part Solution

While politicians debate the merits of modest entitlement modifications, I fear that yesterday's healthcare system is badly outmatched when squaring off with tomorrow's problems. Because the organization, skills, and economic incentives of our healthcare system are overwhelmingly misdirected, additional funding will not solve the problems. Rather, by redirecting the priorities and resources of this system, we could be producing much healthier elders and greater longevity for a far smaller amount than we are now spending.

If we are to solve these problems before reaching an era of crushing chronic-disease epidemics, we must:

1. Commit greater attention and resources to the scientific research required to delay or, if possible, eliminate the diseases of aging.
2. Provide the academic training and continuing education to ensure that healthcare professionals are fully competent at meeting the needs of the new old.
3. Make disease prevention and self-care a national priority.
4. Orient the economic incentives of our healthcare system toward healthy aging.

5. Establish a more humane, respectful, and cost-effective approach to death and dying.

Solution #1: Promote Research Needed to Delay or Eliminate the Diseases of Aging

Beginning in middle age, the risks for most disorders—from arthritis to cancer to heart disease—roughly double every five to seven years. What if we could compress the various diseases of old age into the shortest possible time at the very end of life? An emerging vision in the global scientific community posits that the goal of research should be to delay or prevent aging-related diseases rather than find ways to treat them after the fact with expensive therapies and technologies. In his provocatively titled book *We Live Too Short and Die Too Long,* Stanford Medical School's Dr. Walter Bortz argues that if we could postpone or prevent any of the painful, costly diseases of old age, millions of older men and women would look, feel, and act years younger and trillions of dollars could ultimately be saved.[14]

To envision an aging process freed of protracted disease, gerontologists like to refer to Oliver Wendell Holmes's 1858 poem, *"The Deacon's Masterpiece,"* in which he describes the creation of a "Wonderful One-Hoss Shay" that remained vital and sturdy for one hundred years and a day—and then disintegrated all at once:

Have you heard of the wonderful one-hoss shay,
That was built in such a logical way
It ran a hundred years to a day . . .

Now in building of chaises, I tell you what,
There is always *somewhere* a weakest spot,—
In hub, tire, felloe, in spring or thill,
In panel, or crossbar, or floor, or sill,
In screw, bolt, thoroughbrace—lurking still,

Find it somewhere you must and will,—
Above or below, or within or without,—
And that's the reason, beyond a doubt,
A chaise *breaks down*, but doesn't *wear out*. . . .

So the Deacon inquired of the village folk
Where he could find the strongest oak,
That couldn't be split nor bent nor broke,—
That was for spokes and floor and sills;
He sent for lancewood to make the thills;
The crossbars were ash, from the straightest trees;
The panels of white-wood, that cuts like cheese,
But last like iron for things like these . . .

Colts grew horses, beards turned gray,
Deacon and deaconess dropped away . . .
There are traces of age in the one-hoss shay,
A general flavor of mild decay . . .
All at once the horse stood still . . .
Then something decidedly like a spill,—
And the parson was sitting upon a rock . . .

—What do you think the parson found,
When he got up and stared around?
The poor old chaise in a heap or mound,
As if it had been to the mill and ground!
You see, or course, if you're not a dunce,
How it went to pieces all at once,—
All at once, and nothing first,—
Just as bubbles do when they burst.[15]

Although it's unlikely that, like Holmes's perfectly built carriage, we
will ever be able to remove all disease from human aging, consensus
is emerging among leading medical researchers that with vigorous

efforts in both the public and private sectors, we could conquer many of the age-related diseases and thereby produce long-lived *and* healthy elders.

The National Institute on Aging (NIA), which leads the federal aging research effort, reports that federally funded programs are already making important strides in identifying genetic and environmental factors associated with the diseases of aging. In addition, as we saw in Chapter 2, the pharmaceutical and biotechnology sectors are directing increasing attention and creativity to understanding the relationship between aging and disease.

For example, the war against Alzheimer's is progressing on several fronts. Leading the charge is the National Alzheimer's Association, a voluntary organization dedicated to research and education on the causes, treatments, cures, and prevention of Alzheimer's. Since its founding in 1980, the association has provided more than $70 million in research grants. Until recently, it focused primarily on educating and supporting caregivers, as no treatments were in sight. In 1998, however, as an expression of increased hopefulness that a cure will be found in our lifetimes, the association changed its motto from "Someone to Stand by You," to "A World Without Alzheimer's."

On the pharmaceutical front, efforts are beginning to pay off. Warner-Lambert now markets Cognex and Pfizer markets Aricept, treatments that in a limited number of cases allow the patient to function for about an extra six to nine months. Several major drugmakers are testing a treatment that works by blocking the accumulation of toxic levels of calcium in neurons—one of the ways the neurofibrillary tangles characteristic of Alzheimer's are formed. Researchers in Sweden are even testing compounds that stimulate nerve-cell growth. Others are exploring the effects of estrogen replacement therapy and the use of a new type of anti-inflammatory drug, called Cox-2 inhibitors, both of which may forestall some Alzheimer's symptoms.

Several years ago, a team of geneticists led by Dr. Allen Roses at

Duke University Medical Center announced it had isolated a gene—called APOE4—that is strongly linked with the onset of late-stage Alzheimer's. Doctors will use such genetic markers to identify people most at risk and start them on preventive treatments, as these become available. If some of the potential treatments reach fruition, healthy nerve cells may be injected directly into the brain, where they will grow, make the right connections, and replace dead neurons.

Along with new memory-enhancing drugs, such treatments would also benefit stroke victims and those suffering from spinal injuries, Parkinson's disease, and other neurological disorders. In the future, people may be able to chew pills to fend off dementia the way middle-aged men now ingest baby aspirin to prevent heart attacks. "That's pretty futuristic stuff," says Dr. Zaven Khachaturian, senior medical and scientific advisor to the Alzheimer's Association and the nation's leading authority on the diseases of the aging brain, "but it's entirely possible, assuming sufficient funding is available to develop these breakthroughs."[16]

It is estimated that postponing the onset of Alzheimer's disease by five years would reduce the incidence of this disease by an amazing 50 percent. If these kinds of advances were to occur, half of all the nursing-home beds in America would empty and our overall health costs would plummet.

INSUFFICIENT FUNDING WILL PRODUCE A DARK TOMORROW

The dollars that have been committed to battle the diseases of aging, however, may not be enough to finish the job in our lifetimes. Men and women over 65 already consume a third of all healthcare spending, approximately $342 billion, yet the National Institutes of Health (NIH) spends only 8 percent of its $15.6 billion research budget for aging-related research. This 8 percent includes the entire budget of the National Institute on Aging as well as all aging research conducted by NIH's 23 institutes and research centers. This amounts to an investment of .2 percent of the total healthcare expenditures pertaining to people over the age 65. [17] We are directing huge sums to *treating* chronic diseases, but spending almost nothing to *prevent* them.

The explanation for these lopsided commitments is political as well as economic. As a speaker at the 1995 White House Conference on Aging, I was dismayed to learn that most of the powerful senior lobbying groups would prefer that nearly all available healthcare-related tax dollars go to helping them receive more services *today*. Numerous outspoken seniors at the conference argued—to a very positive reaction from a majority of the delegates—that they'd rather keep the funding aimed at current services from which they will personally benefit, rather than investing in "unknown" future breakthroughs that might occur beyond their lifetimes. Correspondingly, politicians have learned that it's much easier to garner votes by promising short-term benefits than by emphasizing longer-term projects. If such political shortsightedness continues, our futures will be ruined by epidemics of chronic diseases that we could have prevented.

In May 1961, President John F. Kennedy looked to the sky and stated, "I believe this nation should commit itself to achieve the goal, before this decade is out, to landing a man on the moon and returning him safely to earth." [18] Remember how we mobilized all of our science and energy to realize that dream eight years later? Remember how all the excitement—fed by everyone from high school science teachers to the media—aided its realization?

Similarly, in order to avert the chronic disease epidemics looming in our future, we must establish an overarching, long-term commitment to replacing unhealthy aging with healthy aging and devote all of the resources—human and capital—needed to realize this goal, before the threat becomes a reality and we're overwhelmed by the crisis.

Solution #2: Needed: Aging-Ready Healthcare Professionals

Every medical school in the United Kingdom has a department of geriatrics; half of the medical schools in Japan have geriatrics departments—but there are only three such departments in the entire United States: at Mount Sinai Medical Center in New York, the Donald W. Reynolds Center on Aging at the University of Arkansas, and the Veterans Affairs Department of Geriatrics at the University of Oklahoma. In fact, 113 of America's 126 medical schools do not require even a single course in geriatrics, and fewer than 4 percent of medical students take an elective course in the subject.[19]

When the baby boom first hit more than 50 years ago, there weren't enough hospitals or pediatricians. Today, with barely a decade before the boomer tsunami crashes on Medicare's shores, we are heading toward a future dangerously short of high-quality eldercare services and trained geriatricians.

The term "geriatrics" was coined at the turn of the 20th century by Austrian-born physician Ignatz L. Nascher, who practiced medicine in New York City. By Nascher's definition, geriatrics concerns itself with the "preventive, therapeutic, and research aspects of aging-related diseases and conditions."[20] Geriatrics has evolved during this century to encompass the complex needs of older patients, and today there is a strong emphasis on maintaining functional independence, even in the presence of chronic diseases. Yet in closed-door Age Wave focus groups with physicians, I have repeatedly heard doctors lament the high incidence of what they call "do-overs." Because of limited geriatric training, every week physicians make millions of mistakes: misdiagnoses, inappropriate surgeries, incorrect pharmacy prescriptions and complications due to mismanaged polypharmacy. Then, when the outcomes are poor, physicians have to "do over" their intervention strategy and hope for better results. All of these errors, no matter how good the intentions behind them, take their toll—physically, socially, and economically.

If we are to clean up this mess, geriatric competencies are sorely needed. According to the Alliance for Aging Research, a not-for-profit organization in Washington, DC, that promotes scientific and medical research to improve the health of older Americans, "If access to geriatrics-oriented physicians and healthcare personnel were more widely available, more older people would benefit from improved health status, enhanced personal independence, and a substantially lower rate of institutionalization."[21] Dr. Robert Butler, Pulitzer Prize–winning author of *Why Survive?: Growing Old in America* and America's leading geriatrician, agrees: "The result would be a much healthier population of older Americans; dramatically lowered medical, social service, and long-term care costs; and, as a result, a more vital, financially secure 21st century."[22]

With the coming age wave, we should be preparing armies of "aging-ready" healthcare professionals. We are not. From a pool of more than 500,000 physicians, fewer than 9,000 have been trained and certified as geriatricians—less than 2 percent.[23] Although the American Medical Association doesn't like to acknowledge them, Age Wave research has repeatedly uncovered some of the reasons why doctors avoid geriatrics. In focus groups, many comment that it's not glamorous work and it's not a path to riches. Many also complain that they don't particularly like seeing old people and would prefer to spend their time with younger, more attractive patients.

MISGUIDED MEDICARE

This theme was examined in May 1998 at a forum convened by the Senate Special Committee on Aging. Attendees were alarmed to learn that, of almost 100,000 medical residency and fellowship programs that Medicare has helped to support, only 324 were in geriatric medicine. In addition, while Medicare paid nearly $7 billion in graduate medical education costs in fiscal year 1998, only a tiny fraction of those dollars were directed toward the clinical education of physicians who focus on the healthcare needs of older adults.[24]

While there is debate among leaders in this field as to whether we need the 30,000 to 50,000 geriatric specialists that would be comparable to the number of pediatric specialists, there is strong agreement that the average healthcare professional will need an assortment of basic skills in diagnosing, treating, and managing the often complex care of elderly patients. However, it is a sobering fact that most primary-care physicians have received little or no continuing education in geriatrics. Nearly half of the residents in family practice and a majority in psychiatry, internal medicine, physical medicine, and neurology have never even taken a clinical rotation in geriatrics.[25] Current and future physicians are not the only health-care professionals lacking in geriatric skills. The same holds true in nursing, allied health, and pharmacology.

Considering that the average healthcare professional will spend at least 30 minutes out of every working hour with mature adults, allowing them to practice with so few relevant skills is virtually criminal. In essence, we are funding the creation of tomorrow's health-care system for an aging society, but we are neglecting to train our health professionals to work effectively with its patients. The AMA, AARP, the Health Care Financing Administration, Medicare, and all health insurers should *require* physicians, nurses, and other health professionals to attain basic geriatric competencies in order to be eligible for reimbursement. And if managed-care insurers were forced to meet aging-related competency standards in order to qualify for payment from Medicare, geriatric skills would swiftly improve, mistakes and do-overs would shrink, and we'd have better-cared-for elders at a far lower cost.

Solution #3: Make Disease Prevention and Self-Care a National Priority

One of the seldom-discussed problems with our healthcare system is that when many men and women reach maturity, they take very poor care of themselves. This lack of proper self-care winds up being a key factor in many of their eventual struggles with illness. For example, two-thirds of today's elderly don't exercise regularly and approximately 40 percent are overweight. Half don't wear seat belts. Some 75 percent do not regularly comply with their medication regimens. More than half fail to eat healthy and nutritious meals regularly (even among those who can easily afford to), and 4 million elderly men and women (approximately one in eight) remain chronic smokers.[26]

Recent research has consistently shown that we can dramatically influence our health as we age by conscientious self-care. According to the Centers for Disease Control, more than 50 percent of our potential for lifelong health is determined by our personal behaviors.[27] In his book *Successful Aging*, Dr. John Rowe, former professor of geriatrics at Harvard Medical School and currently president of Mount Sinai Medical Center in New York, argues, "It's not just a matter of playing the genetic cards you're dealt. We have the power to shape our own lives. The reality is a much more optimistic scenario than if it were just a matter of picking the right parents."[28] Rowe's views are echoed by Dr. Walter Bortz, in *Dare to Be 100:* "No drug in current or prospective use holds as much promise for sustained health as a lifetime program of physical exercise and proper nutrition."[29]

Regular exercise, proper nutrition, stress management, injury prevention, proper use of medication, quitting smoking, and the appropriate use of healthcare services can definitely help keep your body youthful and disease-free longer. Maintaining a healthy lifestyle can reduce heart disease, hypertension, non-insulin-dependent diabetes mellitus, colon cancer, and osteoporotic fractures—most of the most common diseases of aging. In addition, healthy behaviors have been repeatedly shown to increase bone mass and mineral content and lean muscle mass, as well as improving metabolic rate, balance, coordination, strength, elimination efficiency, and heart/stroke volume and fostering a sense of well-being.

The common response to the age wave by our healthcare system has been to spend more money on "sick care." A more humane and cost-effective approach, however, would be to encourage people to adopt healthier lifestyles and actually prevent or postpone many age-related conditions. If we can control at least some portion of our potential for healthy aging, we have a responsibility to do so. This responsibility is not only to ourselves, but to our families, who will serve as our caregivers—and even to our nation, by helping to avert the "unhealthy aging" crisis it could be facing in the decades ahead.

The economic impact of linking scientific advances with more responsible self-care would be dramatic. By compressing disease into a shorter time frame at the end of life, like Oliver Wendell Holmes's "One Hoss Shay," we would boost the percentage of life that is healthy and productive and plug the drain on the overall healthcare system. For example, it is estimated that postponing physical dependency for older Americans by just one month would save the nation $5 billion in annual healthcare and custodial costs. Similarly, if hip fractures could be delayed five years, we would eliminate 50 percent of such fractures—125,000 per year—and $5 billion in annual costs. A five-year delay in the onset of cardiovascular disease could save an estimated $69 billion per year.[30]

The Healthy Aging Project, launched in 1998, is the Health Care Financing Administration's first serious initiative to examine ways to reduce behavioral risk factors in the elderly. This project will identify and test interventions such as health risk appraisals combined with targeted education programs, arthritis self-management programs, smoking cessation strategies, and home-based geriatric assessments to reduce falls and other environmental hazards that necessitate nursing home admissions. However, I question whether the resources allocated—only $3.7 million in funding—will be sufficient to make a real impact.

Fortunately, some boomers have begun to respond to the public health campaigns of the past decade. The proportion of baby boomers who regularly swim, dance, bicycle, jog, ski, or participate in team sports is twice as large as among the rest of the population.[31] And with the boomers migrating into maturity, the food and beverage industry has experienced a major transformation, as evidenced by the 29 percent drop in per capita consumption of beef between 1975 and 1995. Meanwhile, per capita consumption of leaner poultry rose 250 percent from 1960 to 1995. And compared to 20 years ago, Americans are consuming 21 percent more vegetables and 27 percent more fruit.[32]

DOING WHAT YOU KNOW

As informed as we've all become about the factors that influence health, too many people continue to take too little responsibility for their own well-being. With maturity, the real challenge frequently shifts from *knowing* what to do, to *doing* what you know.

In the 1970s, I wanted to learn everything I could about "wellness" and "peak performance." I read hundreds of books, attended dozens of workshops and training programs. During that same period, I was commissioned by the Nightingale-Conant company to produce a six-audio-tape set, *The Keys to High-Performance Living,* which evolved from the seminars I was then conducting.

Because I was also a buyer of Nightingale-Conant programs, I wound up on several of its targeted mailing lists; whenever a program that matched my customer profile was released, I'd receive a brochure and one of those "customized" offer letters. You can imagine my surprise when, during a particularly stressful and difficult period, I received such a customized letter from the company's president, Dave Nightingale, and read:

Dear <u>Mr. Ken Dychtwald</u>:

Do you feel that you have lost control of your life? Are you suffering from too much stress? Are you finding it harder and harder to stay on your regular fitness program? Are you struggling to balance your work and family responsibilities? Do you feel that you are not achieving your highest potential?

If so, then <u>Dr. Ken Dychtwald</u> can help you! In his new six-tape program, this well-known expert on high-performance living will help you to solve all of your problems and take control of your life again.

Although I didn't buy the set, this message from *me* to *me* provided a potent, existential wake-up call. After all, when it comes to taking proper care of ourselves, we probably already know what to do: The choice is ours.

Solution #4: Orient Economic Incentives Toward Healthy Aging

In ancient China, doctors got paid when people were well. It was the healer's job was to keep the citizenry healthy; if people injured themselves or became ill, the doctor's responsibility was to help cover the costs from his own pocket. The goal was a healthy, productive population, and the system was financially aligned to promote it.

In contrast, throughout modern American history, the financial incentives of our healthcare system have been oriented toward disease rather than health. The sicker people have been, the more tests, procedures, technology, and hospital-bed days they needed, the more money was exchanged. There were few restrictions on the amount of healthcare the doctors could sell and their patients purchase—regardless of the actual outcomes. In fact, within this free-spending medical jubilee, most outcomes weren't even tracked. This approach provided no motivation to produce health and wellness. Exactly the opposite—the more disease, the more profits.

In fact, this really wasn't a healthcare system; it was a disease-management industry that was tough on payers, but very profitable for practitioners, insurers, hospitals, and medical manufacturers. During most of the 20th century, when the U.S. had relatively few old people, this free-spending "fee-for-services" approach seemed effective. However, with the accelerated pace at which our nation has been aging, the out-of-control processes and procedures and their accompanying costs have become staggering.

MANAGED CARE: PROBLEM OR SOLUTION?

In response, the fee-for-service insurance structure has begun transforming into a new model that, while flawed in several ways, actually has the potential to bring us closer to the ancient Chinese approach. The first health maintenance organizations (HMOs) were created in the 1930s with two goals:

1. To better manage the costs of healthcare through careful control and distribution of resources, and
2. To provide doctors and medical institutions with incentives to keep their patients healthy and disease-free.

To date, HMOs have vigorously pursued their first goal—cost containment. But they have done a dismal job of realizing the second, the promotion of health. Unless they turn their serious attention to producing *healthy aging,* they should be stripped of their funding.

The first prepaid health plans, Kaiser Permanente in California and the Health Insurance Plan of Greater New York (HIP) emerged as nonprofit alternatives to traditional, fee-for-service medicine. The capitated group-practice approach to health insurance moved into the mainstream in the 1970s when the Nixon administration advanced legislation that would give the federal government's seal of approval to groups that met predetermined standards and pricing. Under these arrangements, group practices attempted to carefully coordinate all treatment and, wherever possible, refrain from using unnecessary medical services.

Largely spurred by employer enthusiasm for bringing spiraling medical costs under control, managed care spread dramatically during the 1990s. Just a decade ago, less than 10 percent of the insured American public belonged to an HMO or other type of managed care organization (MCO); today more than 75 percent does.

Medicare, too, has begun experimenting with managed care, paying an MCO a monthly rate per enrolled senior beneficiary. Compared with only 1 million participating elders at the beginning of this decade, there are now 4.9 million elders who have come to prefer such advantages as care coordination, coverage for prescription drugs, and zero paperwork offered by such plans.[33]

When MCOs began pursuing Medicare beneficiaries, there was a great deal of concern that these plans might exploit their older members for profit and therefore would not provide the same quality as traditional fee-for-service plans. These worries have so far proven groundless. The American Association of Health Plans conducted a study in 1995, using Health Care Financing Administration data, that concluded that even though Medicare beneficiaries can easily switch plans, only 4 percent return to fee-for-service Medicare after receiving care from a MCO.

Under managed care, out-of-control healthcare costs have been reined in. While fee-for-service rates had escalated 15 percent annually during the 1980s and early 1990s, in 1995 the average premiums for HMOs and preferred provider organizations (PPOs) actually declined by 3.8 percent and 2.1 percent, respectively. Medicare HMO lengths of stay are 17 percent shorter, and total costs are 10.7 percent lower than fee-for-service lengths of stay.[34]

Among some managed-care members, these changes are perceived as insensitive abuses more than accomplishments. In addition, because some for-profit MCOs have been motivated more by profits and shareholder value than member health, we are currently experiencing a powerful consumer backlash. Part of the backlash is justified: The payouts that some MCO executives have received upon selling their companies or taking them public are outrageous. Other aspects of the backlash, however, may be misguided.

Not all managed care organizations are greedy. In fact, 40 percent of MCOs are not-for-profit, and many for-profit MCOs are only modestly profitable. Many people blame MCOs for exercising tight controls on healthcare utilization. Each American would like to believe that he or she can have unlimited access to every possible diagnostic and therapeutic service and technology. The reality, as all other modernized nations have concluded long ago, is that this just isn't possible. Most experts agree that due to the pressures imposed by the aging of our population, in one way or another healthcare costs will have to be tightly managed in the years ahead. If not, skyrocketing healthcare expenditures would bankrupt our economy. But when it comes to healthcare, Americans are so unaccustomed to being told "you can't have it" that many have apparently decided to shoot the messenger.

A SHARPER FOCUS ON HEALTH

Notwithstanding the ongoing concern that some MCOs value profits more than providing care, there is no question that managed care offers a more cost-effective approach, one of its two initial goals. If it is to make a useful contribution to the challenge of our aging society, however, managed care must commit to doing a far better job of realizing its other initial goal, that of preventing disease and keeping people healthy for as much of their long lives as possible.

With each day that passes, they are closing in on this challenge. Now that MCOs have cut the excess costs out of hospitals' services, physicians' salaries, and drug companies' profits, they are beginning to realize that the most expensive remaining element of healthcare is the *diseases of aging*. As their memberships steadily grow older, they are discovering that the sicker their members become, the lower their financial reward. In contrast, the healthier their members remain, the lower the cost of healthcare and the greater their financial reward—similar to the dynamic in ancient China. In response, some MCOs are incorporating preventive health screenings, patient education programs, nutrition therapy, exercise and fitness classes, and alternative therapies such as acupuncture, chiropractic, and massage into their regimes, with some promising results. Should this nascent dynamic advance, patients, practitioners, and insurers would all have their interests and incentives aligned *toward health*—for the first time.

Solution #5: A Humane Approach to Death

Until the 20th century, death was no more strongly associated with old age than it was with any other time of life. One of the riskiest periods was infancy and early childhood. Many healthy young women died in childbirth, and people of all ages were exposed to fatal infectious diseases and trauma. In addition, dying was an integral part of everyday experience. Children observed it regularly. They saw animals killed for food, and they saw family members die not only of old age but also of disease and accidents. Death, like birth, mostly occurred at home. The deathbed scene was a communal experience shared by family and friends.

Nowadays, medical technology makes it possible to sustain human life well beyond the point where death would have occurred in the past. Early in the century, 75 to 80 percent of all deaths took place at home: roughly the same percentage of all deaths now occur in institutions—hospitals, extended-care facilities, and nursing homes. Yet few of these institutions are oriented to deal with the psychological or spiritual dimensions of the dying process. Care of the dying represents a significant gap in our healthcare system. Doctors, whose job it is to cure, see the death of a hospitalized patient as a failure.

Medicare now spends approximately 28 percent of its budget on patients in their last year of life—often when the attempt to prolong life merely means an expensive hospitalized death. While some altruism is at work here, there is a strong dose of capitalistic exploitation involved as well. Some healthcare businesses reap the greatest profits when the dying process is protracted. The average *daily* cost of sustaining an elder dying patient in a critical care ward is $1,500 to $2,500, an amount equivalent to a full year's insurance coverage for a young couple.[35]

In fact, if we allowed elderly patients the dignity of dying a natural death at home, we could save approximately $50 billion per year, which could be used for others who urgently need assistance, such as the more than 20 million uninsured children and adolescents in this country.[36]

DEATH WITH DIGNITY

The emphasis for the dying patient needs to be shifted to "palliative care"—the relief of symptoms, controlling pain, and the provision of emotional and spiritual support for the patient and his or her family. Such treatment requires relatively little apparatus and technology and is much less costly than the procedures currently in place in most hospitals.

The hospice movement is the most prominent modern example of sensitive palliative care for the dying. The term "hospice" was originally used in the Middle Ages to denote a community dedicated to caring for travelers along the way. Derived from the Latin *hospes*, which is the root of such modern words as "hospital" and "hospitality," the word is used today to describe a way of helping people to complete the journey toward death with comfort and dignity.

The modern hospice movement originated in England in 1967 when Dr. Cecily Saunders founded St. Christopher's Hospice in London. In such settings, the physical environment is arranged to be homelike, filled with plants and light. Patients are allowed to wear their own clothing and surround themselves with their possessions, including furniture they may bring from home. Visiting hours are usually allowed around the clock. Young children and pets are welcomed.

Here in the United States, the most common form of hospice program is home care of the dying, spurred by sensitivity for AIDS patients. Hospice home-care programs likewise provide families with the technical, medical, and emotional support that allow them to help their family member through the dying process. The dying patients greatly appreciate both the satisfaction of spending their final days at home and also the loving, noninstitutionalized attention they receive.

THE RIGHT TO DIE

The right for adults to exercise control over the end of own lives has lately become a subject of intense religious and philosophical debate. At one end of the spectrum are those who argue that each of us should be allowed to determine the manner and timing of our death, especially in terminal circumstances. At the other end are those, often motivated by religious or ethical convictions, who say that it's not a private right to decide whether to live or die, that our lives are sacred and we have an obligation not to terminate any life, regardless of suffering.

Changes in philosophical and religious attitudes, as well as other trends in modern society, are beginning to have an impact on the acceptability of passive euthanasia and suicide. As originally used in English, "euthanasia" meant a quiet, gentle, or painless death. *Passive* euthanasia, which is sometimes equated with "letting the patient die," involves refusing or withholding a treatment that would prolong life without reversing the course of the underlying disease. *Active* euthanasia, on the other hand, involves taking some decisive action to hasten a person's death. *Suicide* refers to a circumstance where an individual takes his or her own life.

Proponents of "right to die" legislation argue that under certain circumstances humans can no longer continue living a meaningful life, and that these individuals should be allowed to die peacefully with dignity. Under such circumstances, someone who is considered legally competent to make decisions on his or her own behalf would be able to request that medical treatment be discontinued.

More complex is the case where the individual is no longer conscious or otherwise competent. In such cases, it is suggested that people draw up a "living will" in advance, preferably while they are in good health, which would absolve their doctors and guardians of all legal liability should they discontinue life support.

The right to die becomes much more thorny when it comes to active euthanasia and assisted suicide. While a patient might plead with the physician to administer a fatal injection or perform some other act that would induce death, doctors generally feel that such practice conflicts with traditional medical ethics. Another problem with active euthanasia is that it can be very difficult to guard against potential abuses. Members of the family of a terminally ill or unconscious patient might find it to their advantage to request that his or her life be terminated. Even terminally ill persons themselves, by the very nature of their illnesses, might be incapable of making an objective, rational decision. And there is always a risk of patients being helped to die when a remedy is just around the corner.

While philosophers continue to debate these and other complexities, public opinion has grown increasingly comfortable with the specific option of passive euthanasia. In 1950, a Gallup poll asked whether, if a person had an incurable disease, doctors should be allowed by law to permit the patient's life to end by withholding treatment, if requested by the patient and family. Some 36 percent of respondents approved. When the question was repeated in 1973, those in favor had increased to 53 percent. By 1998 they had grown to 69 percent. [37]

In his book *The Virtues of Aging,* former President Jimmy Carter, a deeply religious man, comments on his personal wishes regarding death:

> We can either face death with fear, anguish, and unnecessary distress among those around us or, through faith and courage, confront the inevitable with equanimity, good humor, and peace. When other members of my family realized that they had a terminal illness, the finest medical care was available to them. But each chose to forgo elaborate artificial life-support systems and, with a few friends and family members at their bedside, they died peacefully. All of them retained their lifelong character and their personal dignity. . . . Rosalynn and I hope to follow in their footsteps, and we have signed living wills that will preclude the artificial prolongation of our lives.[38]

Many aging Americans would do well to follow the Carters' lead by talking openly with family members about their end-of-life wishes and desires and writing down their intentions in a legal living will.

The Challenge Ahead

Whether we grow old sick, frail, and dependent or vital, active, and productive will depend on our ability to dramatically alter the orientation, strategies, skills, and financial incentives of our current healthcare system. The size of the job is daunting and we must get started now. *Modern healthcare has lost its way and needs a new vision and sense of purpose.*

Unless we establish a clear and powerful commitment to aligning key aspects of our research, healthcare practices, insurance reimbursements, and personal lifestyles to promote *healthy aging,* most of us will live long lives, but half of us will hate it. Tithonus will have his revenge.

Tips to Age-Proof Your Life

- Make sure your primary-care physician (and those of your parents) is informed and skilled in wellness and disease prevention and has received sufficient training in geriatric-related competencies.
- Purchase insurance from a company that is committed to scientifically based preventive medicine and wellness programs for you and your family members.
- Take responsibility for your own regimen of self-care. Give your body the loving care and maintenance it will need to go the distance with vigor.
- Create a living will in which your personal wishes regarding prolonged life-support are clearly spelled out for family members and physicians.

CHAPTER SIX

THE CAREGIVING CRUNCH

A few years ago, my mother was hospitalized for the first time in her life. Since my parents moved to Florida in the late 1980s, my mom had been having difficulties with asthma. In 1995, she came down with a bronchial infection that left her unable to breathe. She was rushed to the local hospital where over the next week, with the help of oxygen equipment and IV antibiotics, her condition improved. When she returned home, however, she sounded weary and "old" in a way I had never heard before.

During the following weeks, I called her several times a day. On one of those calls, in the weakest of voices, she said that now my dad wasn't feeling well and she was really worried. My dad has always been a robust man and, despite 20 years of hypertension and 10 years of adult-onset diabetes, he'd seldom been sick and never hospitalized.

At the time of this call, I was in the Washington, DC, airport about to board a plane home to California after six days of meetings around the country. When I asked my mom to explain Dad's problem, she said he'd been having chest pains for several days, and that morning he'd visited his doctor, who'd sent him for an angiogram. Rather than heading west, I suggested, would it make sense if I caught a plane for Florida so that I could be with them that evening? "Oh, no, no," she said. "His doctor is quite sure there's nothing to be alarmed about and the problem can be handled with medications." Feeling concerned and a bit rattled, I took off for California.

After the six-hour ride, I got off the plane and called Florida again from a pay phone. This time, Mom was badly shaken: The angiogram had revealed that my dad's two major coronary arteries were more than 98 percent occluded, and his doctors wouldn't even let him walk out of the hospital for fear that a massive heart attack was imminent. Instead, triple-bypass surgery was scheduled for the day after next.

The following morning, with my carry-on bag over my shoulder, I boarded another plane and headed back east to Florida.

During the first week that I stayed with my parents after Dad's surgery, my children were very upset with me for being away from home so long. Casey (7 years old at the time) was sad that I was missing her parent-teacher visitation night, and Zakary (age 4) was so angry that I wasn't home to play with him that he wouldn't even talk to me when I called.

As familiar as I am with these matters—being both a psychologist and a gerontologist—the feelings accompanying this predicament were all new to me. I was torn between my attempt to be a good and loving *son* while also being a good and loving *father*—and considering that my parents and children live more than 3,000 miles apart, it wasn't easy.

I felt that the very least I could do was to tell my children exactly what was happening. I called home, and this is what I said:

"Hi, guys! I've asked Mom to put you both near the speaker-phone because there are some thoughts that I'd like to share with you. First, I want to tell you how much I love you both and I *really* miss you. I know you are very smart and I hope you will try to understand what I'm about to explain to you.

"While both of you and Mommy are my family, I'm also part of my own mom and dad's family. So I'm in two families at the same time. But both of these families are connected through me, and part of my job is to see to it that we all love and care for each other.

"Right now, Grandpa is very sick and the doctors had to open his chest to fix his heart. I think that what they've done is going to make him better, but it's going to take a while until he feels his strength again. Grandpa is very sad and he has so much pain that he almost cries every time I see him. He's lost a lot of weight, it's very hard for him to move, and he can only talk a few minutes at a time.

"Because she loves him so much, Grandma is working night and day to take care of Grandpa, but it's really tired her out, and remember that she hasn't been feeling that well herself lately. On top of that, Grandma is very, very worried that Grandpa might die, and she definitely doesn't want that to happen.

"Why am I here in Florida and not home with you? Well, when I was a little boy, Grandpa and Grandma were always there for me when I needed them. They always stopped whatever they were doing to take care of me, if I was sick or hurt in any way. Now that they're not well, I intend to let them know how much I love them both. I want to help Grandpa get better and I want to make sure that Grandma's going to be okay, too.

"And so, while I desperately miss you, and I really would love to be with you right now, I hope you will try to understand that while I'm your daddy, I have my own daddy and mommy that I love and they need me a lot right now. I love you and I'll be home as soon as I'm able."

During the next several months, as my dad regained his health and strength, I regularly flew back and forth across the country to care for both my parents and my wife and kids. Since that episode, I have had to step back into this "sandwiched" caregiving role several times to help my parents through subsequent bouts with heart disease and cancer.

Long-distance caregiving is difficult—as is most eldercare, for that matter. Fortunately, my challenges were manageable because my parents recovered their health after their various crises, and my wife and children have been extremely understanding and supportive. Many other caregivers are not as lucky.

In recent years, I have noticed that many friends and associates have been absent more days from work due to parent care than childcare. I have also watched as some of these situations have ended in great misery and cost. This trend—middle-aged parents sacrificing time, energy, and money for their elder loved ones—is dramatically on the upswing. Currently, more than 22 million households actively provide some type of eldercare, and this figure has tripled over the past decade.

If this trend continues, eldercare-giving and its associated responsibilities, sacrifices, and suffering could very well become the social and economic sinkhole of the 21st century.

Am I My Parents' Keeper?

Are we prepared for the impact this caregiving crunch will have on our lives? How will we respond? What will our "modern" values be regarding care of our parents—and ultimately of ourselves? Just as most of our parents cared for us when we needed them, I deeply believe that it is our loving duty to care for them. Due to a variety of factors, however, this will become an increasingly difficult task.

Today, 80 percent of all long-term care is provided by friends and family members outside of hospitals, nursing homes, and other institutions. This caregiving might involve grocery shopping and housecleaning for a disabled parent several hours a week, or helping a loved one who is recuperating from surgery to bathe and dress several days each week for a few months, or it might even mean providing 24-hour attention to a parent struggling with Alzheimer's—seven days a week for 10 years. These kinds of needs will not be met by simply building more hospitals or nursing homes. In this chapter, we will explore the key social, economic, and healthcare trends that are creating a caregiving crunch, including:

- increasing longevity of the chronically ill,
- worsening strain on sandwiched generations,
- insufficient financing for long-term care,
- the absence of integrated and accessible long-term care services, and
- the premature death of men.

I will then outline four solutions to prevent the deepening eldercare sinkhole from swallowing us up.

INCREASING LONGEVITY OF THE CHRONICALLY ILL

As we saw in Chapter 5, until we are able to dramatically compress the period of illness into the last moments of life, aging men and women face an increasing risk of multiple chronic conditions, called co-morbidities. As a person's chronic conditions increase, so do his or her needs for long-term care.

Today, approximately 12 million seniors are limited, to some degree, by chronic health problems. Of these, nearly half are unable to perform basic activities—walking, bathing, preparing meals, managing medication—without help. Last year, some 2.5 million seniors spent time in a nursing home while an estimated 5.5 million used homecare services. Currently, a 65-year-old has a 43 percent chance of entering a nursing home at some point in his or her life. Projecting usage into the 21st century, when the boomers enter old age, a harsh picture arises. By 2040, it is estimated that 5.5 million Americans—more than the entire population of Denmark—will live in nursing homes, and another 12 million—equal to the combined populations of Israel, Singapore, and New Zealand—will require ongoing homecare services.[1]

Providing care to an older loved one is becoming an increasingly long process. According to a recent National Family Caregivers Association study, 62 percent of caregivers report that they have been providing care for five or more years and 75 percent expect that they will continue for another five or more years.[2]

In June 1998, *The New York Times* featured a story about the enormous burden of providing extended care for someone with Alzheimer's disease.[3] Forty-six-year-old Linda Stumm was a wife and mother of two, whose own mother was diagnosed 13 years ago with Alzheimer's. The Stumms could not afford a good nursing home, so the family decided to care for her at home. For the first two years, Linda occasionally stayed home from work to provide the constant care that was needed. Then she gave up her career as a legal secretary and took a part-time position as a school secretary—at half the salary. Eventually, Linda's mom became unable to speak, eat, or even move without help. She spent her days lying on the hospital bed in the living room of her daughter's home.

Expressing her exhaustion from years of caregiving, Linda Stumm reflected, "There are times when I'm so tired I could just cry. Childcare eventually evolves to less and less care—eldercare evolved to more and more. There is no end to this. You know you are going to be changing diapers all the time. It just gets worse." After 13 years of providing care, the family's savings were nearly depleted. The oldest son, an honors student in high school, was hoping to attend the University of Pennsylvania; that dream was evaporating, due to the family's deteriorating financial condition.

The Stumms' plight is not unusual. For every Alzheimer's patient, there are usually three or more close family members whose lives are deeply affected by the emotional, physical, social, and financial burdens of caregiving. Despite their best intentions, the lives of Linda Stumm and her family have been forever altered by this experience.

SANDWICHED GENERATIONS

The combined trends of declining fertility and longer life spans we explored in Chapter 1 have left the average boomer with *more parents than children.* My wife and I have two children, three living parents, one stepparent, and one living grandparent—a total of *two* children and *five* parents. This is not unusual for the "sandwiched generation."

In fact, with the emergence of four-generation families, the future is going to be filled with *double-decker* sandwiched generations. As a result, the average 21st-century American will actually spend more years caring for parents than children.

Notwithstanding men's increasing involvement in child-rearing

and domestic roles, eldercare-giving continues to fall disproportionately on women. The "typical" caregiver is a 45- to 55-year-old
woman who works full-time and spends 18 hours per week caring for
her 77-year-old mother. About 64 percent of sandwiched caregivers
are employed, 52 percent full-time. The contribution of time is not
trivial: Nearly 25 percent of caregiving households provide 40+
hours each week of unpaid, informal care to an older family member.

Of today's eldercare-givers, 73 percent are women, most of
whom bear the brunt of caregiving while working. In 1950, only 38
percent of women aged 45 to 54—the prime years for eldercare-giving—were in the labor force. In 1999, however, 76 percent of women
in this age range were in the work force. To complicate matters, 41
percent of eldercare-givers have children of their own under the age
of 18 living at home. This means that many middle-aged women are
raising children while juggling work and eldercare responsibilities.[4]

In a National Alliance for Caregivers/AARP report, 49 percent
of caregivers said their responsibilities forced them to make adjustments to their daily work schedule, such as going to work late, leaving early, or taking time off during the day. The study also found
that 12 percent of adult-care givers ultimately had to leave the workforce altogether.[5]

The already heavy burden on caregivers will be exacerbated by
the shrinking number of adult children. Today's elder generation
had an average of nearly four children per couple. Boomers have had
only half as many kids—and will therefore have only half as many
available caregiving children when they reach old age. If low birth
and fertility rates continue as expected, tomorrow's elderly will have
not only fewer living children but also fewer grandchildren.

As families become more geographically far-flung, eldercare-
giving becomes even trickier. In 1960, 40 percent of people aged 65+
lived in the household of an adult child. By 1999, this had dropped
to 4 percent. A survey sponsored by the National Council on the
Aging and the Pew Charitable Trust found that nearly 7 million
Americans provide long-distance care to elders at least one hour

away. This number is expected to more than double over the next 15 years.[6]

Eldercare-givers frequently lament that they have much less time for spouses and other family members, and have had to sacrifice vacations and hobbies as well. This point was recently made in an Age Wave focus group by the frustrated husband of a caregiver whose mom had Alzheimer's: "It's harder than if she was working. It's certainly more confining than that. It's all the time, and she barely has the energy to interact with our kids anymore. There aren't any days off. Your life is shot, basically."

This type of complaint is common. As eldercare becomes an unexpectedly long-term demand on boomers, some families may experience new—or, more likely, reruns of old—interpersonal crises. Hard feelings left over from childhood and the unresolved "issues" of many parent-child relationships can flare up when a grown child and elderly parent are forced to resume intimate, day-to-day contact. Counseling may be necessary to cope with strained feelings, and unfortunately, "elder abuse" will likely become a growing psychological and domestic concern in the near future.

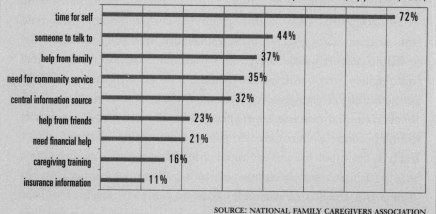

Helpers Looking for a Hand
(what National Family Caregivers Association members feel they need most, by percent, 1997)

time for self	72%
someone to talk to	44%
help from family	37%
need for community service	35%
central information source	32%
help from friends	23%
need financial help	21%
caregiving training	16%
insurance information	11%

SOURCE: NATIONAL FAMILY CAREGIVERS ASSOCIATION

INSUFFICIENT FINANCING FOR LONG-TERM CARE

In the landmark report *Chronic Care in America: A 21st-Century Challenge*, the Robert Wood Johnson Foundation and the University of California, San Francisco's Institute for Health and Aging found that in 1995, $470 billion was spent on medical services for people with chronic conditions, the overwhelming majority of whom were over 65.[7]

Of that money, 76 percent—nearly $360 billion—went toward care of an individual in a nursing home or similar institution. Yet as we saw earlier, only 5 percent of the elderly—fewer than 2 million—are actually in such a facility. It is believed that two to three times that number of elders are being cared for in their own homes—yet *current financing mechanisms do not cover most of their care.* Worse, many people aren't aware of this. In 1996, the Financial Literacy 2000 Project, sponsored by the University of Pennsylvania School of Social Work, surveyed a nationally representative sample of 1,000 adults about their financial knowledge and confidence concerning a range of savings, investment, and health-finance topics. The study found that 53 percent of boomers mistakenly believe that Medicare will pay for the nursing-home care of their parents should they be afflicted with Alzheimer's disease—*it doesn't.* This misperception leads to confusion and frequently results in tragic outcomes.

Medicare was never designed to cover long-term care. Even though most elders would prefer to be cared for in their own homes, Medicare will only provide reimbursement for hospital and physician expenses and some limited support for nursing-home and home-health care. Medicare fully covers just the first 20 days of skilled care; after this, coverage is phased out—ending at 100 days. Even during that time, the amount and type of care financed by the program is restricted to skilled medical care, which most long-term arrangements do not require.

Others believe that they can find ways to shift their costs to Medicaid, an increasingly common strategy that has pushed this public assistance program to the brink of bankruptcy. Medicaid was established in 1965 as a welfare program designed to help the very poor receive nursing-home care. Only those with a maximum of $2,000 in assets were eligible. Over three decades, however, "Medicaid creep" has loosened up the requirements for eligibility, exempting homes, cars, businesses, trusts, annuities, and personal effects from the category of "assets." Although elders are supposed to be impoverished in order to qualify, nearly anyone who wishes to receive free nursing-home care and who can afford a decent lawyer can now be directed through Medicaid's various loopholes. As Stephen Moses, president of the nonprofit Center for Long-Term Care Financing decries, "Virtually anyone, regardless of income or assets, can qualify for Medicaid's long-term care benefits quickly by sheltering or divesting assets."[8]

In fact, an entirely new area of legal practice, Medicaid estate planning, has emerged over the past decade to help guide older adults into artificial impoverishment in order to avoid paying for their own long-term care. A variety of techniques are used to camouflage elders' assets and manipulate their estates so that they will qualify for Medicaid's benefits. For example, in *Avoiding the Medicaid Trap: How Every American Can Beat the Catastrophic Costs of Nursing Home Care*, attorney Armond Budish lists a variety of strategies including moving money in exempt assets; transferring assets directly to children tax-free; paying children for their help; juggling assets between spouses; passing assets to children through a spouse; transferring a home while retaining a life estate; changing wills and title to property; writing a durable power of attorney; setting up a Medicaid trust; and, as a last resort, considering a divorce. [9]

Even though state and federal governments have tried to resist "Medicaid creep" and the exploitation of the program, the protests of senior lobbying groups have prevailed. A federal measure passed in 1996 to criminalize some forms of Medicaid estate planning was undermined when critics complained that it would send some seniors to jail. Attorney General Janet Reno stated that she wouldn't enforce the law, questioning its constitutionality.[10]

Neither Medicare nor Medicaid provides anything approaching a solution to paying for long-term care—yet the costs involved are enormous. While many people's stays in nursing homes are short, the average length of extended care is 2.5 years, and 20 percent of individuals require more than 5 years of care. In 1999, the average out-of-pocket cost was $3,200 per month—or nearly $40,000 per year. According to Paul Hogan, president of Home Instead Senior Care, for those with significant frailty, the cost of care typically exceeds $10,000 per month. Many people either have to pay for this themselves or be driven into poverty and placed in a nursing home, at which point Medicaid does provide some support.[11]

The Center for Long-Term Care Financing's Stephen Moses explains how this dynamic occurred: "In 1965, America was just starting to have a serious problem with long-term care. People were living longer, but dying slower, of chronic illnesses that caused frailty and cognitive impairment. . . . With every good intention, the new federal Medicaid program offered publicly financed long-term nursing-home care. This benefit confronted families with a choice. They could pay out-of-pocket for the homecare and community-based services elders prefer or they could accept nursing-home care paid for by the government. The result was that the market for homecare withered, private long-term care insurance failed to develop, and Medicaid-financed nursing homes flourished."[12]

Although in the 1970s, Medicaid attempted to rein in nursing home costs by limiting the construction of new facilities, the demand persisted and nursing homes simply raised their prices. Since then, the nursing home industry has been running at nearly 95 percent occupancy. The institutional bias of Medicare and Medicaid's financing strategies has inadvertently made millionaires of many nursing home operators while lulling the rest of the population into a dangerous state of financial unpreparedness. Lacking proactive planning, many elders wind up depleting their life's savings—and their children's inheritances—as they tumble into poverty.

Given the pressures of the age wave, if the middle-class masses continue to draw down Medicaid's limited resources, it will be wiped out. We all need to understand that Medicare will not pay for most of our long-term care needs, and Medicaid should be dedicated to supporting the truly poor. As a result, we and our families will be responsible for bridging the gap by self-financing our own long-term care and that of our loved ones. The longer we wait to come to grips with this reality, the harder it will be to do anything about it.

THE ABSENCE OF INTEGRATED, ACCESSIBLE LONG-TERM CARE SERVICES

Acute care is about *curing*, such as mending a broken bone, and is intended to occur within a fixed period of time. Long-term care is about *caring*, usually over an indefinite period of time. As such, it requires an integrated network of professionals across a continuum of disciplines—physicians, nurses, discharge planners, social workers, clergy, recreational therapists, nutritionists, and home-care aids—as well as the active involvement of family and friends.

Unfortunately, most of the available services—from home care agencies to adult daycare centers to geriatric care management—are confusing, fragmented, and difficult to obtain. Unlike childcare, eldercare provides no nine-month preparatory period. All too often, the stroke, heart attack, or cancer diagnosis catches a family off-guard. In addition, a chronically ill elder is likely to experience an unpredictable decline in independence and vitality each year. Consider the following example:

A prominent retired local official in Northern California was discharged from the hospital after suffering from a stroke. He was 83 years old, 20+ pounds overweight, and had a history of diabetes, high blood pressure, and falls. He used two canes and had difficulty sitting, standing, walking, and going to the bathroom. He couldn't drive and was unable to dress himself. Although he lived at home with his wife, she worked full-time, so he was alone from 6:30 a.m. to 7 p.m. on weekdays.

Upon discharge, a home health nurse was ordered for two visits a week and a physical therapist weekly. No additional supportive services were arranged, leaving an ailing elderly man unable to walk, eat, go to the bathroom, or dress himself, at home alone for at least 12 hours each day. He and his wife tried their best to cope with this situation. After he had fallen twice and been found prone on the floor more than 5 hours later, however, the family decided they needed help.

To their frustration and dismay, their health plan was unwilling to increase services. Its position was that the required services were primarily custodial and "nonmedical," and therefore outside the scope of its responsibility. Actually, it wasn't the plan's fault: The plan itself couldn't get reimbursed by Medicare. The family called a local home meal provider, but were told that a waiting list existed. They contacted another organization for a home helper, but were told that a case manager must see them first, and to call the care management agency directly. That agency accepted their call and scheduled an assessment—for a week later. In the interim, no services were provided, and the elderly man's condition further deteriorated.

After the assessment, everyone met and determined that a home helper would be needed five days a week, a physical therapist three times a week, and transportation assistance one to two times a week. The family was chagrined to learn that each of these services was provided by a different agency and they would have to schedule appointments and arrange services themselves. Additionally, each service required a comprehensive initial assessment followed by quarterly reassessments. None of the recommended services were covered by their Medicare-risk plan; the costs rested solely on the family.

As his needs deepened, he was receiving 8 to 10 assessments

every 90 days from several different agencies, none of whom discussed the case with one another.

This example is not rare. I have heard hundreds of similar accounts. The problem lies in the lack of connection between the myriad of independent eldercare providers as well as the fact that so few of these important services are covered by Medicare. During a recent Age Wave focus group on long-term care, a woman reflected on the frustrations she felt trying to navigate through the system after her mother was discharged from the hospital following cancer surgery: "The information we got at the hospital was contradictory, not only from the doctors but also from the caseworkers. One person would say one thing and the next person you talked to would recommend something else. There was a lot of trying to sort through and pull out the consistencies in each one of the persons who were giving you information. It was so frustrating, I could scream!"

The *Chronic Care in America* report found that 47 percent of individuals with long-term care needs do not understand what services they are eligible for, 38 percent do not know who provides which services, and 30 percent found the services that existed confusing or inaccessible.[13] These figures indicate an enormous gap between people's needs and their ability to locate and arrange for appropriate solutions.

Sometimes there is no agency to coordinate eldercare, but just as often there are *too many* agencies, each with its own niche carved out, which creates havoc for people in need. For example, in Fremont, California—population 198,700—there are more than 400 organizations listed in the senior resource directory. Unfortunately, most of these well-intentioned organizations provide very specialized services and seldom communicate with one another. Furthermore, the experts to whom most people turn for information—their doctors or nurses—are usually unfamiliar with the vast majority of community-based programs. Since payments for most of these services fall outside the reimbursement channels of the healthcare system, there is little incentive for healthcare professionals to become more knowledgeable about them. In every city, on every day, elder men and women are falling through the cracks of our incomplete, and all-too-often uncaring, long-term care system.

THE PREMATURE DEATH OF MEN

With very few exceptions, the life expectancy of women worldwide is higher than that of men. In developed countries, the average gap in life expectancy at birth is 7 years. In some it's even greater—Russian women, for instance, outlive men an average of 13 years. Among all 60+ adults in developed countries, there are only 70 men for each 100 women. Among the oldest old, there are only 44 men for each 100 women.[14] As a result, the age wave will also reflect the increasing feminization of the global population.

Since women tend to marry men older than themselves, most women can expect to outlive their husbands by 10 years or more. Unfair as this is to men, it also exacerbates the caregiving crunch by creating legions of widows—often alone and in need of care and support for extended periods. Currently, nearly half of all women over 65 are widows, with five times as many widows as widowers.[15]

Women also tend to have more co-morbidities than men. Studies by the National Center for Health Statistics found that for those 80+ years of age, 70 percent of women and only 53 percent of men had two or more chronic conditions.[16]

For a widowed woman, the death of her husband often triggers a variety of housing, health, and financial difficulties. Elderly women are much less likely to remarry and much more likely to live alone than elderly men. They are more likely to need assistance with daily tasks, and much less likely to have a family member available to provide this help. According to a recent study by the Life Insurance Marketing and Research Association, widows experience a 38 percent decline in household income after their spouse's death, compared to only 26 percent for widowers. The combined stresses of a reduced income and the lack of a spouse to provide care and share responsibilities can be devastating—and studies have repeatedly shown that the recently bereaved are more prone to accidents, injuries, and physical illness. As a result of such factors, women are more likely to need institutional long-term care than are men.[17]

As we can see, the issue of eldercare is like a multi-spoked wheel, involving finance, proximity of caregivers, a myriad of services, longevity, and other factors. But this wheel does not turn smoothly because many of these elements are in disarray and fail to meet the swiftly growing needs of the elderly and their families. How can we address this mounting problem?

How We Can Ease the Caregiving Crunch: The Four-Part Solution

There is a story of a man who goes to sit beside a beautiful yet turbulent river. As he unfolds his blanket and sets out a picnic lunch, he notices that the current is carrying along someone who is crying out for help. The observer quickly dives into the river, fights the current, seizes the victim, and swims him back to safety. Exhausted, the two men collapse on the riverbank; after a while the near-drowned man thanks his savior and goes on his way.

The picnicker dries off and prepares to enjoy his lunch. Before he can take a bite, he hears a piercing cry coming from the river: This time a woman is being pulled down by the current, just like the man before her. The Good Samaritan once again jumps in and with great effort pulls the woman to safety. Afterward, she is so depleted from her ordeal that he shares some of his sandwich with her. She thanks him and leaves.

This same event occurs again and again throughout the afternoon until at last the picnicker finds himself without food, exhausted, and certainly much the worse for wear after pulling so many drowning victims from the river. As the sun sets, he sits back to reflect on the incredible deeds he's been called upon to perform and wonders whether he'll be needed every day to rescue all these drowning men and women. Only then does he glance around and notice that *there's been somebody upstream pushing everyone in.*

As we explored in Chapter 5, the ideal way to alleviate the coming caregiving crunch is *not* to put more lifeguards downstream, but rather to *stop pushing so many people in upstream.* By intensifying aging-related research efforts, improving the geriatric competency of healthcare professionals, educating maturing men and women in self-care, and realigning the economic incentives of healthcare insurance to promote "healthy aging," we raise the likelihood of extending the healthy, independent years of life while compressing morbidity into shorter spans. Just as Oliver Wendell Holmes's "One-Hoss Shay" had little need for care and maintenance, if we could live longer and die shorter, a substantial portion of the caregiving demand would be eliminated.

To bring about this change and rescue ourselves from the social and economic sinkhole that caregiving threatens to become, we must pursue the following solutions:

1. Finance long-term care through private insurance or reverse mortgages.
2. Establish new eldercare-oriented employee benefits.
3. Expand and integrate long-term care programs and services.
4. Develop health-related affirmative action programs for men.

Solution #1:
Finance Long-term Care Through Private Pay Insurance or Reverse Mortgages

According to a recent National Council on the Aging/John Hancock survey on long-term care, "seventy-nine percent of older boomers believe that long-term care is the greatest risk to their standard of living during retirement," but very few are doing anything about it. A key reason is their mistaken belief that long-term care is covered by Medicare or that they can get Medicaid to cover the costs.[18]

Although private long-term care insurance is a far more realistic and secure way to finance these needs, such policies are held by less than 10 percent of the eligible population. When today's elders and their boomer children realize how long-term care can drain an entire lifetime of savings (and expected inheritance) in a few years, and when the government tightens up its controls on Medicaid manipulation, long-term care insurance sales will boom. In the past, the life insurance industry grew based on people's fear of *dying too young*. In the future, long-term care (LTC) insurance will grow based on people's fear of *living too long*.

Global consultants McKinsey and Company have recently concluded that long-term care insurance remains the largest untapped category of financial services growth in the country. As policies become oriented more toward home-based care and keeping people out of nursing homes, and more affordable, we should see a dramatic growth boom in this industry. The McKinsey group projects that the LTC insurance industry will more than triple from $3 billion per year in premiums in 1996 to $10 billion by 2006.[19]

In January 1999, President Clinton proposed a measure to make private LTC insurance available to federal employees, retirees, and relatives. The package also included $6 billion in tax and budget proposals to provide a $1,000 annual tax credit to eldercare-givers. Considering that these caregivers are likely to be spending tens of thousands of dollars every year or forfeiting it in lost work, that part of Clinton's proposal is relatively trivial—$3 a day won't buy you very much of anything. Yet the media coverage it might receive could focus much-needed attention on this serious problem. Additionally, Clinton's plan would make $125 million available to states to assist family-care givers with training, counseling, and respite support. It will also fund a campaign to educate and inform all 39 million beneficiaries that Medicare does *not* cover most long-term care.[20]

Both the public and private sectors have been exploring new approaches to financing long-term care. One innovative approach is the Robert Wood Johnson Partnership for Long Term Care, a "public-private" state-based program (currently in California, Connecticut, Indiana, and New York and set for implementation in all states) that combines asset protection with private long-term care insurance. Its goal is to reach that part of the population that would otherwise spend down or transfer assets to qualify for Medicaid coverage. The program offers "dollar for dollar" trade-offs in which a consumer receives one dollar of asset protection for every dollar of insurance that he or she buys. For example, a 65-year-old woman can purchase long-term care insurance worth $50,000 for an annual premium of $500 to $800 and thereby become eligible for Medicaid while retaining $50,000 in personal assets. According to Mark Meiners of the Center on Aging at the University of Maryland, the program's director, "It's inconceivable that new federal or state health reforms will finance comprehensive long-term care in a time of bulging deficits. But the capacity is lacking in the private sector alone to finance long-term care for the millions of Americans who need it. The blending of state monies and the quality assurance that accompanies state certification with the experience and marketing skills of private insurance makes for a very reasonable, high-quality option."[21]

Other initiatives at the federal level include Ohio Congressman David Hobson's Long-Term Care Insurance Act of 1999, which proposes an above-the-line tax deduction for persons who purchase qualified LTC insurance plans. New Jersey Congressman Christopher Smith's innovative Long-Term Care Advancement Act would permit penalty-free withdrawals from IRAs and 401(k) plans to buy qualified LTC plans. These proposals are currently under review by the House Ways and Means Committee.

These kinds of approaches would, in all likelihood, garner strong public support—especially from boomers. According to the National Council on the Aging/John Hancock's 1999 long-term care survey, 91 percent of respondents favored making LTC insurance premiums tax deductible, 81 percent favored granting a tax deduction to a child or grandchild who buys LTC insurance for a parent or grandparent, and 81 percent favored allowing individuals to pay for LTC insurance premiums using tax-free withdrawals from 401(k) plans or IRAs.[22]

Another possible approach is the reverse mortgage, a concept that originated in the 1970s. Home equity is the single biggest financial asset of most elders, yet it is seldom used as a source of financing for long-term care.

A bank or lending institution could offer older adults an arrangement by which contributions could be made to long-term care financing, drawn from the equity value of their home. In essence, they could continue to live at home while funding their health and lifestyle support needs from their home equity. When a homeowner passes away, the will probated, and the house sold, the insurer would receive the principal and the interest back.

The financing of long-term care will be a growing concern to governments, individuals, and families as the need intensifies while the availability of informal caregivers continues to drop. Innovations in payment strategies should result in better deals and greater flexibility. At the end of the day, however, boomers and their families will foot most of the bill—and only planning, savings, insurance, or reverse mortgages will carry them through.

Solution #2:
Establish New Eldercare-oriented Employee Benefits

As more workers face conflicts between careers and eldercare, employers are beginning to see the cost as a looming social and financial issue. "The bottom line for employers is that 20 to 30 percent of workers care for older relatives," reports the Conference Board, a nonprofit business research organization for senior executives.[23] While workers who miss work to care for children are likely to be in their twenties and thirties, those absent due to eldercare are more likely to be in their forties or fifties—and more senior in rank. The cost of eldercare to American businesses is already estimated at $11.4 billion to $29 billion annually, according to a 1997 survey by the Metropolitan Life Insurance Company, and this expense is destined to multiply.[24]

Yet long-term care benefits are barely on the radar screens of most benefits managers or unions. In a few years, however, employer-sponsored eldercare programs could become the fastest-growing segment of the employee benefit industry.

The situation employers will soon confront is analogous to what they faced in the 1970s with childcare. Until then, it was uncommon for employers to provide any type of childcare benefits, services, or leave. The onrush of baby-boomer women into the workplace, however, put pressure on them to address the childcare issue or lose good workers.

Some companies responded initially by providing greater flextime and extended-leave policies.[25] As the burden of childcare was felt more severely—through employee turnover, absenteeism, decreased productivity, and negative publicity—more companies developed stronger and more attractive benefits. In 1970, less than 20 percent of employers provided childcare benefits. By 1999, nearly 90 percent offered them.

Today, 88 percent of companies allow workers to take time off from work for childcare obligations; 68 percent allow them to periodically change starting/ending time; 55 percent permit workers to work at home occasionally; 37 percent allow employees to share jobs; and 36 percent provide information to help locate childcare in the community. Additionally, 50 percent of companies have dependent-care assistance plans that help employees pay for childcare with pretax dollars.

In contrast, eldercare remains the sleeping giant. A 1997 report by the American Business Collaborative found that of all resources devoted to work/family programs, 95 percent were targeted to childcare, only 5 percent to eldercare.[26]

Some concerned companies, such as IBM, Johnson and Johnson, and Hewlett-Packard, are just beginning to institute programs in this area. A survey of 1,057 major U.S. employers revealed that 23 percent offered modest eldercare benefits in 1998, more than twice the number in 1990. These initial programs typically included some information and referral services and unpaid family leave. The flex-time that is permitted for childcare generally does not apply for eldercare, though employers appear to informally support workers who need to adjust schedules.[27]

The impact of such programs can be significant. More than 6,000 Aetna Insurance employees have used their eldercare consul-tation and referral service since it was established in 1988. Aetna estimates that for every dollar invested in the benefits, the company saves $3 in the form of increased productivity and reduced absen-teeism. This level of savings has been affirmed in a new study pre-pared for Metropolitan Life Insurance Company showing that employers stand to save $3 to $5 for every dollar they spend helping employees find eldercare resources.

While very few companies currently offer eldercare insurance, those who do have seen a positive response. Since Hewlett-Packard began offering LTC insurance as a feature of its employee benefit package five years ago, more than 10,000 employees have purchased policies. The Hewlett-Packard model is unusual in that it is a self-insured plan—that is, the company is at risk for the medical claims of policyholders. To reduce its risk, the company has priced the pol-icy to make it attractive to a younger age group. In the individual sales market, the typical purchaser is usually an older adult in the mid- to late sixties, but at H-P the typical purchaser is in his or her late forties to early fifties. With younger policyholders, both the price and claims are significantly reduced. Currently, the average annual rate for long-term care insurance for a 65-year-old is $1,800, but only $435 for a 45-year-old.

Two years ago, the California Public Employees Retirement Sys-tem (CalPERS) developed a long-term care insurance program and offered it to employees, retirees, and family members. In less than 18 months, more than 100,000 policies were written—making the CalPERS plan the most active in the country. In fact, from 1996 to 1999, more LTC insurance policies were issued for CalPERS members than for everyone else in the state of California.

Although employer-supported long-term care benefits have a long way to go, the number of policies sold in the employer market has grown from 20,000 in 1988 to over 650,000 in 1996.[28]

Solution #3:
Expand and Integrate Long-term Care Programs and Services

Decades ago, nearly all long-term care was provided in hospitals. This is still the case in Japan, where the average hospital stay is 45 days compared with 5 1/2 in the U.S. Of the more than 700,000 elderly Japanese hospitalized today, nearly half have been in the wards for more than six months—most for lack of a better place to go.[29]

By contrast, socialized countries like Denmark and Sweden already have an effective and well-supported home- and community-based care system. In these countries, social care services enable many elderly people, even those with disabilities, to live independently. It is not uncommon for Scandinavian home helpers to visit the elderly several times a day.

As we have seen, our primary focus in the U.S. has not been on community- or home-based care but on hospital-based services and nursing-home care. The past 30 years have taught us, however, that nursing homes are not the solution most consumers are seeking. In addition, industry experts have come to believe that one-fifth to one-third of institutionalized elders shouldn't be there in the first place. Their needs would be better served within the community by adult daycare programs and, whenever possible, in their own homes supported by homecare nurses, physical therapists, and specially trained homecare aides.

Unfortunately, America's current long-term care service system is fragmented, often dysfunctional, and biased toward nursing homes. With the coming age wave, we face worsening problems of availability and quality. In response, we need to integrate our health-care and social service systems into a seamless continuum that provides institutional and home-based medical and custodial care, as well as respite for the family. And we must find a way to deliver this care and support in each community without bankrupting the economy.

The good news is that some of these pieces are already in place, although they need nourishment and better orchestration. The Aging Network—linking more than 600 government-supported Area Agencies on Aging (AAA) with tens of thousands of community organizations—has launched programs in nearly every community across the country to support eldercare-givers. For example:

- The National Adult Day Services Association coordinates and provides a variety of adult daycare activities.
- The Caregiver Assistance Network offers support and information to family members caring for older adults and disabled persons nationwide.
- Internet-based Caregiver Survival Resources provides a regularly updated clearinghouse of links to caregiver resources nationwide.
- Aging Network Services personally selects a geriatric care manager to help with eldercare. Its membership network consists of 250 master's-level social workers throughout the United States. Careful consideration is given to matching the specialties of the local care manager to the particular needs of the client family.
- The National Federation of Interfaith Volunteer Caregivers promotes, in all congregations throughout the United States,

the ministry of caregiving to disabled persons and their families.

- The National Family Caregivers Association is a charitable organization dedicated to family caregivers. Through its information and education services, NFCA strives to minimize the deterioration of a caregiver's quality of life and raise public awareness.
- The National Institute of Senior Centers coordinates the activities of nearly 15,000 senior centers, serving millions of older adults. Such centers are community focal points where older adults can access information and services and participate in educational, recreational, and cultural activities. Many also serve nutritious meals.[30]

A few federal demonstration projects also provide models for integrated care. The Program of All-Inclusive Care for the Elderly, or PACE, pioneered by On Lok Senior Health Services in San Francisco 16 years ago, has shown the financial benefits of keeping the elderly at home. PACE takes "nursing home eligible" individuals hampered by functional frailty and, through the efforts of a team of case managers, physicians, therapists, nutritionists, and home health aides, helps them continue to live at home. PACE has proven to be so successful that it transitioned from a demonstration program to a full-fledged Medicare HMO in 1998.

Other models seek to show the advantages of lower-cost alternatives to nursing home care. Social health maintenance organizations (S/HMOs) are currently being piloted in six locations: SCAN Health Plan in Long Beach, California; Kaiser Foundation Health Plan in Portland, Oregon; ElderPlan in Brooklyn, New York; and EverCare in Atlanta, Baltimore, and Westborough, Massachusetts. Each combines case management and social support with all-inclusive payments for a cross-section of the older population. While these S/HMOs are still in the demonstration phase, the hope is that this integrated-care model can eventually be broadly developed.

Because a large portion of eldercare is paid for out-of-pocket, numerous entrepreneurial companies are offering enhanced and expanded homecare services, varied housing options, new LTC insurance products, better care coordination, and other products and services.

In a recent Age Wave focus group, a middle-aged caregiver commented on some of the services she would really appreciate: "To pack Dad up and get him outside the house or have someone come in and stay with him while I went out would be very helpful. If I could have a least one day a week when I didn't have to be worried about Dad, I think I could recharge my batteries. Also, if I could find someone reliable who could help me with ordinary, day-to-day housecleaning, grocery store shopping, and dry-cleaning errands, it would take a lot of pressure off me. How about a service that would coordinate the deliveries from the drugstore, supermarket, and medical supply store? I'm not a big believer that computers are going to take over everything, but if grocery products were online and I could go click, click, click, and then have my order delivered, that would be great."

Some companies are carving out specific niches along the long-term care continuum:

- LifeSource Nutrition Solutions, based in Emeryville, California, provides appetizing, home-delivered food to individuals with specific chronic conditions such as diabetes, coronary artery disease, and congestive heart failure.[31]
- CHCS, a national organization headquartered in Weston, Florida, has developed into the nation's largest geriatric care management company, contracting with HMOs, long-term care insurance companies, and families to oversee and coordinate all aspects of home-based eldercare in communities throughout the country.
- LifeMasters® is one of the dozens of Supported/SelfCareSM disease management firms that contract with health plans to help patients manage and live with chronic conditions.

- Home Instead Senior Care is a nationwide franchise of non-medical homecare services; with 144 offices in 31 states, it is one of the largest and fastest-growing such companies in the country.
- Recent years have seen a surge of growth in "assisted living" residences that provide an attractive alternative to nursing homes for those who are able to maintain more independence. In spite of massive construction, however, projections show a shortage of available facilities in the coming years.

Solution #4:
Develop Health-related "Affirmative Action" Programs for Men

Although a tragedy unto itself, the premature death of men also leaves tens of millions of elder women to depend on their friends and adult children for support and care. If men didn't die so much earlier than women, couples could help *care for each other* in their later years. One of the more obvious ways to relieve some of the burden on sandwiched caregivers would be to *improve the longevity of men*.

Men have a great deal to learn from women when it comes to improving their health. In recent decades, women have developed a strong track record of self-care and health activism. During their childbearing years and in the role of caregivers, women come into contact with health services in a way men often do not. Women are the principal purchasers of self-help books, exercise equipment, health club memberships, and a wide range of other health-related products and services. Women are also far more likely than men to modify their diets, join an exercise class, or participate in preventive health screenings. Since it began in the 1960s, the "women's health movement" has also helped elevate public awareness, create better-attuned healthcare practitioners, and attract greater amounts of funding for important women's health concerns.

Considering men's inferior health and longevity, it's a shame that no similar men's health movement has taken flight. Experts reflect that it's probably men's self-consciousness that keeps them from doing more about the health problems that threaten their lives, as well as socialization that discourages them from complaining or seeking assistance.

Researchers at the National Institutes of Health and numerous universities have repeatedly shown that male morbidity and longevity are influenced by *alterable* lifestyle habits and can be improved by stopping smoking and excessive alcohol consumption, eating more nutritious meals, exercising regularly, avoiding occupational hazards when possible, and conscientiously using healthcare services. It is estimated that as much as 70 percent of the illnesses than men struggle with could be prevented by regular checkups and better self-care. Yet most men tend to avoid regular physician visits and ignore health problems until they become serious. Declaring "I haven't been to a doctor in years" or viewing self-examination as akin to hypochondria is typical, and sometimes deadly, behavior among men. Older men are often reluctant to go public with their health afflictions for fear that they might lose their pride, status, or jobs.

In this era of publicly driven funding priorities, unless men start calling out for more help, they're not likely to get it. The result: The gap between male and female longevity could widen, producing an even greater caregiving burden on adult children.

If male longevity is to be improved, nothing short of a revolution in men's health is required. To initiate such a movement, there is much to be learned from the women's health movement. In the 1960s, Barbara Seaman was a health columnist for magazines such as *Bride's* and *Ladies' Home Journal.* When the first oral contraceptives appeared, readers deluged Seaman with questions about birth-control pills. In response, she began an investigation that culminated in the publication of *The Doctors' Case Against the Pill,* a 1969 exposé claiming that the pill could cause fatal strokes, heart disease, diabetes, depression, and other ailments. All the media attention she received helped to ignite a political movement focusing on women's health.[32]

Around the same time, the Boston Women's Health Collective formed. The original 12 members, brought together during a workshop on women's health, charged themselves with compiling a list of ob/gyn doctors in the Boston area who were responsive to women's reproductive health questions. Failing to find enough to fill even a couple of pages, they decided to undertake the research themselves.

In 1970, the collective's research papers were published in an underground, newsprint edition. After it sold 250,000 copies, Simon and Schuster published the first commercial edition of *Our Bodies, Ourselves,* as they named the collection in 1973. Since then, nearly 4 million copies have been sold in 17 different languages, including Braille. A quarter of a century after *The Doctors' Case* and *Our Bodies, Ourselves,* most universities now have established programs in women's health, governments across the world have created offices of women's health, and almost half of all U.S. medical students are female.

Perhaps nowhere is the movement's impact so powerful as in publicizing the risks and treatments of breast cancer. In the mid-1990s, breast cancer activists began sporting pink ribbons to make the public aware of the death toll. Since then, breast cancer has metamorphosed from a medical diagnosis into a potent political cause. Along the way, celebrity patients and their friends, scientific findings, and personal stories have catapulted the ailment into the headlines perhaps more often than any other single affliction besides AIDS. This public attention has led to more widespread use of mammograms, enhanced professional sensitivities, and greater research funding.

There are some signs that a men's health movement might be emerging. In the last several years, well-known public figures such as Norman Schwarzkopf, Arnold Palmer, Andrew Grove, Harry Belafonte, and Michael Milken have spoken up about their struggles with prostate cancer, and Michael Korda's *Man to Man* recounting his experience became a breakthrough best-seller in the late 1990s. In 1998, Bob Dole extolled the benefits of Viagra on national television, something difficult to imagine coming from other politicians of his era. Ronald Reagan has written forthrightly about his struggle with Alzheimer's.

More boomer men are taking an interest in how to care for their bodies. The cover of a recent issue of *Men's Health* exclaimed, "Give Yourself the Finger"; although jocular in tone, the article provided valuable instructions on self-examination for testicular cancer—something that would have been almost unheard of in the leading men's sports and hobby magazines a few years ago.

To achieve greater gender health equality, we need to:

- Increase research into the physiological and behavioral factors that influence the mortality of men.
- Increase public education on men's health issues such as prostate cancer.
- Motivate men to take better care of themselves.
- Encourage doctors' offices and insurance companies to be more responsive to men's needs and styles of communication.
- Enlist public figures in a campaign to raise public awareness of the social and economic value of greater male longevity.

Shoring Up the Sinkhole

Until the era of healthy aging arrives, numerous disabilities and frailties will accompany age power. Yet our current healthcare and social service systems were not designed with the elderly and their caregivers in mind. The components of these systems are not integrated, are extremely difficult to navigate, and require out-of-pocket costs that most families are not prepared to pay for. Unless changes occur, the social, emotional, and economic resources of our families will be drained by having to provide or finance decades of long-term care.

The 21st century will require better information, products, respite, support services, and affordable financing for long-term care. The caregiving crunch can be eased if government, nonprofits, businesses, and individuals set in motion the right corrections now.

Tips to Age-proof Your Life

- Talk with your parents about their preparedness for chronic health problems. Take steps to protect their savings—and your inheritance—through proper insurance coverage and/or estate management. If you believe that poverty may be imminent, consult an expert to establish the proper preparations for Medicaid.
- Expect that you might require some form of at-home, long-term care in your old age, and find a long-term care insurance policy that will allow you and your family to be protected at a reasonable cost.
- Familiarize yourself with long-term care services in your and your parents' communities before they're actually needed. Use your company's benefits office, the library, or the Internet to stay abreast of available services.
- Pay extra attention to the health and medical needs of the men in your family—the healthier elder men remain, the less of a caregiving burden is likely to fall on adult children.

CHAPTER SEVEN

FINANCIAL WAKE-UP CALL

The household savings rate in South Korea is nearly 25 percent. In Japan it is 12 to 15 percent; in Europe, 10 percent. In the U.S., the household savings rate dipped from 11.7 percent in the 1950s to 10.8 percent in the 1970s, then plummeted to 5.9 percent in the 1980s. By the 1990s, total personal savings, including what families save on their own as well as employer pension contributions, has averaged only 4.9 percent of disposable income. Excluding pensions, the rate is much lower—a virtually useless 1 to 2 percent.

Even if government entitlements continue, the current approaches to financing retirement will fail for the boomer generation. Too many people, living too many years and having saved far too little, will place increasing tax demands on smaller working generations.

If we continue down the path we're on, when the dust settles, some of today's middle-aged generation will make out just fine. Approximately one-third of boomers are earning large salaries, have invested wisely, and will benefit from their share of the ten trillion dollars in inheritances that their parents will leave behind. Another third, however, will be forced to extend their work lives at least five years beyond current expectations before they might enjoy a satisfactory retirement. If they're fortunate enough to receive some inheritance, they might even live comfortably in maturity. Yet a sizable segment of boomers— as much as one-third (and a group disproportionately female)—has virtually no savings, no investments, no pensions, and, in all likelihood, will receive no inheritance windfall. Today, these 25 million boomers have average household net assets of less than $1,000.[1]

According to former Secretary of Commerce Peter G. Peterson,

"Even the optimists admit that a bleak future awaits the estimated one third of all boomers who are expected neither to accumulate financial assets nor to received a private pension. Among these will be many of today's burgeoning number of divorced and single mothers."[2]

Unless dramatic changes are made soon, not only will a third of today's middle-agers become tomorrow's impoverished elders— 20+ million, in contrast to the 4 million poor among today's elderly—but the programs from which the rest of us expect to bene-fit will be diverted to save them.[3]

Part of the problem is that in most discussions regarding the boomers' financial security in retirement, the emphasis is placed on Social Security's viability. Because such a large segment of this gen-eration has done so little financial preparation for retirement, the emphasis should be placed *equally* on savings and pensions.

Two interconnected elements are therefore creating the boomers' financial insecurity:

- The *economics* of old-age entitlements don't add up. Politi-cians are playing a game of "pyramid power" with our future.
- Many boomers are caught in a dangerous state of *financial paralysis* and are not taking the necessary steps to plan for their financial futures.

Old-Age Entitlements Just Don't Add Up

Politicians and special interest groups are winning public adula-tion for proclaiming that Social Security and Medicare are easily fix-able and can be made to last with a few simple tweaks. Don't believe it. *Between 2010 and 2030, the size of the 65+ population will grow by more than 75 percent, while the population paying payroll taxes will rise less than 5 percent.* In the year 2013, just two years after the first baby boomers begin turning 65, the annual surplus of Social Security tax revenues over outlays will turn negative. By 2030, when all the surviving boomers will have reached 65, Social Security alone will be running an *annual* cash deficit of $666 billion. Although it is often touted that Social Security has been accumulating a gigantic surplus to cover future liabilities, the trust fund's resources will cover only a tiny fraction, perhaps 10 percent, of these future outlays.[4]

The General Accounting Office (GAO), not known for hysterical proclamations, stated the situation plainly in its report of July 11, 1997: "The bottom line? The Old Age and Survivors and Disability Insurance program is out of balance, and the private pension system will not provide adequate benefits for a majority of workers. Over the long run, Social Security receipts will fall far short of expenditures, and the problem will get worse over time because people are living longer, retiring earlier, and real Social Security benefits have increased.[5]

According to the GAO, without corrective action the trust funds will be depleted by 2029, and Social Security's revenues will be sufficient to fund only 70 to 77 percent of benefits. If Medicare Hospital Insurance is included, and if both programs continue according to current law, the combined cash deficit in 2030 alone will be $1.7 trillion.

Consider the magnitude of the tax increases that would have to be levied on today's generation Xers to fund the boomers' retirement. If benefits remain at the current level, by 2040 the cost of Social Security as a share of the average worker's payroll is expected to double from today's 11.5 percent to more than 22 percent. If you add both parts of Medicare, which currently cost the equivalent of 2.9 percent of payroll but are growing so rapidly that they could eventually surpass Social Security in size, we'd be looking at a tariff of 40 percent or more of every worker's paycheck just to cover the cost of old-age entitlements.

Although former President Jimmy Carter has always been a strong supporter of all aspects of Social Security's programs, he offered some sobering reflections in his recent book, *The Virtues of Aging:* "Most political leaders have only recently acknowledged what many experts have long recognized: The future of the American Social Security system is in serious trouble. . . . Today, about half of the federal budget goes to pay for programs for the elderly. If basic changes are not made in entitlement programs, it has been predicted that by 2013 the entire federal budget will be going to pay for the elderly and for interest on the federal debt."[6]

To better understand how we got into this predicament, let's briefly review the original purpose and structure of this once-great program.

THE CONTRACT BETWEEN THE GENERATIONS

For FDR's "social insurance" to work, it initially needed to provide instant benefits for those already over the age of 65—only 6 percent of the population when the program began providing payments in 1937. Realizing that it would be impossible to tax those already old enough to receive benefits, the Roosevelt administration taxed those who were still working—the younger generations. With the average life expectancy only 63, and with 40 workers paying in per each recipient, it seemed a sensible thing at the time.

Representatives of the senior lobby, largely composed of AARP, repeatedly assert at conferences, before congressional panels, and in the media that whatever the economic and social consequences, American workers are duty-bound to fulfill their side of this "contract between generations." But what exactly was that "contract"?

For the first 12 years after payouts began in 1937, the top contribution to Social Security was about 2 percent of the maximum taxable individual income ($3,000), or $60. Just $30 per year was contributed by each employee, with another $30 matched by his or her employer. By 1940, the average annual benefit payment was a modest $157.66.[7] Social Security was not intended to subsidize a comfortable retirement for the masses: It was meant to provide a small financial safety net that would complement the individual financial planning that citizens were expected to do on their own. As

FDR himself stated, "We have tried to frame a law which will give some measure of protection to the average citizen and to his family against the loss of a job and against poverty-ridden old age."[8] Several years later, in his Message to Congress, Roosevelt emphasized Social Security's limited role in an individual's overall financial planning: "We shall make the most lasting progress if we recognize that Social Security can furnish only a base upon which each one of our citizens may build his individual security through his own individual efforts."[9]

This limited intergenerational transfer of funds, providing a modest financial safety net, was the actual *pact* that many of today's seniors argue is the debt owed them by our government. However, in recent debates, owing largely to the growth in age power, the original deal has been revised again and again—almost always in favor of seniors.

At its inception, Social Security provided old-age benefits only to workers in commerce and industry—about 60 percent of the workforce. In 1939, coverage was extended to provide benefits for some family members and survivors. In the 1950s, state and local governments were given the option of expanding coverage to their own employees, and in 1956 the Disability Insurance Program was added, providing income for disabled workers. Then in 1965, Medicare further increased the benefits. Beginning in 1975, the entitlements got another boost when benefits were automatically tied to the Consumer Price Index (CPI) to ensure protection against inflation. In 1999, the average annual benefit was $9,360—up more than 1,300 percent in real dollars since 1937.[10]

Meanwhile, the initial ratio of 40 productive workers to each retiree has steadily shrunk from 16 in 1950 to only 3.3 today. By 2040, it is projected that there will only be 2 workers, and perhaps as few as 1.6, to support each boomer retiree, who could be living as many as 20 to 40 years in retirement. To pay the ever-growing bill, the Federal Insurance Contributions Act (FICA) obliges workers and their employers to contribute 12.4 percent of the first $72,600 of taxable income. Add to this the 2.9 percent[11] Medicare tax rate imposed on all taxable wages, and the total burden for a two-income middle-class couple earning $60,000 has grown to $9,180 per year, representing a 7,650 percent increase in contributions when compared to the original deal of $120 per couple. Even in inflation-adjustment dollars, the increase has been 570 percent. Today's maximum Social Security tax for a two-income, 25-year-old couple is just over $18,000.[12]

It's obvious that the dynamics, costs, and rewards of today's entitlement benefits bear no resemblance to the contract made more than 60 years ago. Moreover, the majority of today's beneficiaries are receiving *far more* than they ever paid in FICA contributions, just as today's workers continue to contribute more and more to support them. Given current life expectancy, the average one-earner couple retiring in 1999 will receive about $123,000 *more* out of Social Security than they and their employers ever paid into it, plus interest. Add in Medicare, remove the employer's contribution, and the average windfall rises to $310,000 more than they put in. Because so much of Social Security is tax-free, and because retirees no longer pay FICA taxes, a typical retired couple on Social Security in 1999 with $30,000 in total cash income—including Social Security—paid, on average, only $936 in federal taxes.[13] Meanwhile, their daughter and son-in-law, working while raising two children on the same income of $30,000 per year, had a total federal tax burden nearly seven times greater, $6,360, including both the FICA tax they paid and that paid by their employers.[14] Very few industrial nations tilt their tax systems in favor of the elderly as much as the United States.

SHELL GAMES AND PONZI SCHEMES

But wait, the problem is worse: There really isn't *any* money in the Social Security Trust Fund. The federal government created the fund in 1937 as a fail-safe against a Social Security shortfall—but that isn't how it has been maintained.

Old Age and Survivors and Disability Insurance receipts are

accumulated in a special government fund that by law is allowed to invest only in a special class of U.S. Treasury securities. Yet this money is *not* saved for a rainy day. Instead, the government legally uses it to finance deficit spending in other areas and leaves an IOU in its place. According to economist William G. Shipman of the Cato Institute, "In common usage, a trust fund is an estate of money and securities held in trust for its beneficiaries. The Social Security Trust Fund is *quite different.* When taxes exceed benefits, the federal government lends itself the excess in return for an interest-paying bond, an IOU that it issues to itself. The funds are *not* invested for the benefit of present or future retirees. The government spends its new funds on unrelated projects such as bridge repairs, defense, or food stamps.[15] In 1998, the total amount that the government had "borrowed" from the fund was $100 billion.[16]

Several years ago, I saw an entertaining movie, *King of the Gypsies,* starring a young Eric Roberts. It portrayed modern-day urban Gypsies as a collection of charmers, misfits, and tribal elders. In one touching scene, after the Gypsy elder passed away, members of Gypsy tribes from far and near come to his home to pay their respects. According to their custom, anyone who owed a debt to this powerful man is honor-bound to deposit the amount in his coffin, where it will stay forever. Hundreds of bills, coins, and jewels are left by mourners until the body is barely visible. Just before the coffin is sealed, the Gypsy elder's conniving grandson (Roberts) requests a few moments alone with his beloved grandpa to pay his final respects.

As soon as everyone has left the room, the grandson takes all of the cash and riches out of the coffin, hides it in a sack, then writes a check for the total value of the booty he has taken. He places the check over the heart of his grandfather, and seals the coffin.

This is how the government has used the Social Security Trust Fund. If you go to sleep tonight believing the fund works in any other way, you might as well put a tooth under your pillow and await a visit from the tooth fairy.

Haeworth Robertson, former Social Security chief actuary, recently published a powerful book offering his personal views on the Social Security system. The book's title: *The Big Lie*. Robertson is "mad as hell," as he exclaims in the preface. What about?

> . . . all the lies and hypocrisies surrounding the selling of Social Security to the public for the past 60 years. It was easy to disregard the first half-truth, to overlook an omission here and there, to ignore the first lie, and to give the benefit of the doubt to government officials and policy makers who seem to be well intentioned but didn't get the facts straight. But the cumulative effect of 20 years of personal experience with these deceptions is more than I can tolerate any longer. I am compelled to speak out as forcefully as possible about one of the greatest frauds ever perpetrated on the American public. . . . As Social Security's problems mount, and as the public becomes more disenchanted with it, a giant propaganda machine turns out more and more lies to lull the public into a false sense of security that is destroying their will and ability to create their own financially sound retirement.[17]

The Social Security system is, in fact, very much like a Ponzi scheme, also known as a pyramid financing scheme—illegal in all 50 states. In this arrangement, early investors are paid off with cash taken in from later investors.

Charles Ponzi was an Italian immigrant who moved to Boston in 1919. Through his Financial Exchange of Boston, Ponzi concocted a scheme whereby he promised investors a 50 percent return on their money within 45 days. Ponzi explained that he could achieve this by purchasing international postage coupons in countries where the exchange rate was low, then reselling them in other countries where there were higher rates. Within six months, Ponzi's offer had lured 20,000 investors to give him $10 million, while he pacified earlier investors with money he received from the most recent ones. At its peak, Ponzi's operation had a daily cash flow of $250,000—an incredibly large sum in those days. Ponzi's scheme was exposed by *The Boston Globe* in 1920 and he was arrested, convicted of fraud, and sentenced to prison. Later deported to Italy, he eventually died a pauper in Rio de Janeiro.

Pyramid schemes work best when a large pool of new entrants contributes to the arrangement. The reason that the Social Security Trust Fund is currently overflowing has little to do with how much seniors have contributed. Rather, it's due to the 3.8 children each of them had—the boomers—who are now in their prime earning years and are contributing mightily to their elders' financial security. The boomer generation's size and tax-paying power is about the best thing that could have happened to their parents' retirement security. They might as well be called "the pyramid generation." In contrast, their own fertility rate has halved compared to their parents'—approximately 1.9 children per couple—and virtually guarantees that the subsequent generation will not be large enough to support them in the same fashion.

When elder boomers reach entitlement age, where will the Treasury find the cash? According to Charles Morris in *The AARP*, "The government will have to raise the cash either through increased taxes or by borrowing, in sums that could raise interest rates and increase the cost of buying houses and cars. The cash to pay off the bonds held by the trust funds can only be raised from a new generation of workers and businesses."[18]

The federal government has already promised $8.3 trillion in future Social Security benefits beyond the value of the taxes that today's adults will have paid. This figure is more than 250 times greater than the much-decried "unfunded liabilities" of all private-sector pension plans in America. If Social Security were held fiscally accountable the way private pensions are, the annual federal deficit would instantly rise by $675 billion. If unfunded federal-employee pensions and Medicare were added to the mix, the annual deficit would rise by more than $1 trillion.

Many Boomers Are Caught in a Dangerous State of Financial Paralysis

Given how well educated and self-help-oriented they are, it is ironic that so many boomers are *financially illiterate*. And because so many purchases, especially those involving immediate gratification, have become easy and even mindless, boomers as a generation are not balancing their current and *future* needs. Considering that half of all boomer households currently have a total net worth of less than $10,000, unless changes are made soon, many will eventually find themselves old and broke.[19]

To explore the depth and breadth of the boomers' economic confusions, the Financial Literacy 2000 Project, sponsored by the University of Pennsylvania School of Social Work, recently surveyed a nationally representative sample of 1,000 adults about their financial knowledge. Under the direction of gerontologist and economist Dr. Neal Cutler, the survey found that most boomers (80 percent) know that when you purchase shares of a mutual fund, your money is invested in several different stocks and bonds; that you don't have to pay income tax on the earnings and growth in individual retirement accounts until the money is withdrawn for retirement (79 percent); and that compound interest is better than simple interest (75 percent). That, however, is where the financial literacy stops.[20]

More than half of boomers did not know that if you elect early Social Security retirement at 62, you still must wait until 65 to qualify for Medicare, and more than half mistakenly believed that Medicare would cover the costs of their parents' long-term care, should they need it. While boomers are bullish on mutual funds, 71 percent reported that they did not feel confident in choosing one. Similarly, a recent poll conducted by Scudder Kemper Investments found that, "despite the fact that two-thirds of boomers say they are worried about having enough money in the future, 64 percent have no idea how much money they will need, and only 14 percent consider themselves to be experienced investors."[21]

Part of the problem is that too few boomers are long-range planners, and many are overwhelmed trying to meet the demands of family and work. Several years ago, the Administration on Aging conducted focus groups with baby boomers, and heard over and over, "I'm so busy working, my wife's working, one of my kids is having trouble in school and my mother needs help. I have so many things that I'm dealing with and juggling now, I'm just not able to plan for the future." This is reinforced by a recent study conducted by the research group Public Agenda that found that only 20 percent of working-age adults are "planners" who conscientiously save toward a specific financial goal. The rest of the population is made up of "strugglers," "impulsives," and "deniers" who don't plan for the future at all.[22]

Compounding their financial paralysis, many boomers are now coming to realize that Social Security and Medicare were not designed to match their generation's size and extended longevity. And because of the boomer cohort's long-standing distrust of government's promises, no matter how hard today's seniors try to convince them of Social Security and Medicare's goodness and stability, their confidence in the program's future solvency is nearly nonexistent. According to a recent Age Wave/Roper poll, more than 90 percent of the boomer generation believes that "the government has made financial promises to us that it will not be able to keep."[23]

The Road to Boomer Financial Security

Because the problems of tomorrow's financial security are complex, involving demographic, economic, psychological, and social elements, the solutions will come from all corners. These four commonsense changes would help to create a more secure tomorrow for aging boomers and subsequent generations:

1. Increase personal savings rates.
2. Make pensions more portable and flexible to match the boomers' mobile lifestyles.
3. Affluence-test and target entitlements to match the diverse needs of tomorrow's elders.
4. Privatize portions of Social Security to generate better returns.

Solution #1:
Increase Personal Savings Rates

For generations, our forebears believed that thrift, like cleanliness, was next to godliness. Because there were so few social safety nets, an individual who didn't save would have to suffer the consequences. Even one generation ago, for the parents of the boomers, living off credit was simply not acceptable—if you didn't have it, you didn't spend it. The Depression left them with a bit of healthy paranoia about debt and savings. As noted by J. Walker Smith and Ann Clurman in *Rocking the Ages*, "People paid with cash. Mortgage interest rates were low; refinancing was unknown. Credit cards had not been invented."[24] Today's seniors have always had a much higher regard for delayed gratification than their children. Their generation's mind-set reflects the kind of financial common sense that is all but lost today.

For the boomers, living in debt has become acceptable, even stylish. Unshadowed by the Depression, they came of age during a particularly prosperous period. According to Smith and Clurman, "Economic optimism freed them from worry about basic survival. . . . Boomers have always spent all of their money and even gone happily into debt, because they were confident that there was plenty more where it came from. Boomers . . . learned to spend, and to spend for instant gratification—get it now, no lines, no waiting."[25] This self-indulgence has run wild during the past two decades—and the credit card industry has had a field day.

In *The Overspent American: Upscaling, Downshifting, and the New Consumer,* Harvard professor Juliet B. Schor captures some of the debt madness that has seized our nation:

> Nearly all Americans borrow to buy their homes, and most automobiles are bought on time. Add to this the credit card balances, finance company loans, department store debts, and debts to individuals, and you begin to get an idea of the pervasiveness of household debt (about $5.5 trillion in late 1997). . . . As I write these words, the fraction of Americans' disposable income that goes toward debt servicing continues to rise; it has now reached 18 percent.
>
> The rise in indebtedness is in large part due to credit cards. Between 1990 and 1996, credit card debt doubled. Credit cards, with interest rates reaching nearly 20 percent, are a remarkably lucrative part of the loan business. Debtors pay an average of $1,000 a year in interest and fees alone. And the companies look increasingly like "credit pushers," soliciting heavily and beyond their traditional creditworthy base."[26]

In January of 1960, Americans carried an average of less than one credit card per person and owed $56 million in credit card debt. By January 1970, the numbers had jumped to an average of 3 credit cards per person and an outstanding total debt of $127 million. The average baby boomer now carries between 5 and 10 credit cards and owes approximately $4,000 in outstanding unsecured debt; as a result, $1.324 trillion was owed nationwide in January of 1999.[27] Although credit cards provide many conveniences and useful functions, they are now being abused by many people. With all of the "pre-approved" direct-mail solicitations flooding the market—3 bil-

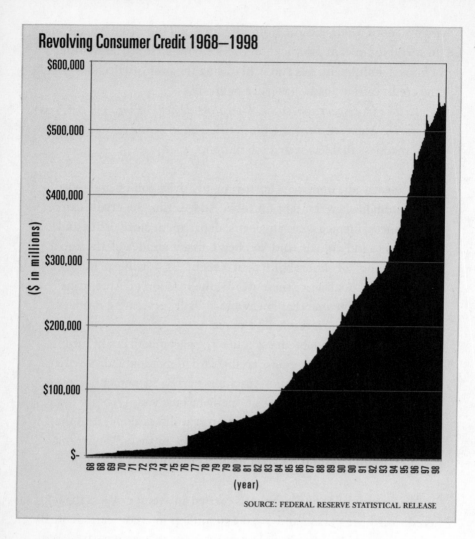

Revolving Consumer Credit 1968–1998

SOURCE: FEDERAL RESERVE STATISTICAL RELEASE

lion pieces in 1998 alone—moderate-income Americans are among the most heavily targeted. Some boomers (we all know a few) hold literally dozens of credit cards carrying tens of thousands of dollars in high-interest debt. Americans have more credit cards, over a billion, than the rest of the world's population combined.

THIS CARD MAY BE HAZARDOUS TO YOUR HEALTH

Many nations, including America, have a hallowed tradition of consumer warning labels. For nearly half a century, a movie ratings system has given parents some ability to monitor what their kids may see. In the 1950s, comic books began to be stamped with a "comics code" that denoted the absence of excessive violence. In the late 1960s and early 1970s, cigarettes, other forms of tobacco, and alcohol were forced to carry now-familiar warnings. Similarly, in the 1970s and '80s, we began to apprise consumers of risks that certain children's toys carried. Today, as pharmaceutical companies have begun to advertise directly to consumers, they too are legally required to advise buyers of potential risks. And yet no precautions accompany all of these credit card solicitations.

More than 1.1 million Americans now declare bankruptcy each year—triple the bankruptcy rate of 20 years ago—reflecting a trend that many economists link to runaway credit card debt.[28] Rather than backing off from soliciting individuals who are at risk, the banks have responded by lobbying Congress for laws that will make it more difficult to file personal bankruptcy.

But if overspent consumers need to own up to their responsibilities, credit card issuers should do the same. Financially strapped consumers who accept those "pre-approved" solicitations are often surprised to discover that their card issuers may raise interest rates, add additional fees, apply monthly payments in ways that maintain high-interest balances, or even change payment terms virtually at will. "Balance transfers" sometimes come with hidden charges and typically feature unusually high interest rates after an initial introductory period. Few consumers understand the effects of compounded interest and how little of a minimum payment goes toward actually reducing compounding debt.

Credit card companies should be required to plainly spell out these matters in their mailings. For example, credit card mailings that promise rock-bottom introductory interest rates should be required on the same page to specify what the rates will rise to, rather than simply leaving consumers to do the calculations themselves. Mail solicitations should specify in plain wording that rates may rise at any time and that cash advances carry far higher rates to which payments are not applied until lower-interest balances are paid off. Finally, there is the question of exploitation. Credit card companies should exercise some restraint in the amount of debt they allow a card user to accumulate. Just as automobile drivers and their passengers are obligated to obey speed limits and wear seat belts, and pharmaceutical users are restrained from overusing or abusing certain drugs, many men and women are overdosing on debt—and the card companies set no limits.

LEARNING TO SAVE

When the boomers began turning 50 in 1996, newspapers and magazines throughout the country started featuring special articles on their aging-related challenges. Most boomers were shocked when experts predicted that they would need to have saved $1 million to $1.5 million per household by the time they retire, if they hope to maintain their standard of living.

Study after study revealed that the overwhelming majority of boomers are quite a distance from this level of financial preparedness. Because of the power of compounding, however, there is good reason to pay down debt and intensify savings and investments as soon as possible. A recent study by *Fortune* magazine pointed out that if a 40-year-old couple decides to go out to dinner and a movie twice a month instead of four times and instead invests $150 each month into a 401(k) plan, these contributions will grow to $169,500 by the time they retire. Further, if the same couple were to pay off their credit card bills when they first arrive instead of incurring finance charges, they will have another $121,400 for their later life-financial security.[29]

Another reason that boomers should immediately improve their financial planning is that various lifestyle challenges—such as education for their children, eldercare for their parents, and retirement funding for themselves—are likely to collide at around the same point in their lives.

For example, my wife and I had our children nearly 15 years later than the ages at which our parents had us. When my children reach college age, if they choose a private institution and also pursue some graduate education, it will cost a quarter of a million dollars in cash *each*. It's also likely that tax support for college scholarships and loans will continue to dwindle because the government's resources will be depleted by elder-related demands. Already the government funds only 11 percent of all college costs, compared to 46 percent in 1950. And since I will be in my late fifties at that time, I will be approaching retirement age. At the same time, there's a good chance that I will be called upon to provide eldercare to one of my parents or in-laws. In the Scudder Kemper study, only 8 percent of boomers say they are prepared to pay tens of thousands of dollars for their parents' eldercare.[30]

TUNE IN, TURN ON, MAX OUT

To elevate the boomers' financial literacy, a massive, multiyear public education campaign is necessary. However, there is a distinct leadership vacuum in this critically important area. When José Piñera, Chile's then-30-year-old minister of labor and social security undertook to improve his country's economy in the late 1970s, an essential element of his transformative process was his regular appearances on television news programs. Couched in easy-to-comprehend terms, his discourses and explanations were designed to upgrade every citizen's understanding of the impact of economic forces on his or her life and raise awareness of the steps each would need to take to improve lifetime financial security.

In stark contrast, our own government has taken a very passive role in this regard. While many insurance companies and brokerage firms have been promoting financial planning recently, it's hard for the average worker to separate the truth from advertising and promotions. Just as the government has used nationwide programs to improve public health and physical fitness, it is time for a public "fiscal fitness" campaign. Broad-based *financial literacy* should be a goal of short- and long-term national policy.

In addition to motivating boomers to break their debt habit and increase their savings, it would be wise to guide younger generations to start saving as soon as they can. As recently as the mid-'70s, grade schools offered courses in "home economics," based on the now-outdated notion that young women would soon be home baking cakes and mending socks. We should revive "home economics" for a new purpose: teaching young students about personal finance management. States should mandate that such courses become a standard part of the educational curriculum. The advantage of inculcating a savings mentality at an early age is that the individual gets the full benefit of the power of compounding. If a worker starts saving just $25 a week at age 25 and earns 10 percent on his or her investment, that would add up to a retirement nest egg worth $694,000 by age 65.

If we are to avert a future financial disaster, it is essential that boomers break free of their financial paralysis and intensify their personal savings and investment programs in preparation for their own later-life challenges and the inevitable decline in government entitlements.

Solution #2:
Make Pensions More Portable and Flexible to Match Boomers' Mobile Lifestyles

Boomers who are hoping that pension funds may close the gap in their savings need to look again. After government entitlements, pensions are the second major source of retirement income, but they are not what they once were. Private pensions grew rapidly between 1900 and 1920, until about one worker in six was covered.[31] Growth in pension coverage was frozen during the Great Depression, but grew once more between 1940 and 1970 until leveling off at just under half the workforce. During the 1960s and 1970s, experts forecast that private pensions would become a universally available supplement to Social Security. This has not happened. Instead, pensions have become increasingly inaccessible or irrelevant. Four factors are contributing to this problem:

a) Absence of coverage

Approximately half of all workers are not covered by any type of pension program. According to the Employee Benefit Research Institute, 53 million workers, including 33 million working in small businesses, do not participate in a retirement plan and in all likelihood will never be covered. Although businesses with fewer than 100 workers provide 40 million jobs, 80 percent offer no pension coverage.

b) The shift from defined benefits to defined contribution

While many of today's elders receive *guaranteed* benefit retirement pensions, for boomers the game has been switched in a critical way. In the past, employers were responsible for providing pension coverage: Whether it was a flat-benefit, career-average, or final-pay plan, employers agreed to provide their employees with lifetime benefits based on a predetermined formula.

Today, through the "now-you-see-it, now-you-don't" transition to "defined contribution" plans such as 401(k)s, employers are off the hook and have made workers responsible for their own pension decisions. While many employers provide some matching funds, each employee is left to become his or her own expert on asset allocation. Should investment decisions be misdirected, or should there be a decline in the stock market, the employer is not responsible for guaranteeing security of any sort.

c) Vesting hurdles and the absence of pension portability

Most pension vesting standards require 5 to 10 years of employment for eligibility. However, the average boomer changes jobs every 3 or 4 years. This pattern of frequent job changes is continuing with genXers. Between the ages of 18 and 32 alone, the average person now holds nine different jobs. As reflected by 27-year-old software developer Ben Shichman, "My father started working for AT&T as soon as he graduated from college and he just retired last year at 55. I don't know anyone my age who is likely to have the same situation. These days, 3 or 4 years is the longest anyone stays at one company. . . . It's no longer a sign of weakness to leave a job after a short stint. Now, it shows that you're ambitious."[32] As a result of such frequent job changes, fewer than half of today's workers working for the one-half of all companies that offer pension plans will ever actually receive a pension from these employers. Net result: Only one-quarter of workers are likely to receive a pension from an employer.

d) 401(k) "leakage"

According to the Employee Benefit Research Institute, approximately 40 percent of all workers are offered a 401(k)-type plan, and of those 75 percent participate. Other tax-deferred savings plans include 403(b) for nonprofit workers or thrift savings plans (TSP) for federal employees. Beyond the fact that 25 percent of 401(k)-eligible employees don't even use them, many others are liquidating theirs prematurely. Since most plans allow workers to borrow from their accounts, millions of cash-strapped employees are diverting these funds for immediate needs—referred to as 401(k) "leakage"—even though tax laws discourage using pension assets for nonretirement purposes. Currently, only 20 percent of individuals who receive lump-sum distributions roll the entire amount into another tax-qualified vehicle.[33] Despite penalties and tax liabilities, many workers are cashing out their accounts, further eroding their retirement security. By giving workers the freedom to manage their own retirement security without making sure they behave responsibly, we are shaping tomorrow's elder poverty today.

Traditional pension plans worked best in an era when most people remained with one employer for the majority of their working lives. Given the aforementioned limits in pension coverage, the shift away from defined benefits, the absence of portability, 401(k) leakage, and job mobility, boomers are at risk of jumping on a pension bandwagon that is falling apart as it rides. Instead, we need pension plans that include a much larger group of people and that each worker can carry throughout his career, regardless of employment changes. And to help the boomer generation avoid a poverty-stricken old age, it may even become necessary to *mandate* participation in these mobile plans while intensifying disincentives to deplete them prematurely.

The federal government has a definite interest in promoting expanded pension coverage, which will help workers meet their own retirement income needs and will also increase national savings. Although Americans often feel reluctant to import ideas, particularly economic ones, several other countries are paving the way for key innovations and improvements in pension coverage. For example:

- Australia has made employee-funded pensions *mandatory*, increasing coverage from less than 40 percent to nearly 90 percent of the workforce. By 2002, all Australian workers will be required to set aside 9 percent of their income annually in a retirement income plan of their choice. These mandatory savings may be enhanced by additional tax-favored voluntary contributions. And by making pensions completely portable, Australians can continue saving despite changes of job. Accordingly, private savings in superannuation funds have gone through the roof, climbing from Au$40 billion (approximately US$28 billion) in 1985 to Au$304 billion (US$240 billion) as of June 1997.[34]

  Today, the average Australian retiree's future looks bright. As economists Daniel Mitchell and Robert O'Quinn point out, "average-wage workers who made no voluntary contributions and earned only 4 percent in real returns each year (a modest figure, since the average over the last 10 years has been 5.5 percent) will be able to retire with nearly twice as much income as they would have had under the old government-run system."[35]

- In Chile, a *mandatory* 10 percent of monthly wages is deposited by the employer into a pension savings account (PSA), which is managed by a private administration company, Administradoras de Fondos de Pensiones (AFP). Every worker is allowed to invest up to an additional 10 percent of his wages in a portable pension fund. The AFP in turn oversees the operation of a variety of mutual-type funds that invest in low-risk and diversified stocks and bonds. Therefore each worker's pension is simply the amount that he or she has been able to accumulate over the years. The PSAs are totally portable, and each worker receives a passbook and a tri-monthly statement reporting balance and fund performance.

  Unlike practice in the United States, Chilean employees own the assets in their private pension funds. The larger the desired pension, the more the worker can contribute each month above the required 10 percent. After 20 years, the worker is free to use the capital from his PSA to purchase an annuity from a private life-insurance company, which guarantees a fixed income for life, or he can leave the money in the PSA and make predetermined withdrawals. In Chile today, pensions are 50 to 100 percent higher than they were prior to privatization. If an older Chilean is without funds, the government will provide a "safety net" pension to help him or her avoid poverty in the later years.[36]

- The Swiss have been innovating as well. According to their constitution, the goal of the social security system is a retirement income equaling 60 percent of final salary, through a combination of private and public pension plans. About 2.3 million Swiss, 90 percent of the workforce, contribute to the occupational pension program, with assets placed in managed funds. This *required* contribution is a fixed percentage of salary and increases with age, and the employer pays half of the total contribution. For example, men under 34 and women under 31 give 7 percent, while men over 55 and women over 52 contribute 18 percent of monthly income. In return, workers are guaranteed that their individual pension accounts will earn a return of no less than 4 percent per year.[37]

Although these international experiments are not without their problems, the United States would be wise to study these systems and to adapt one that fits our own nation's character and needs. If the millions of American workers who either do not participate in or lack access to a 401(k)-type plan had been required five years ago to save as little as 5 percent of their salary, given an average annual mutual-fund return of 15 percent, more than $1 trillion in savings would have been created.

Solution #3:
Affluence-test and Target Entitlements to Match the Diverse Needs of Tomorrow's Elders

As we saw in Chapter 1, the financial security of elders has never been better than at this moment. During the past half-century, due to the dramatic growth in their savings, investments, and property values, not to mention all the government entitlements they receive, seniors have experienced a terrific reversal of fortune. As a result, the percentage of elders living in poverty is at an all-time low, while the percentage who are rich has reached an all-time high. Somewhere between 750,000 and 1 million seniors are now estimated to be millionaires, yet continue to receive government entitlements and senior discounts.

Today's senior generation includes a hefty percentage of solidly middle-class households. As reported in *The Economist*, "In 1997, an estimated $48.1 billion in Social Security benefits will go to households with incomes between $50,000 and $100,000. Another $15.5 billion—almost exactly what the government spends on income support for all families on welfare—will be sent to households with incomes of more than $100,000."[38]

Does it make sense for young workers to be heavily taxed to provide entitlements to those elders who really don't need them? "Do we deserve such special treatment?" asks former President Jimmy Carter in *The Virtues of Aging*. "The fact is that I and more than a million other Social Security beneficiaries would be considered quite wealthy, while many of the Americans supporting us may be struggling to make ends meet."[39]

On one end of the continuum, millions of seniors don't need government entitlements to live in security and comfort; on the other, some struggle to survive with insufficient support.

If we look at the senior population by age, race, and income, we find a profile of heterogeneous needs. A little over half of seniors—about 18.2 million people—are 65 to 74 years old. Their average household income is $25,292, and, as we've seen, having paid off their homes, finished putting their kids through college, maintained reasonably good health, and become recipients of tens of thousands of dollars in government entitlements and senior discounts each year, they have retained a high level of discretionary income. This group's poverty level is only 9.2 percent—roughly half that of American children, and much lower than the national average. In fact, this segment contains more millionaires than any other age group. Among the 16.3 million members of the 75+ population, however, the picture begins to change. Their average household income falls to $17,079 and their poverty level rises to approximately 12.4 percent.[40]

If we further examine older Americans by gender and ethnicity, a disturbing portrait emerges. African-American and Hispanic elders are two to three times more likely to be poor than their white counterparts, and elderly nonwhite widows over age 75 are struggling with a near 50 percent poverty level.[41]

A TIP FROM ROBIN HOOD:
GIVE LESS TO THE RICH AND MORE TO THE POOR

For decades, means testing has been rejected in favor of programs that purport to provide universal benefits. There is a pervasive anxiety that means testing would expose a wide segment of the elder population to financial vulnerability. Perhaps we need to redefine means testing so that it's clear that the focus would be not on depleting the resources of those in need, but instead on triaging entitlement dollars away from those wealthy older adults who don't need them at all. So that there is no confusion on this point, let's also change the name of this approach to "*affluence testing.*"

Variations of affluence testing have already begun creeping into practice. In a sense, income taxes on Social Security benefits already provide a limited affluence test. Social Security benefits are subject to income tax if current income exceeds $25,000 for a single person or $32,000 for a married couple. Also, taxes currently apply to only a portion of benefits—up to 85 percent—depending on adjusted gross income. Modifying these provisions further, by making 100 percent of benefits subject to income tax above certain income levels, would achieve an effect similar to an affluence-tested benefit reduction.

Former Secretary of Commerce Pete Peterson has proposed an "affluence test that would reduce entitlement benefits to all households with incomes over $40,000—or more than $5,000 above the U.S. median household income." Under Peterson's plan, households with lower incomes would retain all government benefits, while "higher-income households would lose 10 percent of all benefits that raised their income above $40,000, and 10 percent for each additional $10,000 in income." For example, within this scheme, a household with $120,000 in income and $10,000 in federal benefits would lose $8,500, or 85 percent of benefits—the maximum benefit withholding rate.[42]

In order to support the millions who will be truly needy, some type of affluence testing will become necessary as the boomers age.

Whether Peterson's formula or some other equation is selected, demographic and economic pressures will force the targeting of tax-supported entitlements. This will frustrate, but not shock, the boomers: As we have seen, nearly every aspect of their lives has been "means tested"—acceptance to college, availability of scholarships, access to homes, employment placement, and income taxes have all been based on individual strengths and limitations, not on everyone receiving equal treatment.

Of course, those elder boomers who will lose the most benefits and receive the lowest rate of return on their contributions will actually be the ones who have paid the highest taxes and supported the greatest number of retirees. This may not be an entirely happy outcome, but it will be necessary to rescue those who are truly in need and to maintain a program whose books are balanced in an era of radically different age demographics.

Solution #4: Privatize Portions of Social Security to Generate Better Returns

Compared to almost every other type of long-term investment program, the paybacks from Social Security are very weak. The average American worker retiring in 1950 at age 65 received a real annual rate of return of about 20 percent on all FICA taxes—but workers retiring at age 65 in 2005 and beyond will reap a real annual return of less than 2 percent.[43] Given the times we live in, this is unacceptable. By privatizing some portion of the Social Security funds, it is extremely likely that a better return can be achieved.

WHAT IS PRIVATIZATION?

In much the same way that most people fail to understand how Social Security works, many misunderstand what is meant by "privatization." For some, the concept brings to mind fearful images of elder boomers jumping off buildings on Wall Street when the stock market crashes, scuttling their retirement savings. For our purposes here, privatization of some portion of Social Security would mean a controlled and limited government investment in carefully selected and regulated mutual funds based on many of the same principles that govern 401(k) plans—instead of continuing to direct all investments into low-risk, low-return U.S. Treasury securities.

Even before privatization emerged as a hot issue in Social Security debates, the value of mutual funds as both an institutional and an individual tool was already long established. Moreover, the idea of governments investing pension money in the stock market is hardly new. The federal government already engages in private investments for its pension programs for federal workers. States, too, have been investing public pension and school funds in the equity and bond markets for years with double-digit annual returns. Some examples:

- The California Public Employees Retirement System (CalPERS) is one of the largest holders of equities in the world. It controls about $150 billion, including $103 billion (two-thirds) in equities.
- The New York State Comptroller's Office controls the retirement funds for New York State employees, as well as those of police and firefighters in the state—some $104.9 billion in assets, of which $63.3 billion, or 60 percent, is in the form of equities.
- The Employees Retirement System of Texas, combined with various other state-administered retirement trusts, controls $116.2 billion in investable assets, of which $56.9 billion (49 percent) consists of equities.
- The Florida Department of Insurance administers the state employees' retirement fund, and allows employees to determine how their assets will be invested. Of about $79.6 billion in "classifiable investments," this fund has $40.4 billion, or 51 percent, in equities.

- Pennsylvania's State Employees' Retirement Systems (SERS) controls roughly $38.9 billion in assets, including $21.9 billion (56 percent) in equities.

INTERNATIONAL EXPERIMENTS IN PRIVATIZATION

Because the United Kingdom has an economic and political environment similar to our own, it provides a good case study for U.S. policy planners looking at Social Security privatization. In 1970, pension assets in both Britain and the U.S. amounted to 17 percent of GDP. By 1990, British pension funds had reached 55 percent of GDP, compared with 43 percent in the United States, and 73 percent of British workers were enrolled in private plans.[44]

With up to 80 percent of these funds invested in equities, the gross rate of return for median private pension funds from 1986 to 1995 was 13.3 percent a year. Based on 1997 projections, the average British worker making average wages and paying a minimum of contributions could accumulate a personal fund worth $208,000 upon retirement at 65 and secure a tax-free pension of $1,120 per month. Peter Lilly, the United Kingdom's former social security secretary, calculates, "If returns are 1 percent higher than assumed, pensioners will get nearly 30 percent above the basic pension. If the yield is 2 percent higher, the pension could be over 70 percent higher."[45]

This approach has caught on: Fully or partially privatized systems exist or are being implemented in numerous countries, including Argentina, Australia, Chile, Colombia, Italy, Mexico, Peru, Singapore, and Sweden.

While many Americans are strongly opposed to privatizing all of Social Security, in the last decade most have growth quite comfortable with the idea of *partial* privatization. Eight in ten Americans support the idea, according to a recent survey conducted for the Associated Press. Among adults aged 18 to 34, the support runs as high as 90 percent.[46]

Some experts have suggested that additional confidence in this approach could be achieved if the federal government designed special boards to handle Social Security investments; these boards would operate semi-autonomously—not unlike the Federal Reserve—to keep the process free from political bias. "Under the President's plan, an apolitical board would select private-sector investment managers through a competitive bidding process. Investments would be limited to broad-based index funds, eliminating the possibility of individual stock picking or market-timing concerns," noted Lawrence Summers and Janet Yellen in the *Wall Street Journal*.[47]

A NOTE OF CAUTION

In this era of annual double-digit stock growth, boomers will insist on benefiting from the results of a more aggressive investment program than Social Security is providing. A word of caution should be offered. Just as the Great Depression has left many seniors overly *pessimistic* and even paranoid about the stock market, so have decades of prosperity and a long-running bull market left the average boomer overly *optimistic*.

While there is a good chance that the boomers' own active spending and investing will continue to drive the Dow upwards for years, the market could deflate considerably when they begin retiring and spending down their savings. If the boomers' retirement security is *too* dependent on the unpredictable ups and downs of the market, in their senior years they may suffer the ultimate effect of their generational gravity as their elevated investments come falling back to earth. Therefore, privatization should be a sensible part of our Social Security investment, but certainly not the whole of it.

Toward Financial Security

The future of Social Security, Medicare, and employer pensions are unmistakably in jeopardy. This is not because boomers disrespect their elders or because of some failing in the founding vision behind these programs. The problem is that current government entitlements and pensions were masterfully designed in an era when there were dozens of workers supporting each recipient, people died relatively young, most workers were diligent savers, and the government and employers were widely trusted. We now live in an era where there are very few workers to support each retiree, most people die very old, savings rates have plummeted, and the government as well as employers' promises are not generally trusted.

Expecting tax-supported government entitlements to compose a significant part of boomers' retirement income would be a huge mistake. We must intensify our individual and collective efforts to plan a diversified approach to savings, investments, and insurance *now*, if all boomers—not just the high earners—are to have any hope of achieving financial security in their maturity.

Tips to Age-proof Your Life

- Pay down your high-interest debt as soon as possible.
- Start saving at least 10 percent of your monthly income.
- Maximize all allowable tax-protected savings programs, such as 401(k)s, to take advantage of compounding growth.
- Plan ahead for the day when you must simultaneously support your children's education and your parents' eldercare, in addition to funding your own retirement.

CHAPTER EIGHT

INTERGENERATIONAL RELATIONS: MELTING POT OR GERASSIC PARK?

In an evolving, fluid society such as ours, there are wisely conceived checks and balances that prevent any particular group from dominating the political and social agendas. The public and for-profit sectors keep each other at least somewhat in check. Labor and management still battle to keep each other's interests in balance. Likewise, the political parties.

The rise of age power, however, poses a new and perplexing problem. Living in an era when life expectancy was 35 and less than 2 percent of the population was over 65, our founders never anticipated the challenges of managing the relative contributions and demands of three to four living generations—particularly when the elder generation had grown so large and powerful.

As each of these generations competes for its share of the American pie, our social institutions and policymakers must learn a new and complex skill: how to manage a *multigenerational melting pot*. And since today's elders have amassed a much greater concentration of political clout than younger cohorts, distributing the nation's limited resources is likely to become a thorny challenge.

While we normally assume that the groups with the greatest differences in social perspectives and political demands would be liberals and conservatives, in the years ahead, new political action lines will be drawn between age groups and generations. Although the coexistence of three or four living generations offers the unprecedented possibility of a wonderful range of intergenerational friendships, mentorships, and learning opportunities, the absence of such positive relationships could lead to insensitivity, bickering, fierce competition for limited resources, and social *"age wars."*

Developing a philosophy and a new set of ground rules for intergenerational relations presents a novel set of considerations. First, we must establish a basic understanding of each generation's composition, style, and identity. Next, it's critical to take stock of the relative power and influence among the different generations. Only then can we create programs that will bring each generation's needs, interests, contributions, and demands into greater balance in the 21st century.

Generational Identity

Generational identity is a relatively new dynamic, brought about in part by the rapid changes in technology, media, and social mores that have given each generation its own set of experiences and values. In the past, groups could be identified by social class, race, religion, or political affiliation; today, individuals have an enormous connection to the era in which they grew up and the generation with whom they have shared so many experiences springing from pop culture, world events, politics, and technology.

Historians, sociologists, and market researchers have recently begun to develop an insightful analysis of generational perspectives. The following chart characterizing the different generations is drawn from *Rocking the Ages,* by Yankelovich researchers J. Walker Smith and Ann Clurman:[1]

Generational Identities

	Matures	Boomers	Xers
Defining ideas	Duty	Individuality	Diversity
Celebrating	Victory	Youth	Savvy
Success because	Fought hard and won	Were born, therefore should be a winner	Have two jobs
Style	Team player	Self-absorbed	Entrepreneur
Rewards because	You've earned it	You deserve it	You need it
Work is	An inevitable obligation	An exciting adventure	A difficult challenge
Leisure is	Reward for hard work	The point of life	Relief
Education is	A dream	A birthright	A way to get ahead
Future	Rainy day to work for	"Now" is more important	Uncertain but manageable
Managing money	Save	Spend	Hedge
"Program" means	Social program	Cult deprogrammers	Software programs
Go watch	*The Best Years of Our Lives*	*The Big Chill*	*Reality Bites*
The "in" crowd	Rat Pack Nightclubs Hep Zoot suit Kansas City Jazz	"Leader of the Pack" Rock clubs Groovy Bell-bottoms San Francisco Rock 'n' roll	Brat Pack Rave clubs Edgy Flannel Seattle Alternative

For our purposes here, I will draw upon Age Wave's research as well as the Yankelovich insights to highlight some of the identifying characteristics of 65-, 45-, and 25-year-olds in order to set the stage for some of the intergenerational challenges ahead. I have not included the youngest age group—sometimes called the ".com generation"—because it's still too early to analyze its nature.

THE VIEW FROM 65

As we have already examined, while some 65+ men and women have low incomes, are frail, or both, they are in the minority. Echoing the positive changes they've made in their life spans and bank accounts, this group in general feels self-confident and involved with life. Today's older generation also has the advantage of enormous size and steady, predictable growth. Every morning when the elderly wake up, they have a larger, stronger team than they had the night before. And since the life expectancy at 65 is higher than at birth, the average 65-year-old of today can expect to live another 18 years.

Team Players Who Trust Authority

Many of today's elders fought in an "honorable" war, and those who returned came back heroes. GI loans provided a terrific boost to help them get started in their households and careers, just as military pensions continue to provide strong support for millions of elder vets.

In his recent book *The Greatest Generation*, Tom Brokaw extols the special qualities of this cohort: "They came of age during the Great Depression and the Second World War and went on to build modern America—men and women whose everyday lives of duty, achievement, and courage gave us the world we have today."[2]

Teamwork is how this generation got things done. When their individual needs went unmet, they organized into groups, clubs, and unions to maximize their bargaining power. Their values held that shared work and sacrifice led to the best results, while individuals who put their personal agendas before that of the group were considered selfish and destined to achieve poor results. This generation's members were much more willing to delay their own rewards. As Smith and Clurman point out, "Matures believed that a lifetime of commitment was required to accomplish their goals. Duty came before pleasure. The job to be done required that they postpone their own gratification."[3]

Throughout their working years, most of their employers were committed to honoring agreements and either stood by their workers or were forced to do so by unions. Employment benefits usually reflected a paternalistic approach to retirement security that rewarded aging employees with employer-guaranteed benefit programs for life—and in some cases for the lives of their spouses after they passed away.

These experiences have left today's older adults with a high degree of confidence in the government, large employers, and traditional authority figures and institutions, from unions to doctors to politicians to church leaders. Overall, they feel that the government has given them a fair deal, and most are inclined to believe that, at the end of the day, political leaders and employers will honor their commitments.

Seeking Security

Understandably, 65-year-olds are concerned about what matters most to them at this stage in their lives. As we might expect, issues of crime control and personal safety are very important. And since 44 percent of 65+ men and women are single, many battle loneliness and social isolation daily.[4] They are particularly anxious about living on fixed incomes. Their declining health frightens them, and they worry about being able to pay for long-term care, should they need it.

From the point of view of a 65-year-old, financial security has to do with the stability of government entitlements, the vitality of their investments, interest rates on savings, taxes, the value of their home equity, and the rising cost of out-of-pocket healthcare. Not surprisingly, their political agenda is characterized by intense, continued support for Social Security and Medicare.

Racial Makeup

Racially, today's elders are the most homogeneous of all living Americans: 89 percent are white, only 8.3 percent are African-American, 2.3 percent are of Asian origin, and .5 percent are American Indian. About 5.2 percent are Hispanic, an ethnic designation that cuts across racial lines.[5]

Politically Wired

As we have seen, today's elderly have become the 800-pound gorilla of generational politics: They vote their own issues in large numbers, write letters, lobby, protest, and are not shy about calling on their connections when they want attention paid to their needs.

THE VIEW FROM 45

As we have explored in earlier chapters, members of the middlescent boomer generation are often involved in an exciting, productive, yet hectic and overextended stage of life. Both men and women are juggling careers and parenting. While this generation's enormous size has allowed it to dominate the consumer and media marketplaces for decades, boomers are realizing that this size will become a severe liability as they line up for government entitlements in their maturity.

Distrust of Authority

In stark contrast to their elders, boomers are distrustful of government, employers, and other authority figures. They came of age in a peculiar era during which young people watched their favorite political leaders being gunned down. Some were sent off to fight in an unpopular war and were often treated as pariahs on their return. Boomers' political awareness was shaped by the Watergate era, and many have felt deceived by politicians ever since.

Modern employers have had no sacred pact with the middlescent generation, regularly laying off tens of thousands while giving their CEOs huge bonuses. Moreover, pension programs have shifted from paternalistic "guaranteed benefit" arrangements to "defined contribution" plans in which workers are basically told, "You're on your own."

Looking Out for Number One

Compounding their suspicion of authority, boomers—more than any previous cohort—were encouraged to be intellectually and socially individualistic. Rather than learning teamwork and uniformity, every boomer was told at home, in school, and through thousands of commercial messages to "be special," "do your own thing," "pursue your inner dreams," "think for yourself," and "look out for number one."

In contrast to earlier generations who were more inclined to align with their neighborhood, platoon, employer, church, or political party, boomers have grown up with an overriding commitment to *themselves,* their immediate families, and their own *inner drives.* According to Yankelovich's Smith and Clurman, "Matures and Boomers reflect two distinctly different value systems. For Matures, as we've seen, worth is measured in objective, external terms. Boomers look inward and evaluate their achievements in terms of personal fulfillment."[6]

Seeking Security: A Different Blend of Ingredients

As we examined in Chapter 7, boomers are becoming concerned about paying down their debts, stepping up their savings and investments, managing their cash flow to pay for home mortgages (or rent), and having the resources to pay for both college tuition and eldercare. In addition, since many boomers are beginning to plan for retirement, they are anxious to gain some sense of what they might expect from pensions and government entitlements.

Racial Makeup

Racially, today's middle-agers are a bit more heterogeneous than their elders: 83 percent are white, 12 percent are African-American, and 4 percent are Asian. Among these middle-agers, 9 percent are Hispanic.

Politically Unplugged

Boomer politics have always been more involved with *"causes"* than political parties. Boomers are less likely to identify themselves as Democrats or Republicans than their parents, and more likely to vote for issues and individuals than to take a party line. In contrast to their rebellious youth, when idealistic social issues ruled the day, these days the average boomer's social and political concerns tend to be locally focused on school and community concerns and workplace dynamics.

THE VIEW FROM 25

The generational perspective of today's 25-year-olds is very different from that of elders or boomers. Just starting their careers and adult relationships, they wonder daily if they'll ever fall in love and get married. They worry that there won't be any good jobs available to them or that they will lose their jobs unexpectedly. They're concerned about becoming pregnant or contracting a sexually transmitted disease.

Diversity in all its forms is a fundamental character trait of generation X. Largely due to the proliferation of the media, they have been exposed to a wide range of social, political, sexual, and racial styles. More than any previous group, Xers are "samplers," picking and choosing language, role models, and social philosophies from a wide range of choices. In fact, this generation is so diverse that its most distinct characteristic may be the *lack* of a unifying generational identity.

It is in their relationship with technology that Xers are especially different. As noted by the Yankelovich research:

Information and electronic technologies have always been fundamental to how they live, work, and play. Technology defines their vocabulary. It ties together their finances, their communications, their calendars, their entertainment. It creates the bonds and connections of their communities and families—particularly cell phones and beepers and voice mail. It permeates every nook and cranny—they've never driven a car without an on-board computer; they've never had a job without a PC on their desk.[7]

Seeking Security

For 25-year-olds, financial security is a mixed bag, marked by concerns about job stability, the irrelevance of most pension programs, and avoidance of excessive debt. They are anxious that low income and high taxes will keep them from affording a home and that Social Security might not be around when they retire. According to genXer Mark Jannot, "My status crystallized for me one morning last fall. First, the newspaper reported that Social Security will be dead broke by the year 2029. By subtracting my birth year, 1965, from 2029, I realized that the year the geezer dole goes belly-up, I'll be 64, ready to feed at the entitlement trough myself."[8]

Racial Makeup

The young adult generation is more racially and culturally diverse than the nation's middle-aged or elder cohorts: 78 percent are white, 16 percent are African-American, and 5 percent are Asian. Ethnically, about 13 percent are Hispanic. This greater diversity can be traced to higher birthrates among minorities of childbearing age and the large number of young people in recent waves of immigrants, especially Hispanics and Asians.

Tribal Politics

While elders make smart use of the traditional political system and boomers support causes, Xer politics are characterized by a weak pulse, fragmentation, and a diverse range of issues that are orchestrated by small, clannish groups rather than big associations. For example, in 1993 some Xers formed a small but interesting advocacy organization called Third Millennium. Where AARP counts more than 32 million members, Third Millennium has only 3,000. Similar twentysomething-oriented political groups such as Lead or Leave and Rock the Vote have failed to attract significant followings.

Intergenerational Justice

We now have multiple adult generations—each with its own psychology, sociology, entertainment, political style, vernacular, and identity. The challenge is to create parity and fair exchanges between them.

As noted earlier, today's elders are well organized into a large, powerful voting bloc in a way that 45-year-olds and 25-year-olds are not. In fact, while mature men and women have AARP and its army of lobbyists to defend their needs, middle-aged and young people have no comparable club or entity dedicated to fighting their battles.

Due largely to elders' increasing political clout, since 1965 total federal spending on Americans over 65 has increased from 16 percent of the budget to 33 percent. Comprising just 13 percent of the population, elders receive four times as much federal money as those under 18, who comprise 26 percent. Considering that *for every $1 of tax revenues that Washington spends on seniors, it devotes only 11 cents to each child*, it's obvious that elders have seized control of society's purse strings.[9]

According to Georges Minois in *The History of Old Age*, "Nothing in political or moral theory implies that a group which votes more heavily than its percentage of the population because it has low costs of time, and votes disproportionately because of the focus and homogeneity of its interests, is morally entitled to the political power that these attributes confer."[10]

MIT's Lester Thurow agrees that such unrestrained age power could have a destructive effect: "All successful societies need to make long-term investments in education, infrastructure, and the basic research that leads to growth industries like biotechnology and new business opportunities on the Internet. How is this going to happen when the largest and most powerful voting bloc is the elderly, who know that they stand no chance of seeing the benefits of these investments?"[11]

Thurow's concerns are real: During the past 20 years, government investments in infrastructure, education, and research and development have fallen from 24 percent to 15 percent of the federal budget. During that same period, government spending on entitlements for the elderly has grown by 253 percent in real dollars. If a government cannot cut benefits that go to a disproportionately powerful segment of its voters, it is destined for a serious crisis.

This is a very disturbing circumstance for a nation that prides itself on better tomorrows.

THOUGHTFUL RESTRAINT NEEDED

My daughter is a healthy, athletic 12-year-old, and my son is equally fit and frisky at age 9. Sometimes, for fun, they like to wrestle. I have to remind my daughter that she is much stronger than her brother and could really hurt him if she fully exerted herself. Although it's hard for her to accept, she must restrain herself when they wrestle just to make it an almost fair fight.

Similarly, if the different generations are going to negotiate an equitable distribution of resources, the elderly will have to exercise some conscious restraint and a renewed commitment to fair play. Otherwise the old will inadvertently demolish the young and harm everyone's future in the process.

AGE WARS—BETWEEN WHOM?

In recent years, the media have become fascinated with the prospect of "age wars" in which generations would supposedly do battle with one another over scarce resources. That danger is real, but not yet set in cement.

If there are battles, they probably will not be between today's elders and the boomers. For the time being, the boomers have too much concern and regard for their elders. In nearly every research study that's conducted, boomers express respect for their parents' and grandparents' generations. *Yet both elders and Xers seem to be annoyed with the boomers.*

For example, in January 1996, AARP's *Modern Maturity* devoted an entire issue to the baby boomers as a way of welcoming the first of this generation into maturity. I wondered how the members of AARP—whose average dues-payer is 68 years old—would react to the boomers entering their private club. Promptly in the May/June issue, the "Letters to the Editor" section was filled with nasty comments from seniors to boomers. Some examples: "You are selfish twits." "You act as if you know everything—and you don't." "You go out and do meaningful work in an office and let uneducated, uncaring people take care of your kids. You are too busy 'being me' to have the time for them." "Your selfishness knows no end."

Similar frustrations toward boomers are expressed by the twentysomething generation. Many Xers feel bitter over the social messes that the boomers have left in their wake. Forget what the idealistic boomers proclaimed, Xers say, and look at what they've actually accomplished: Divorce. Homelessness. Holes in the ozone layer. Drug addiction. Downsizing and layoffs. Soaring debt. Urban gangs. Senseless violence.

Because there are so many boomers, they are able to support their elders' needs, albeit with some distress. In a few years, however, as boomers become the new elders, their generational weight will place an unbearable strain on the Xers. If the situation continues, in 10 to 15 years, generation X and those whose follow will become increasingly outraged at the burden the *new old* will place on their future.

Younger generations, growing percentages of whom will be non-white, will have grown up in a different world than most of today's elders or the boomers. It's not likely that they will quietly agree to pay for millions of boomers' greens fees, middle-class lifestyles, and medical expenses. Moreover, as we have explored in Chapter 2, the 70 million or so boomers who will survive into old age may live years, even decades, longer than currently anticipated.

The result: *Younger Americans will rebel and the newly elder boomers will become the target of their frustrations*—even though most of these serious problems and injustices will have been instituted by earlier generations.

Can We Weave a New Set of Unifying Patterns Among the Generations?

Whether we're heading toward intergenerational conflicts or a new paradigm of multigenerational relations in which everyone gains will be a central social challenge of the 21st century.

Fortunately, there are important adjustments we can start making today that could very well turn a potential social disaster into a new era of intergenerational cooperation. They can be summed up as follows:

1. Drawing on wisdom and generativity to create a new purpose for elderhood.
2. Crossing age lines to forge a multigenerational melting pot.
3. Taming the two-headed giant, or, scaling AARP down to size.
4. The importance of Elderheroes.

Solution #1:
Wisdom and Generativity: A New Purpose for Elderhood

In some ways, the biggest challenges facing aging Americans will be *psychological.* America has always considered itself a young nation, a new society—not an old one. While we have created a wonderful new third of life for tens of millions of men and women, we have done a far less effective job of envisioning a new sense of purpose to go with it.

Right now, the prevailing model is that when you age, you retreat and retire. While some elders live productive and useful lives, many do not: The average retiree watches 43 hours of television per week, 85 percent of today's elders do not work, and older Americans volunteer less than any other adult age group.[12] It would seem that these millions of mature men and women are matriculating into a kind of "elder wasteland."

This dynamic is both unfortunate and unsustainable: Modern society desperately needs to replant the experience, wisdom, and resources of the elderly into the fields of tomorrow. We need new roles for maturity that not only allow people to grow and contribute, but also make young people feel good about giving up a sizable portion of their income to their elders.

Unfortunately, most authorities on human development have focused little attention on the challenges and purpose of maturity. Sigmund Freund—whose work influenced much of modern counseling, psychology, and even advertising—believed that the basic configuration of one's personality and character occur within the first two decades of life, with the majority of formative activity in the first five years. According to modern adult development theorist Dr. Daniel Levinson of Yale, "Freud was inclined to regard adulthood primarily as a scene in which the early unconscious conflicts were re-enacted, rather than a time of further development."[13] This notion of a flower that blooms once in the spring, then wilts and fades, may have made sense in Freud's era, when the life expectancy was only around 50.

Freud's ideas were advanced by Carl Jung, who made an insightful attempt to imagine the role and purpose of old age. In his essay, "The Stages of Life," Jung divided the life span into four phases: childhood (infancy to age 12), youth (12 to 40), maturity (40 to 65), and old age (65 and older).[14] According to Jung, as the child grows into adulthood, it's necessary to make practical decisions that will influence the course of the second lifestage. Jung appreciated that many of the pragmatic choices the young make on the path to adulthood can't be lasting ones because the personality isn't fully developed until later in life.

Jung theorized that the next great opportunity for fundamental change in one's life comes at about age 40 (which would equate with approximately 50 today). Rather than enter into a decline, he believed, the middle-aged individual must embark on a whole new process of development, called "individuation," which would extend over the remainder of the life cycle. Jung also proposed that old age provided a new stage of discovery and development, with the individual cultivating aspects that were submerged or neglected during earlier life.

Some of Jung's ideas were taken up decades later by adult development pioneer Erik Erikson. After years of research and review, Erikson concluded that each successive stage of life must involve letting go of certain concerns and responsibilities, along with the assumption of new, more mature challenges.[15]

Erikson perceived that each lifestage was marked by a crisis or task that must be resolved in order for the individual to move on successfully to the next. The first five stages he delineated are elaborations on Freud's psychosexual stages of childhood development; the last three characterize the challenges and responsibilities of adulthood and maturity. Moreover, Erikson believed that each developmental task was defined in terms of a dichotomy, which could have either a desirable or an undesirable outcome.

ERIKSON'S STAGES OF LIFE

Stages	Psychosocial Crises	Basic Strengths
I. Infancy	Basic Trust vs. Basic Mistrust	Hope
II. Early Childhood	Autonomy vs. Shame, Doubt	Will
III. Play Age	Initiative vs. Guilt	Purpose
IV. School Age	Industry vs. Inferiority	Competence
V. Adolescence	Identity vs. Identity Confusion	Fidelity
VI. Young Adulthood	Intimacy vs. Isolation	Love
VII. Adulthood	Generativity vs. Stagnation	Care
VIII. Old Age	Integrity vs. Despair	Wisdom

According to this model, childhood concludes with the completion of puberty at stage five, and the maturing individual must begin to settle on an occupational identity, connecting previous roles and skills with the social and occupational behavior of the day. Emerging from this search for identity, in stage six the young adult seeks to fuse his identity with others. If he cannot achieve intimate relationships, he will become isolated and self-absorbed.

According to Erikson, stage seven, adulthood, is devoted to producing something that will outlive itself, through either parenthood, one's work, or the guiding of the next generation. Because so much of an individual's adult productivity occurs during this stage, its successful completion is critical to achieving a sense of fulfillment.

During Erikson's eighth stage, maturity, the individual becomes increasingly aware of the approach of death, and begins to evaluate his life and accomplishments. During this period, he or she strives for "ego integrity." "Old age demands that one garner and lean on all previous experience, maintaining awareness and creativity with a new grace," Erikson wrote. "We can look back over a long past, and so doing helps us understand our lives and the world we live in."[16] In this eighth stage, the key psychological achievement is *wisdom*, fueled by *generativity*—the desire to give back. While failure to achieve this integration results in despair and a sense of meaninglessness, Erikson felt that this stage of life afforded the special opportunity to complete nature's life cycle by allowing each individual to contribute what he or she has learned back to society.

Erikson was concerned about the growing uselessness of elders in modern society. He felt strongly that the whole society suffers—not just the individual—as elders are removed from the tapestry of intergenerational life: "When no challenges are offered, a sense of stagnation may well take over. Others, of course, may welcome this as a promise of respite, but if one should withdraw altogether from generativity, from creativity, from caring for and with others entirely, that would be worse than death."[17]

As fate would have it, Erik Erikson and his wife and long-standing collaborator, Joan Erikson, lived extremely long lives. Writing after his death at 92 in 1994, Joan (also in her nineties) attempted to sort out the elements of another, ninth stage of life:

> When Erik wrote *The Life Cycle Completed*, his ninth decade had not yet begun. Although at age 80 we began to acknowledge our elderly status, I believe we never faced its challenges realistically until we were close to 90. . . . At 90 we woke up in foreign territory. . . . Even the best-cared-for bodies begin to weaken and do not function as they once did. . . . As independence and control are challenged, self-esteem and confidence weaken.[18]

Although Joan Erikson's writing on the full purpose of life's ninth stage was incomplete when she passed away in 1997 at 95, she had come to believe that "gero-transcendence" might be the goal. She reflected that in this more spiritual lifestage, the individual experiences a shift from a materialistic, rational perspective to a more cosmic and transcendent vision. Perhaps in the years ahead, as the number of 80-, 90-, and 100-year-olds multiplies, the Eriksons' pioneering work will be carried forward by a new generation of social scientists.

Solution #2:
Across Age Lines: Forging a Multigenerational Melting Pot

In earlier centuries, it was very common for members of all age groups to live, work, and socialize together. The fragmentation of modern times, however, has eroded the myriad of intergenerational contacts that used to be a natural part of life. And it appears that many elders are so busy dealing with their own interests and priorities that they're not very concerned with understanding the challenges of today's younger generations.

During the speak-out on the first evening of the White House Conference on Aging in 1995, a steady stream of mature men and women took the microphone to assert that aging was hard, unfair, and impoverishing, and that substantially more entitlement funding was needed to solve its problems. For hours, these speakers were cheered on by the elder audience. Then, when a young female college student stood in front of the microphone to state, "I love my grandparents and want them to be secure. But please don't demand so much funding that there'll be nothing left for my generation," she was roundly booed from the podium. My stomach knotted again and again over the next several days as senior advocates demanded more benefits and protections with little regard for the effect on younger generations.

Most of today's elders—removed from schools, households with children, and the workplace—have little contact with young people. As a result, many develop their views about today's youth from the media. Judging merely from the proliferation of vitriolic shows like those hosted by Ricki Lake, Jerry Springer, and Jenny Jones, as well as numerous "reality TV" programs, it's hard not to conclude that a growing number of young people are, in many ways, degenerate. From this reference point, increasing numbers of elders have come to view young people with skepticism—even fear.

Likewise, if you open up one of your children's schoolbooks and look in the index under "aging" or "elderly," what will you find? Nothing. Pick up the high school texts that are shaping your children's ideas and, once again, explore the index for aging-related issues. You won't find them. Indeed, your children's lives contain very few connections with the world of the aged. As a result, many young people form their impressions of the elderly from occasional visits with relatives or from the media. Unfortunately, sitcoms and commercials that kids are likely to watch often portray the elderly as out of tune with the times, frail, set in their ways, or nonexistent.

THE NEED FOR AN ELDER CORPS

Beyond the growing age segregation, two parallel wrongs exist in our society: One is the growing wasteland of so many older people sitting idle in their homes, and the other is the fact that we have 20+ million young people considered at risk, and without enough funding or human resources to support them. Their parents are not fully present to handle the job because a third of those kids are being born out of wedlock and half are coming into families where there's only one parent.

What if we took these two *wrongs* and brought them together through a National Elder Corps? We'd be making an incredible *right*. We'd also be establishing a new "Eriksonian" model for millions of not-yet-old Americans who are beginning to set personal goals and social priorities for the future. An Elder Corps would exemplify and pass on the ideals of wisdom and generativity that are so desperately needed in our culture. In fact, intergenerational social programs have already begun to grow—but they lack the national infrastructure, promotion, participation, and funding necessary to flourish.

The seed for such programs was actually planted in the spring of 1963 by President John F. Kennedy. While delivering a speech on aging, he decried the "wall of inertia" that existed between old people and their communities. To break it down, Kennedy proposed the equivalent of a domestic Peace Corps, which would provide a wide range of opportunities for community service, paying particular attention to bringing the old and young together.

Unfortunately, Kennedy's plan for a National Service Corps never made it out of Congress. In 1965, however, President Lyndon Johnson used federal funding to launch his own approach to senior service. The most impressive programs to spring from Johnson's Office of Economic Opportunity were the Foster Grandparent and Green Thumb programs. Through Foster Grandparents, seniors were paired with troubled and disadvantaged youths, while Green Thumb, sponsored by the National Farmers Union, involved seniors in highway beautification and other service programs.

During the same period, the Small Business Administration created the Service Corps of Retired Executives (SCORE), a nonprofit organization designed to assist young entrepreneurs. In 1967, another federally funded program called Serve and Enrich Retirement by Volunteer Experience (SERVE) began with 23 older volunteers working with children and young adults at a residential home for the mentally retarded. Within two years, SERVE had recruited more than 1,500 volunteers working in 90 agencies. SERVE's initial successes lead to the creation of the Retired and Senior Volunteer Program (RSVP) in 1969.

Over the decades, these programs have evolved and expanded. Currently, Foster Grandparents provides help to more than 80,000 children and teenagers and their families, and contributes more than 20 million hours annually. Last year, 300,000 entrepreneurs were mentored by SCORE volunteers, and during the past 30 years, RSVP has become the largest senior service organization in the country with 450,000 participants who contribute more than 80 million hours of service.

Beyond government-sponsored activities, a wide variety of elder volunteer programs has emerged in communities nationwide. For example:

- Generations Together at the University of Pittsburgh develops educational programs that couple young and elderly for tutoring, community service, and other activities. About 800 older adults and 8,000 youths in western Pennsylvania participate in its programs each year.
- A national coalition linking programs such as United Way, Big Brothers/Big Sisters of America, National Urban League, Boy/Girl Scouts, and AARP, Generations United focuses on advancing intergenerational programming, policies and issues. Along with a national office in Washington, DC, the association has bureaus in 23 states working to increase interaction between people of different generations.
- The Older Adult Service and Information System (OASIS), headquartered in St. Louis, coordinates 5,500 older adult volunteers in 17 cities who tutor 12,000 students one hour per week.
- In Los Angeles, the Family Friends Project matches seniors with families who have chronically ill or otherwise vulnerable children. For instance, 74-year-old retired teacher Cecelia Manzo was paired with the Figueroa family, who were struggling with nine children, including a boy with leukemia. Manzo, who is single and childless, has become an extended member of their family as she helps with the boy's transportation, education, and interactions with doctors.
- The Phone Pal program started in 1989 in Cowley, Kansas, enlists senior volunteers to phone latchkey children before and after school each day.

- Ann Arbor's public schools have launched an intergenerational website production project that joins at-risk teenagers with seniors. The website focuses on lifestyle choices made during the teen years and includes discussions of their long-term effects.
- After working out licensing and malpractice insurance issues, retired physician Jack McConnell opened Volunteers in Medicine in late 1994. In two years, the clinic has built a staff of more than 35 retired doctors and nurses as well as 200 other volunteers, each donating at least one day a week. The clinic has treated more than 7,000 patients and has been replicated in 10 other communities.
- The Rheedlen Center for Children and Families in New York City's Harlem has reached out to homebound seniors who are unable to shop; they are visited each week by two-member youth teams who bring fresh fruits, vegetables, and other food.
- At the DuPont Corporation, 7,000 older and retired workers serve as mentors to young workers. Protégés select mentors whose skills and background can help them learn the ropes. Other corporations with mentoring programs include AT&T, Merrill Lynch, Federal Express, Charles Schwab, and Barnett Bank.

Some intergenerational programs are just for fun. Elderhostel now offers a popular course for grandparents and their grandchildren that takes a six-day tour of Washington, DC. The New Jersey YMHA-YWHA sponsors a weekend for grandparents and grandchildren at the end of each summer. The Sierra Club now offers tours and camping trips for grandparents and grandkids.

These kinds of activities give elders the "Eriksonian" opportunities to transfer culture, knowledge, skills, and values to the next generation. In many ways, older adults are a perfect match for volunteer assignments. They are experienced workers, have learned about life through trial and error, tend to be reliable, and have a great deal of free time. Indeed, many retirees are discovering that so much free time can be depressing. Fifty-five percent of the respondents to a recent Harris poll reported that they felt somewhat useless after retirement and yearned to be involved in more meaningful activities.

When I recently had the opportunity to ask former President Jimmy Carter—whose charitable activities we'll look at later—if he felt that most retirees were giving back enough, he responded, "No! I don't think so, and it's not a deliberate attitude of selfishness. It's primarily the timidity that we feel in taking an unpredictable step into a greater life. There's always a hesitancy about reaching out to someone else in an attitude of friendship. I think that's the main thing, that we get too timid to share part of our lives with strangers or with people whom we don't understand, and we build an increasingly diminishing cocoon within which we survive. I think too many people are reluctant to try something new and to realize that even if you're 85 years old, you can still have a life that's constantly expanding in excitement, in adventure, in joy, in pleasure, and in gratification."[19]

While the gains made by all of these senior service programs are truly impressive, much more is needed if we are to prevent intergenerational strife. The time is past for an assortment of underfunded and underpublicized service programs. We need corporate and government sectors to join forces to recruit and sponsor retirees in order to create a full-blown National Elder Corps: 5 to 10 million people who are ready to become mentors in the workplace, guides to latchkey children, coteachers in our community centers, and leaders in their communities.

These elder volunteers would have a chance to reignite our society's flickering sense of community and impart a powerful base of values that we're about to lose. By giving of themselves in this fashion, they not only can help fix America but can connect with its youth. And they themselves would reap the gratification of meeting what Erikson felt was life's final challenge: "I am what survives of me."

Solution #3:
Taming the Two-Headed Giant:
Scaling AARP Down to Size

Over the years I have come to know many of AARP's executives, researchers, and lobbyists. They are an extremely bright, caring, and dedicated group. I have repeatedly observed the organization in action, however, and am appalled that its leaders claim to be "representing" their 32 million members. AARP's own studies show that only about 15 percent of the membership—about 5 million people—join to align with the lobbying and political programs.

The most publicized example of how out of touch AARP leaders can be occurred a few years ago when the Clinton administration attempted to provide national healthcare. As noted in Chapter 1, AARP not only supported the doomed plan but helped draft it. A subsequent AARP opinion poll revealed that 82 percent of its members opposed the plan.[20]

During the past 25 years, I have participated in nearly a thousand meetings, conferences, media interviews, and public debates on aging-related themes. I have watched AARP use its muscle and sponsorship resources to set the priorities and shape the debates in the majority of these meetings. Within the study of aging and the needs of America's mature adults, AARP is omnipresent—and no other organization can hold a candle to its capabilities.

Most debates about the aging of America are enmeshed in what I'll call *AARPthink*. I am reminded of George Orwell's *1984,* in which he described the use of *Newspeak* to influence—even limit—meaning and thought. Orwell was sounding a warning that true democratic ideals and liberty could only be maintained when a wide range of thoughts, ideas, and disagreements were allowed to flourish. Similarly, diverse public interests will not be served when one group with a distinct point of view—*AARPthink*—monopolistically positions itself as representing the needs and concerns of the entire mature population.

While the association's initial focus was the insurance problems of disenfranchised retirees, for several decades it has been recruiting *pre-retirees* into the fold as well. Working older adults now represent 41 percent of the membership.[21] As though it were a political party unto itself, AARP has repeatedly redefined its field of interest to encompass a wider range of subjects. An examination of its 1995 public policy agenda, "Toward a Just and Caring Society," reveals the group's interest in influencing policy on everything from raising gasoline taxes to boosting government spending for AIDS research, from the need for antilock brakes on oversize trucks to rent control.

Although no one has ever successfully challenged AARP's power, more and more people are growing annoyed at its practices. Several years ago, *Consumer's Research* magazine published a deeply critical review of AARP's activities, which declared, "Claiming that their own interests reflect the interests of tens of millions of seniors, organizations led by the American Association of Retired Persons are quick to oppose policymakers who seek fundamental reform of programs for the aged. They try to lull working-age Americans into complacency about the impending bankruptcy of Social Security and Medicare while frightening the elderly about constructive efforts to resolve the crisis."[22]

Recently, the National Taxpayers Union published its own evaluation of the AARP. After extensive analysis, it concluded that the association is "profoundly undemocratic by almost any measure."[23]

LET THE TWO HEADS HAVE THEIR OWN BODIES

As we noted in Chapter 1, AARP wants to be viewed as an altruistic advocate for the rights of the elderly at the same time that it co-markets a wide range of products and services to that very group. In addition, AARP refuses to own up to the fact that its members have become an active, vital, and financially powerful group and to stop characterizing them as the impoverished retirees they might have been back in 1958.

Reflecting its different interests, AARP's activities should be separated into *two enterprises:* one a not-for-profit advocacy and social service organization, and the other a for-profit affinity marketing organization. Each head should occupy its own body.

AARP's commercial enterprises should be stripped of their not-for-profit status and forced to abide by the same rules, postage rates, taxes, market forces, and competition as other businesses. In fact, its reach and might is so unrivaled that if it were a company, AARP would in all likelihood be broken up on antitrust grounds.

Once the commercial ventures were separated, the remaining social service and advocacy programs would shrink to a fraction of their current size and would lose their monopoly of policy debates. Finally, I would like to see AARP take a cue from Erik Erikson and focus less on taking and more on *giving back*. For this organization to continue to be eligible to receive tens of millions of dollars of federal support, they should devote at least half of their resources to helping the young: The Elder Corps I previously described could be born from the new AARP.

Solution #4:
The Need for Elderheroes

When we're young, we inhabit a make-believe world of heroes and heroines. As mythology expert Joseph Campbell taught, our various heroes contribute to the ever-evolving impressions of who we would like to become as we continue to grow. The problem is, most of the popular heroes in sports, fashion, business, community leadership, media, and even the family *have been young*. As we move into middlescence and maturity, it becomes harder to find new heroes and heroines to illuminate the journey ahead.

Last summer my wife and I journeyed to Houston to participate in one of Jimmy Carter's Habitat for Humanity home-building projects.[24] The experience was unusual in ways that I would never have imagined. I'd gotten the idea to join the Habitat build while meeting with President Carter in Atlanta, where he had invited me to help brainstorm the topics for his new book, *The Virtues of Aging.*

On a hot Sunday in early June, I arrived at an initial gathering of all the volunteer workers at the Houston Convention Center. Some 5,000 people had come from all over the world. I was anxious because I had never really built anything in my life, other than putting up an occasional shelf. During the orientation, we learned that the plan was to build 100 houses from scratch in five days. There would be approximately 40 people per house crew, and about a thousand of the volunteers would provide meals and first aid.

During the welcome presentation, President Carter reminded everyone that he was there to work. While he would make a point of getting to every house to visit with every worker before the week was over, he requested that people not come by the house on which he was working to visit or to socialize because he had "a job to do," and he hoped that they understood that they had one, too.

Like all other workers, I had to bring my own tools, and pay the $250 fee to work for no pay for five days. Each house had four crew leaders who knew how to build. In fact, a third of the people working on the site were professional construction workers. (If you're a construction worker, working on a Habitat project is like a spiritual pilgrimage.) Beyond that, another 10 or 15 workers were fairly capable, and probably 10 more had no home-building skills whatsoever, but kept busy removing garbage and bringing supplies and water.

I showed up at six-thirty Monday morning, and was thrilled to learn that I'd be working on house #1 with Jimmy and Rosalynn Carter. We all gathered in a circle while President Carter said a prayer, and right from the beginning you could tell that this was going to be a different kind of week. Then we got to work. At six-thirty in the morning it was already 96 degrees, and the humidity was 95 percent. Although I'm in pretty good shape, I felt like I was either going to have a stroke or throw my back out in the first 15 minutes. We began with a 1,100-square-foot slab of cement that had already been poured and set. With little fanfare, we all began lifting and hammering beams and walls; within just a few hours, the framing was up.

By around nine, I was ready to go AWOL. If you've never swung a hammer for more than half an hour, try swinging one for two straight hours in 100-degree heat. I've never been in a more punishing physical environment, and it was only the morning of the first day. As I was hammering, I couldn't help noticing that President Carter was *really* hammering—boom, boom, boom! As he was down on his knees with his hammer, I was thinking, "Where does this guy get his energy?" But, I figured, it was still early, and he was used to this; he grew up in the heat of Georgia. He'd tire soon.

By one o'clock, I'd already had four breaks, including a quick lunch, and was completely exhausted. But President Carter kept pounding—steady, powerful hammering—and the temperature had risen to 104. Then we had to start cutting wood, but had only two power saws available. I noticed that President Carter was doing all of his cutting by hand. If you've ever cut through a two-by-four, you feel pretty proud of yourself. But he was on his *twentieth* board and his energy was unrelenting. By around four-thirty, everybody was totally spent. Nearly all my fingers were damaged and bleeding. But President Carter kept right on working into the night. I went back to my room to grab a bite and crash. The next thing I knew, the alarm was going off, and it was time to return to the site.

Throughout the second day, all eyes were watching the Carter house to see when our roof went up. I was now fascinated that our progress was being driven by this "old" man who said little. I could see that his leadership style involved never barking at people or being critical, but rather making everybody on the site work to keep pace with him.

Wade and Shalina Gibson, the young couple who, with their three children, were going live in the house, worked also. You could see it dawning on this low-income, African-American couple that they were soon going to have their own house, and that the work crew was being led by a former president, who was on his knees tacking in their trimwork, and a former first lady, who was busy framing in the windows.

To pass the time while working, I'd ask my workmates. "Why are you here?" Almost everybody had the same answer: They didn't feel right unless they did something to help other people. And it wasn't about writing a check; it was about giving a chunk of your life and time and effort. The majority of the workers were over 50 years of age, uncomplaining older people who were hammering away in the heat.

By the end of the fourth day, while the plumbing and electrical fixtures were being installed by volunteer contractors, we started laying down sod and planting trees. On the last day the carpeting and appliances went in. At two-thirty on Friday afternoon—on schedule—President and Mrs. Carter brought us all inside for a little ceremony. The 40 of us stood in a circle in the living room holding hands. And it hit everybody at the same time what we had done.

Exhausted and filthy but with full hearts, we huddled in a circle as President Carter presided over a makeshift service. He said a prayer, then turned to Wade and Shalina and gave them a white linen–covered Bible—the first book for their new house. The gesture was so powerful; the emotional intensity in the room went up a notch, if possible.

Then Carter said to Wade, "Do you know what Jesus did?"

Wade replied, "He died for our sins."

"But do you know what he did as a young man?" Carter asked. "He was a carpenter, he worked with his hands. And so, by allowing us to build this house for you, in a small way you've allowed us to do the work of the Lord."

All of a sudden, Wade—who is a very big, tough, 250-pound guy with two gold front teeth—started to cry. And he reached out to Carter and, sobbing, put his arms around him. Then Shalina started crying, and soon we all stood there crying.

Before our group broke up, President Carter stressed that those of us who are more fortunate should never forget others who are less so. He spoke of the blessing of giving, how the harder he and Mrs. Carter work, the more they feel blessed by the results. Giving of themselves, he said, made them stronger. When I later asked President Carter what motivated his involvement in so many charitable activities, he explained, "Every time we thought we were making a sacrifice for others, it has turned out to be one of our greatest blessings. In other words, we have gotten more out of it than we have put into it. You just try it, even if it's nothing more than going to a public hospital and rocking a baby for two hours a week. It's an *expansion of life*, an encounter with new people who are potentially friends. And so, it's a learning process, an exciting process that gives you new and expanding life experiences."

Even though I come from a different generation and a different religious orientation than Carter, working by his side gave me the feeling that I was in the presence of a great man, a *large man*, and his age seemed more an *empowerment* than a diminishment. His wrinkles and gray hair didn't make me feel that he was less of a man, but more of one. In many ways, Carter and his "post-career" activities are the embodiment of Erikson's vision of wisdom and generativity.

Jimmy and Rosalynn Carter are not alone. As we have seen, in every town, in every apartment building, church, gym, and community center, we can find new role models of productive aging. *Maturity has never had so many high-spirited, motivated men and women who, with their deeds and actions, are clearing a new and more hopeful path to our future.* These are the real heroes of aging—and by honoring and calling attention to them, we provide healthy models to whom all of us can look for direction as we grow older.

Tips to Age-proof Your Life

- Think carefully about who you want to be in your elder years, and about what skills and life experiences will allow you to help and remain connected with others.

- Before you join AARP, consider whether your dues will go toward causes that you believe are for the good of all society and whether the organization projects an image of aging that you approve of.
- Learn whether your community and workplace are making use of the resources of older people and how you can involve yourself and your family in these activities.
- Avoid thinking of your own retirement as an extended vacation, and remember that in order to be worthwhile, old age should ideally be a time of continued growth, generosity, wisdom, and love.

CONCLUSION:
THE AGE OF POWER

By now it will be obvious that America is becoming a gerontocracy, and that four outcomes are certain:

1. More of us will live longer than in any previous generation;
2. The epicenter of economic and political power will shift from the young to the old;
3. We will need to change our current mind-set about how to spend our extra years of life; and
4. How we decide to behave as elders will, in all likelihood, become the most important challenge we will face in our lives.

BOOMER DESTINY

In the decades ahead, the boomers will complete America's transformation into a gerontocracy as they take control of the nation's social and economic power. From this demographically and politically dominant position, they will have the potential to realize their full intellectual, social, and political influence, not as baby boomers but as elders.

In youth, boomers were self-indulgent in their priorities. In their late teens and twenties, many shared an idealistic commitment to society. During the past several decades of career building and child-rearing, many of their early ideals have been submerged. As boomers shed the skin of youth, however, they could be migrating into the *most powerful years of their lives.*

If they can step outside their generational tendency toward self-centeredness and wield this power with wisdom and generativity, they could rise to their greatest height and make a remarkable success of history's first multiethnic, multiracial, and multigenerational melting pot. Or if, like silver-haired velociraptors, they use their size and influence to bully younger generations and gobble up all of the available resources, we will find ourselves in a Gerassic Park of our own making.

If this generation evolves to a deepened appreciation of the effect it has on others and can learn to exemplify a new kind of wise, mature leadership, when the boomers' time on earth is over, perhaps they will be remembered not just as the *largest* generation in history, but the *finest*.

The choice is ours.

NOTES

CHAPTER ONE

1. Kristen Bole, "Graying Japan Poses Golden Opportunity," *San Francisco Business Times,* December 16, 1996.
2. Carl Haub, Population Reference Bureau, conversation with the author, Washington, DC, May 10, 1999.
3. Wendy Koch, "U.S. Is a World Leader in Population Surge: Immigrants Make Up One-third of Growth," *San Francisco Examiner,* May 8, 1997.
4. Jean Bourgeois-Pichat, "The Unprecedented Shortage of Births in Europe: Below-Replacement Fertility in Industrial Societies, Causes and Consequences," *Population and Development Review,* supplement to vol. 12 (1986), pp. 3–25.
5. Therese Hesketh and Wei Xing Zhu, "The One Child Family Policy: The Good, the Bad, and the Ugly; Health in China, part 3," *British Medical Journal* 314, no. 7095 (June 7, 1997), p. 1685.
6. Michael Specter, "Population Implosion Worries a Graying Europe, *New York Times,* July 10, 1998.
7. Ibid.
8. Jim Impoco, "Baby Bust Is Worrying Japan," *San Francisco Chronicle,* January 23, 1991.
9. Specter, *NYT.*
10. Barbara Beck, "The Economics of Ageing: The Luxury of Longer Life," *Economist,* January 27, 1996.
11. Ben Wattenberg, "The Population Explosion Is Over," *New York Times Magazine,* November 23, 1997.
12. Increase Mather, *Dignity and Duty of Aged Servants of the Lord* (Boston: B. Green, 1716), p. 52.
13. Benjamin Franklin [Richard Saunders, pseud.], *The Way to Wealth* (Philadelphia: by the author, July 7, 1757).
14. Cortlandt Van Rensselaer, *Old Age: A Funeral Sermon* (Washington, DC: by the author, 1841), pp. 10–11.
15. David Hackett Fischer, *Growing Old in America* (New York: Oxford University Press, 1977), p. 52.

16. Philip J. Greven, *Four Generations: Population, Land, and Family in Colonial Andover, Massachusetts* (Ithaca, NY: Cornell University Press, 1970), pp. 143–144.

17. Dr. William Osler, "Valedictory Address at Commencement at Johns Hopkins University," *Journal of the American Medical Association*, February 22, 1905, pp. 706–710.

18. Anthony Trollope, *The Fixed Period* (London: Oxford University Press, 1882), pp. 2–3.

19. F. Spencer Baldwin, "Retirement Systems for Municipal Employees," *Annals of the American Academy of Political and Social Science* 38 (Philadelphia: University of Pennsylvania Press, 1911), p. 6.

20. Nathan Allen, "The Physiological Laws of Human Increase," *Transactions of the American Medical Association* (Philadelphia: AMA, 1870), p. 26.

21. W. Andrew Achenbaum, *Old Age in the New Land: The American Experience Since 1790* (Baltimore: Johns Hopkins University Press, 1978), p. 51.

22. Fischer, *Growing Old in America*, pp. 90–94.

23. Employee Benefit Research Institute, *EBRI Databook on Employee Benefits* (Washington, DC: EBRI, 1997), www.ebri.org.

24. Irving Bluestone, "Working-Class Hero," *Time*, December 7, 1998, p. 157.

25. Ken McDonnell, Employee Benefit Research Institute, conversation with the author, Washington, DC, May 3, 1999.

26. Theda Skocpol, "Delivering for Young Families: The Resonance of the GI Bill," *American Prospect*, September/October 1996.

27. C. Eugene Steuerle, "Prepared Statement Before the Senate Finance Committee," *General Revenue Financing of Social Security* (Washington, DC: GPO, February 9, 1999).

28. National Association of Realtors Research Group, "Existing Home Sales—Annual," http://nar.realtor.com/databank/home.htm.

29. U.S. Bureau of the Census, Current Population Reports, Series P60-201, *Poverty in the United States 1997*, Joseph Delaker and Mary Naifeh (Washington, DC: GPO, 1998), p. vi.

30. Data here and in the following bullet points, unless otherwise noted, were culled from Federal Reserve Board, "Family Finances in the U.S.," and from U.S. Department of Labor, Bureau of Labor Statistics, *1997 Consumer Expenditure Survey* (Washington, DC: GPO, 1998), see http://stats.bls.gov/csxhome.htm.

31. U.S. Bureau of the Census, "Housing Vacancies and Homeownership, First Quarter, 1999," (Washington, DC: GPO, 1999), http://www.census.gov/hhes/www/hvs.html.

32. Mediamark Research Inc., *MRI Market Segmentation Studies* (New York: Mediamark, 1999), http://www.mediamark.com/.

33. Health Insurance Association of America, *Source Book of Health Insurance Data, 1998* (Annapolis, MD: HIAA, February 1998).

34. Mediamark, *MRI Market Segmentation Studies.*

35. Health Care Financing Administration, *National Health Care Expenditures* (Washington, DC: HCFA, 1999), http://www.hcfa.gov/stats/nhe-oact/nhe.htim.

36. National Center for Health Statistics, *National Health Care Survey* (Hyattsville, MD: NCHS, 1999), http://www.cdc.gov/nchswww/about/major/nhcs/nhcs.htm.

37. Representative Peter DeFazio, *PALNI: Congressional Record* (Washington, DC: GPO, June 25, 1997), http://www.palni.edu/ gpo/.

38. For more on AARP, see Jeffrey H. Birnbaum, "Washington's Most Powerful Man . . . ," *Fortune,* May 12, 1997; Jill Young Miller, "When AARP Speaks, Washington Sits Up and Listens," *Sunday Gazette Mail* February 15, 1998; and Charles R. Morris, *The AARP* (New York: Times Books, 1996).

39. Jeffrey H. Birnbaum, "The Influence Merchants," *Fortune,* December 7, 1998.

40. Morris, *The AARP,* pp. 53–55.

CHAPTER TWO

1. To better appreciate the future pursuit of life extension, it would be helpful to understand the difference between "life span" and "life expectancy." Life span is defined as the number of years an individual may expect to live if nothing intervenes to cut short his or her life. While more and more people are surviving into old age, there is no sign yet that the limit of human life—its span—has been extended significantly. Death seems to be programmed into the organism, and this process sets an upper limit on life span for each species: one day for mayflies, four months for grasshoppers, 3 years for hummingbirds, just under 30 years for dogs, 200 years for the Galapagos tortoise, and 120 years for humans. Life expectancy, on the other hand, is simply the average number of years to which humans are living at any particular time in history. To illustrate the difference between life span and life expectancy, imagine that half the members of a certain species die at age 50 and the other half live to 100. The life span for that species would then be 100 years, and the average life expectancy 75. One of the key reasons that the average life expectancy has been so low in past centuries is the fact that so many children used to die in the first months and years of life—a dynamic that pulled the average down.

2. Quoted in John Langone, *Long Life* (Boston: Little, Brown, 1978), p. 23.

3. Serge Voronoff, *Rejuvenation by Grafting* [translation edited by Fred. F. Imianitoff.] (London: G. Allen & Unwin Ltd., 1925), p. 17.

4. Ibid., p. 22.

5. Ibid., pp. 78–79.

6. IMS Health Inc., "IMS Health Forecasts Viagra Sales to Reach $1 Billion in First Year," *Market Research* (Westport, CT: IMS, 1998), http://www.imshealth.com/html/in_arc/07_06_1998_27.htm.

7. It's also getting easier for doctors to prescribe pharmaceuticals for unconventional treatments. A federal law passed in December 1997, Section 401 of the 1997 FDA Modernization Act, allows drug companies to promote "off label" uses directly to physicians as long as there is some medical evidence to back up the claim.

8. U.S. Department of Health and Human Services, National Institutes of Health, National Institute on Aging, "Two New Studies Suggest that Caloric Restriction in Monkeys May Extend Their Life and Health," NIA Public Information Office, October 2, 1997.

9. Barbara Levine, Ph.D., and Maureen Mulhern, "Phytochemicals: Natural Disease Fighters," *Newsweek*, November 1998 (Winter, Special Edition).

10. Sharon Begley, "Beyond Vitamins," *Newsweek*, April 25, 1994.

11. Geoffrey Cowley, "Attention: Aging Men," *Newsweek*, September 16, 1996.

12. "Estrogen and Heart Health: More Data, More Confusion," *Harvard Heart Letter*, November 1, 1998.

13. Nananda F. Col, M.D., and John B. Wong, M.D., "Patient-Specific Decisions About Hormone Replacement Therapy in Postmenopausal Women," *Journal of the American Medical Association* Vol. 277, No. 14, April 7, 1997; and Mi Young Hwang, "No Bones About Osteoporosis: Postmenopausal Women Face Difficult Dilemma of Choosing Estrogen or Other Therapies," *Journal of the American Medical Association* Vol. 279, No. 18, May 13, 1998.

14. Stephen Rae, "Natural Age Eraser," *Men's Health*, July 1996.

15. Russel Reiter and Jo Robinson, *Melatonin: Your Body's Natural Wonder Drug* (New York: Bantam, 1996).

16. Rick Weiss, "Aging: New Answers to Old Questions," *National Geographic*, November 1997.

17. Bill Lawren, "Youth Serums: What Works, What Won't," *American Health for Women*, July 17, 1997.

18. Alex Kuczynsi, "Anti-Aging Potion or Poison," *New York Times*, April 12, 1998.

19. Ibid.

20. Thomas Maier, "Hormones: A Growing Concern," *Newsday*, November 17, 1998.

21. Intel cofounder Gordon Moore prophesied in 1965 that the computing power of silicon chips would double every 18 to 24 months. He was right.

22. Scientific developments throughout the world are contributing to our understanding of the complexities of the human gene. For example, in January 1999 the country of Iceland announced that it had decided to sell the rights to the entire population's genetic code (including all 270,000 residents) to a

biotechnology company in order to advance the progress of genetic research. Due to the fact that Icelanders are one of the most homogenous populations in the world, with genealogical records that go back hundreds of years, this genetic data should prove to be enormously valuable. For further reading, see John Schwartz, "With Gene Plan, Iceland Dives into a Controversy," *International Herald Tribune,* January 13, 1999.

23. Ricki Lewis, "Telomere Tales," *BioScience,* December 1998.

24. Ibid. See also Andrea G. Bodnar, et al., "Extension of Life Span by Introduction of Telomerase into Normal Human Cells," *Science,* January 16, 1998. Active research programs for telomerase inducer drugs are being conducted by the University of Texas's Southwestern University Medical Center and Cold Spring Harbor Laboratory on Long Island, New York, as well as by several biotech and pharmaceutical firms.

25. Steve Sternberg, "Pacemaker Pioneers's 'Long Shot' Has Lasted 40 Years," *USA Today,* October 19, 1998.

26. U.S. Department of Health and Human Services, Centers for Disease Control, National Center for Health Statistics, *Advance Data from Vital and Health Statistics* No. 291, "1995 Summary: National Hospital Discharge Survey," E.J. Graves and M.F. Owings (Hyattsville, MD: NCHS, 1997).

27. Gavin Evans, "Man Made," *Guardian* (Manchester), September 2, 1998.

28. Iain S. Bruce, "Just How Close Are We to Creating the Cyborg?" *Scotsman* (Edinburgh), December 1, 1998.

29. United Kingdom, Medical Research Council (MRC), Institute of Hearing Research, *Evaluation of the National Cochlear Implant Programme,* "Cochlear Implantation in the U.K. 1990–1994," A.Q. Summerfield and D.H. Marshall (London: HMSO, 1995).

30. Stephen Baker, "A Transplant Breakthrough ... with One Big Catch," *BusinessWeek,* April 7, 1997.

31. Richard Knox, "Pig-Cell Transplants Said to Ease Disease," *Boston Globe,* March 1, 1997.

32. Baker, *BusinessWeek.* We haven't even begun to tackle the ethical issues surrounding the creation of "chimeras"—transgenic animals. Already, animals engineered with human genes have been patented in the U.S., while the European Patent Office has received its own applications for chimeric mutant animals. Although the Thirteenth Amendment outlawed slavery, it is unlikely that the architects of that amendment could have imagined a future in which body parts and genes would be created, bought, and sold in the service of human market demand.

33. Mohammad Zahirul Haque, "Cloning and Other Discoveries that Will Change Your Earthly Life," *Economic Review,* February 1998.

34. Ed Susman, "Organs Grown Outside Body Work in Dogs," United Press International, June 1, 1998.

35. It is obvious that scientific knowledge and government regulatory agencies

will not be able to keep up with all of the thousands of anti-aging therapeutics that are appearing throughout the world. While the promise of these therapies is undeniably attractive, we are still years away from knowing just what their ultimate effect on the human organism will be. Even though I have always identified with the "early adapters" in almost every area of social and technological advance, I do NOT believe that it is safe yet for individuals to self-prescribe the various hormonal, phytochemical, and herbal therapeutics that have been discussed in this chapter.

CHAPTER THREE

1. Due to immigration, there are now 78 million American boomers.
2. J. Walker Smith and Ann Clurman, *Rocking the Ages: The Yankelovich Report on Generational Marketing* (New York: HarperCollins, 1997), p. 23.
3. "Prosperity," *Time,* January 10, 1955.
4. Landon Y. Jones, *Great Expectations: America and the Baby Boom Generation* (New York: Ballantine, 1980), p. 42.
5. Ibid., p. 140.
6. Media Dynamics, *TV Dimensions '99* (New York: Media Dynamics, 1999), http://www.mediadynamicsinc.com.
7. Morris, *The AARP,* p. 179.
8. Jones, *Great Expectations,* pp. 70–88.
9. Ibid. pp. 263–265.
10. Sidney Zion, "Outlasting Rock," *New York Times,* June 21, 1981.
11. U.S. Department of Education, National Center for Education Statistics, *Digest of Education Statistics, 1996,* tables 168 and 194 (based on the IPEDS/HEGIS "Fall Enrollment" surveys), and conversation with Stanford University Undergraduate Admissions Office, May 10, 1999.
12. U.S. Bureau of the Census, Current Population Reports, Series P23-194, *Population Profile of the United States 1997* (Washington DC: GPO, 1998).
13. Nancy Romanenko, "Daddy Dearest: He's More Involved Than Ever Before," Gannett News Service, June 19, 1998.
14. D. Moore, *The Gallup Poll* 61, no. 43 (Princeton, NJ: Gallup, 1997). Also see *Research Alert,* May 1, 1997.
15. James T. Bond, Ellen Galinsky, and Jennifer E. Swanberg, Families and Work Institute, *The 1997 National Study of the Changing Workforce* (New York: FWI, 1998).
16. J. D. Zahniser, *And Then She Said: Quotations by Women for Every Occasion* (St. Paul: Caillech Press, 1990).
17. Catalyst, *Two Careers, One Marriage: Making It Work in the Workplace,* no. D-39 (New York: Catalyst, 1998).
18. Harry Dent, *The Roaring 2000s* (New York: Simon & Schuster, 1998), p. 31.
19. Smith and Clurman, *Rocking the Ages,* p. 17.

20. Alzheimer's Association, "Research" and "The Facts," http://www.alz.org/research/index.htm.

21. National Association of Area Agencies on Aging, *1998–99 National Directory for Eldercare Information & Referral* (Washington, DC: NAAAA, 1999).

22. Lawrence A. Weinbach, Committee for Economic Development, *Who Will Pay for Your Retirement? The Looming Crisis* (Washington, DC: CED, 1995).

23. Media Dynamics, *TV Dimensions '99*.

24. Adapted from Ray Bradbury, "A Sound of Thunder," *The Golden Apples of the Sun* (New York: Avon Books, 1990).

CHAPTER FOUR

1. Susan Littwin, *The Postponed Generation* (New York: Morrow, 1986).

2. Granville Stanley Hall, *Adolescence* (New York: Arno Press, 1969).

3. Erik H. Erikson, *Childhood and Society* (New York: Norton, 1993).

4. Roger L. Gould, *Transformations* (New York: Simon & Schuster, 1978).

5. Roper Starch Worldwide, *The Boomer Balancing Act: Baby Boomers Talk About Life and the American Dream* (Harrison, NY: RSW, 1996). See also, "Roper Survey Finds Baby Boomers Redefining the 'American Dream,'" *American Marketplace*, October 3, 1996.

6. David Van Biema, "The Journey of Our Lives," *Life*, October, 1991.

7. See John W. Rowe and Robert L. Kahn, *Successful Aging* (New York: Pantheon, 1998).

8. Erica Goode, "New Study Finds Middle Age Is Prime of Life," *New York Times*, February 16, 1999.

9. Rose, Jonathan, "From Bismarck to Roosevelt," *Scholastic Update*, December 13, 1985.

10. Katie Louchheim, *The Making of the New Deal* (Cambridge, MA: Harvard University Press, 1983), as quoted by Wilbur J. Cohen.

11. Center for Strategic and International Studies, CSIS Panel Report, *The 21st Century Retirement Security Plan* (Washington, DC: CSIS, March 1999), http://www.csis.org/pubs/ pubsheal.htm1#ncrp.

12. Japanese Ministry of Health and Welfare, Statistics Bureau, Management and Coordination Agency, *Vital Statistics 1998* (Tokyo: MHW, 1999).

13. Employee Benefit Research Institute, *Employee Benefits, Retirement Patterns, and Implications for Increased Work Life*, EBRI Issue Brief 184 (Washington, DC: EBRI, April 1997).

14. F. Thomas Juster and Robert T. Willis, Institute for Social Research, University of Michigan, *The Health and Retirement Study* (Ann Arbor, MI:ISR, 1999), http://www.umich.edu/~hrswww/.

15. John Brugger, conversation with the author, February 25, 1999. See also http://www.monsanto.com/monsanto/.

16. Claude Pepper, OpEd, *New York Times*, July 26, 1977.

17. José Piñera, Cato Institute, *Empowering Workers: The Privatization of Social Security in Chile* (Washington, DC: Cato, December, 1996). See also http://www.cato.org/dailys/12-17-97.html.

18. Bernard Weinraub, "Where Father Doesn't Know Best," *New York Times*, November 1, 1998.

19. Ibid.

20. Lisa Schwarzbaum, "Women of a Certain Rage," *Entertainment Weekly*, October 11, 1996.

21. High Yield Marketing, *Ageism in Advertising: A Study of Advertising Attitudes Towards Maturing and Mature Consumers* (St. Paul: HYM, 1995), www.highyieldmarketing.com. See also "New Study: Ad Agencies Are Ageist At Own Expense," *Aging Today*, September/October 1995.

22. Melanie Wells, "Ad Land's Age Old Problem: Age Bias Cases Gush from Fountain of Youth Culture," *USA Today*, March 18, 1997.

23. "Age Bias Still Lurks," Bulletin Board, *Washington Times*, January 20, 1999.

24 George J. Church, "Unmasking Age Bias," *Time*, September 7, 1998. See also Fair Employment Council of Greater Washington, *No Foot in the Door: An Experimental Study of Employment Discrimination Against Older Workers* (Washington, DC: FEC, December 1997).

25. Dennis Coleman, "Baby Boom to Baby Bust: Flexible Work Options for Older Workers," *Benefits Quarterly*, Fourth Quarter 1998.

26. Tait Trussell and Joan McQueeney Mitric, "Report Advocates Older Employees," Maturity News Service, May 15, 1994. See also Commonwealth Fund, http://www.commonwealthfund.org/ newnav.asp.

27. Ben Wattenberg, "We're Not Just Adding Years, but More Life to Them, Too," Newspaper Enterprise Association, December 8, 1997.

28. Lisa R. Davis and Greg Marchildon, "New AARP Study Finds 'Boomer' Views of Future, Retirement Vary," U.S. Newswire, June 2, 1998. It's obvious that we'll need new words to describe work and retirement when multiple retirements become commonplace.

29. Rowe and Kahn, *Successful Aging*.

30. U.S. Department of Labor, Employment and Training Administration, *Work-based Learning* (Washington, DC: GPO, 1998).

31. U.S. Department of Education, National Center for Education Statistics, *Digest of Education Statistics, 1998* (Washington DC: GPO, 1999).

32. "Welcoming Older Students," *USA Today*, November 1, 1993.

33. U.S. Department of Education, National Center for Education Statistics, Table 171, *Digest of Education Statistics, 1997* (Washington DC: GPO, 1998), http://nces.ed.gov/pubsearch/pub info.asp?pubid=1999036.

34. Elizabeth Sheley, "Why Give Employee Sabbaticals?" *HR Magazine*, March 1996. See also Society for Human Resource Management, http://www.shrm.org/index.html.

CHAPTER FIVE

1. *The World Almanac and Book of Facts* (Mahwah, NJ: World Almanac Books, 1998), p. 615.

2. U.S. Bureau of the Census, International Programs Center, International Data Base, http://www.census.gov/ipc/www/ idbnew.html.

3. National Center for Health Statistics, *Health, United States, 1998, with Socioeconomic Status and Health Chartbook* (Hyattsville, MD: NCHS, 1999), http://www.cdc.gov/nchswww/ products/pubs/pubd/hus/hus.htm.

4. Ellen Graham, "Weighing the Benefits of Buying Insurance for Extended Elder Care," *Wall Street Journal*, March 31, 1999.

5. Health Care Financing Administration, Healthy Aging Project, 1999, http://www.hcfa.gov/quality/3b.htm.

6. U.S. Bureau of the Census, Current Population Reports, Special Studies, P23-190, *65+ in the United States* (Washington, DC: GPO, 1996). Although in the past few years there has been a slight trend toward declining frailty, the improvements are not sufficient to halt the steady and disconcerting growth in the number of very old and very sick men and women. Americans with chronic conditions are now living longer than ever before.

7.

LEADING CAUSES OF DEATH, 65+

Diseases of heart	597,000
Malignant neoplasms [cancer]	355,000
Cerebrovascular disease	125,000
Chronic obstructive pulmonary disease	76,000
Pneumonia and influenza	69,000
Diabetes mellitus	47,000
Unintentional injuries	31,000
Alzheimer's disease	21,100
Nephritis, nephrotic syndrome, and nephrosis	21,000
Septicemia	17,500

SOURCE: U.S. BUREAU OF THE CENSUS, 65+ IN THE UNITED STATES.

LEADING CHRONIC CONDITIONS, 65+

Disease	Prevalence
Arthritis	50.2%
High blood pressure (hypertension)	36.4%
Heart disease	32.5%
Hearing impairment	28.6%
Cataracts	16.6%
Deformity or orthopedic impairment	16.6%
Chronic sinusitis	15.1%
Diabetes	10.1%
Tinnitus	9.0%

SOURCE: AMERICAN CANCER SOCIETY, WWW3.CANCER.ORG, 1997

8. American Heart Association, "Statistics, Economic Cost of Cardiovascular Diseases," http://www.americanheart.org/statistics/10econom.html.
9. American Cancer Society, "Cancer Information, Statistics, 1999 Cancer Facts and Figures," http://www3.cancer.org/cancerinfo/acs_frame.asp?frame=statmenu.html.
10. Daniel Haney, "Lifetime Cost of a Stroke," Associated Press, February 8, 1997.
11. American Federation for Aging Research, *Putting Aging on Hold: Delaying the Disease of Old Age* (New York: AFAR, 1995).
12. Alzheimer's Association, "The Facts," and "Statistics/Prevalence," http://www.alz.org/facts/index.htm.
13. Zaven Khachaturian, *Alzheimer's Disease* (Boca Raton, FL: CRC Press, 1996).
14. Walter M. Bortz, *We Love Too Short and Die Too Long* (New York: Bantam Books, 1991).
15. Oliver Wendell Holmes, *The Poetical Works of Oliver Wendell Holmes* (Boston: Houghton Mifflin, 1975).

16. Zaven Khachaturian, conversation with the author, January 1999.

17. National Institutes of Health, Office of Financial Management, Budget, http://www4.od.nih.gov/ofm/. Although many NIH projects could have a direct impact on the diseases of late life, the aging-specific funding remains minute.

18. John F. Kennedy's address to U.S. Congress, May 25, 1961.

19. AFAR, *Putting Aging on Hold*.

20. Ignatz Leo Nascher, *Geriatrics: The Diseases of Old Age and Their Treatment* . . . (Philadelphia: Blakiston, 1916).

21. Alliance for Aging Research, *Will You Still Treat Me When I'm 65?* (Washington, DC: AAR, 1996).

22. Robert N. Butler, *Why Survive?* (New York: Harper & Row, 1975).

23. John Murphy, speaking to the U.S. Senate Special Committee on Aging, May 20, 1998.

24. Ibid.

25. Kathleen Lohr, et. al., ed., Institute of Medicine, *The Nation's Physician Workforce: Options for Balancing Supply and Requirements* (Washington, DC: National Academy Press, 1995), p. 23.

26. Centers for Disease Control, National Center for Health Statistics, "National Survey of Personal Health Practices and Consequences," http://www.dc.gov/nchswww/products/catalogs/subject/nsphpc/nsphpc.htm#description1.

27. Ibid.

28. Rowe and Kahn, *Successful Aging*, p. 28.

29. Walter Bortz, *Dare to Be 100* (New York: Simon & Schuster, 1996), p. 10.

30. AFAR, *Putting Aging on Hold*, p. 5.

31. Alison Wellner, "Getting Old and Staying Fit," *American Demographics*, March 1, 1998.

32. U.S. Department of Agriculture, Economic Research Service, *America's Eating Habits: Changes and Consequences*, Elizabeth Frazão, ed. (Washington, DC: GPO, 1999), http://www. econ.ag.gov/.

33. Health Care Financing Administration and Office for Strategic Planning, *A Profile of Medicare: Chartbook, 1998* (Washington DC: GPO, 1999), http://www.hfa.gov/pubforms/chartbk.pdf.

34. American Association of Health Plans, *Managed Care Facts* (Washington, DC: AAHP, 1999), http://www.aahp.org/menus/ index1.cfm.

35. Alliance for Aging Research, *Seven Deadly Myths: Uncovering the Facts About the High Cost of the Last Year of Life* (Washington, DC: AAR, 1997), http://www.agingresearch.org/Resources/aging_frame.htm.

36. Ibid.

37. William Claiborne, "Doctor Assisted Suicide Is Backed in Poll," *Washington Post*, July 30, 1998.

38. Jimmy Carter, *The Virtues of Aging* (New York: Ballantine, 1998), pp. 85–86.

CHAPTER SIX

1. E. Hing and B. Bloom, National Center for Health Statistics, Series 13, no. 104, *Long-Term Care for the Functionally Dependent Elderly, Vital and Health Statistics* (Hyattsville, MD: Public Health Service, 1990).

2. National Family Caregivers Association, *Caregiver Member Survey 1997: A Profile of Caregiving* (Kensington, MD: NFCA, November 1997), http://www.nfcacares.org/.

3. Sara Rimer, "Families Bear a Bigger Share of Long-Term Care for the Frail Elderly," *New York Times,* June 8, 1998.

4. National Alliance for Caregiving and Equitable Foundation, *The Caregiving Boom: Baby Boomer Women Giving Care* (Bethesda, MD: NAC, 1998), http://www.caregiving.org/content/ reports/babyboomer.pdf.

5. National Alliance for Caregiving and AARP, *Family Caregiving in the U.S.: Finding from a National Survey* (Bethesda, MD: NAC, 1997), http://www.caregiving.org/content/reports/finalreport.pdf.

6. National Council on the Aging (NCOA) and Pew Charitable Trust, "7 Million Provide Long-Distance Care to Elders," March 12, 1997, http://ncoa.org/news/archives/7millLTC031297. htm.

7. Institute for Health and Aging, University of California, San Francisco, *Chronic Care in America: A 21st Century Challenge* (Princeton, NJ: Robert Wood Johnson Foundation, November 1996), http://www.rwjf.org/library/chrcare/.

8. Stephen Moses, "Aging Anomalies Analyzed," *LTC Bullets,* April 9, 1999, http://www.centerltc.com/. See also University of Pennsylvania, School of Social Work, Boettner Center of Financial Gerontology, http://www.ssw.upenn.edu/.

9. Armond Budish, *Avoiding the Medicaid Trap* (New York: Henry Holt, 1989), p. 34.

10. "Loopholes Let Wealthy Seniors Access Medicaid Funds," *USA Today,* May 27, 1998.

11. Paul Hogan, conversation with the author, March 16, 1999, Omaha, Nebraska.

12. Stephen Moses, *LTC Choice: A Simple, Cost-Free Solution to the Long-Term Care Financing Puzzle* (Seattle: Center for Long-term Care Financing, September 1, 1998), pp. 5–6.

13. Institute for Health & Aging, UCSF, *Chronic Care in America.*

14. U.S. Bureau of the Census, International Programs Center, IB/98-3, *Gender and Aging: Caregiving,* Victoria Velkoff and Valerie Lawson (Washington, DC: GPO, December 1998), http://www.census.gov/ipc/prod/ib-9803.pdf.

15. Ibid.

16. National Center for Health Statistics, *Health, United States, 1998, Socioeconomic Status and Health Chartbook* (Washington, DC: GPO, 1999).

17. Life Insurance Marketing and Research Association International, *What Do You Do Now?* (Hartford, CT: LIMRA, 1999), http://www.limra.com/wn9899/index.htm.

18. National Council on the Aging and John Hancock Financial Services, "Study Finds Long-Term Care Generation Gap," March 23, 1999, http://ncoa.org/news/ltc/ generation_gap.htm.

19. Mark Francis, "Market Segmentation Key to LTC Sales," *National Underwriter*, May 10, 1999.

20. See also Howard Gleckman, "A Golden (Years) Opportunity," *BusinessWeek*, March 29, 1999.

21. Mark R. Meiners, conversation with the author, February 14, 1999. See also Meiners's testimony to the U.S. House Committee on Ways & Means, Subcommittee on Health, on coordinated care options for seniors, April 29, 1997.

22. NCOA and John Hancock Financial Services, "Study Finds Long-Term Care Generation Gap."

23. Elizabeth Miranda, Conference Board, *Work/Family: Redefining the Business Case* (New York: CB, December 1993).

24. "Eldercare Tasks Cost Business $11 Billion a Year: Workplace Programs Can Bring Significant Reduction," *Employee Benefit Plan Review*, September 1997.

25. Employee Benefit Research Institute, Consumer Education Series, *Fundamentals of Employee Benefit Programs*, 5th ed. (Washington, DC: EBRI, 1993).

26. T. Childs, IBM Corporation, "Remarks at the American Society on Aging Annual Meeting," *Aging Today*, May 1998.

27. Families and Work Institute, *1998 Business Work-Life Study* (New York: FWI, 1998), http://www.familiesandwork.org/ summary/worklife.pdf.

28. Health Insurance Association of America, *Long-Term Care Insurance: Policy and Research Findings* (Washington, DC: HIAA, 1998).

29. "A Look at Japan's Health System," Associated Press, January 3, 1999.

30. The following service organizations, among many others, can offer additional information:

Organization	Phone	Web Site
Alzheimer's Association	(800) 272-3900 (312) 335-8700	www.alz.org
American Association of Homes and Services for the Aged	(202) 783-2242	www.aahsa.org

American Diabetes Association	(800) 342-2383	www.diabetes.org
American Heart Association (Stroke Connection)	(800) AHA-USA1	www.amhrt.org
Assisted Living Federation of America	(703) 691-8100	www.alfa.org
Children of Aging Parents	(800) 227-7294	www.careguide.net
Children of Parkinsonians	(760) 773-5628	N/A
Epilepsy Foundation of America	(800) EFA-1000	www.efa.org
Family Caregiver Alliance	(415) 434-3388	www.caregiver.org
Family Caregiver Focus	(715) 356-9241	N/A
Intercommunity Caregivers	(303) 778-5984	N/A
National Adult Day Services Association	(202) 479-6984	www.ncoa.org/nadsa
National Alliance for the Mentally Ill	(800) 950-NAMI	N/A
National Caregiving Foundation	(800) 930-1357	N/A
National Family Caregivers Association	(800) 896-3650	www.nfcacares.org
National Hospice Organization	(800) 658-8898	www.nho.org
National Respite Locator Service	(800) 773-5433	N/A

31. An Age Wave Company, www.lifesourcenutrition.com.
32. See also Charles Mann, "Women's Health Research Blossoms: Closing Gender Disparities in Medical Research and Treatment," *Science,* August 11, 1995.

CHAPTER SEVEN

1. Weinbach, *Who Will Pay for Your Retirement?* Please note that these figures do not include gains on property, stocks, or other asset appreciation.
2. Peter G. Peterson, *Will America Grow Up Before It Grows Old?* (New York: Random House, 1996), p. 73.
3. U.S. Bureau of the Census, *Poverty in the United States 1997.*
4. See U.S. Social Security Administration, Office of the Chief Actuary, *The 1999 OASDI Trustees Report* (Washington, DC: GPO, March 30, 1999), http://gopher.ssa.gov/OACT/TR/TR99/index.html; and Len Burman, Urban Institute, *Policy Challenges Posed by the Aging of America* (Washington, DC: UI, May 1998), http://www.urban.org/health/oldpol.html.
5. General Accounting Office, HEHS-97-81, "Retirement Income: Implications of Demographic Trends for Social Security and Pension Reform, 1997," http://frwebgate.access.gpo.gov/cgi-bin/multidb.cgi.
6. Carter, *The Virtues of Aging,* pp. 27–29.
7. The contributions to Social Security actually increased on a sliding scale during this period, as follows:

Years	Employees	Employers
1937–1939	1.0%	1.0%
1940–1942	1.5%	1.5%
1943–1945	2.0%	2.0%
1946–1948	2.5%	2.5%
1949	3.0%	3.0%

SOURCE: SOCIAL SECURITY ACT OF 1935.

8. President Roosevelt's statement upon signing the Social Security Act of 1935, August 14, 1935.
9. President Roosevelt's address to the U.S. Congress, January 16, 1939.
10. For a history of Social Security and current benefit information, see SSA's website, especially "Highlights of Social Security Data, January 1999," at http://www.ssa.gov/.

11. Employers and employees *each* pay 1.45 percent.

12. U.S. Social Security Administration, Office of the Chief Actuary, "Historical and Current FICA Rates," http://www.ssa.gov/OACT/srch.html.

13. See also C. Eugene Steuerle's address to the Senate Finance Committee regarding general revenue financing of Social Security, February 9, 1999; Gary Hendricks, American Academy of Actuaries, *Financing the Retirement of Future Generations* (Washington, DC: AAA, 1998); Mike Causey, "For Some Retirees, Too Much of a Good Thing?" *Washington Post,* May 1, 1998; Evan Thomas, "Social Insecurity," *Newsweek,* January 20, 1997; Tom Redburn, "Promises to Keep: Rethinking the Future of Social Security," *New York Times,* January 19, 1997; and Peter Passell, "Can Retirees' Safety Net Be Saved?" *New York Times,* February 18, 1996.

14. Peter G. Peterson, "Will America Grow Up Before It Grows Old?" as excerpted in *Atlantic Monthly,* May 1996.

15. Melissa Hieger and William Shipman, Cato Institute, Cato Project on Social Security Privatization, SSP no. 10, *Common Objections to a Market-Based Social Security System: A Response* (Washington, DC: Cato Institute, July 22, 1997), http://www.socialsecurity.org/pubs/ssps/ssp10.html.

16. Frederick Breimyer and Michael ter Maat, "Social Security Reform: A Necessary Opportunity," *ABA Banking Journal,* December 1998.

17. A. Haeworth Robertson, *The Big Lie: What Every Boomer Should Know About Social Security and Medicare* (Washington, DC: Retirement Policy Institute, 1997), pp. xi–xii.

18. Morris, *The AARP,* p. 83.

19. U.S. Bureau of the Census, "Asset Ownership of Households, 1993," http://www.census.gov/hhes/www/wealth.html.

20. Neal Cutler, "The False Alarms and Blaring Sirens of Financial Literacy: Middle-Agers' Knowledge of Retirement Income, Health Finance, and Long-Term Care," *Generations,* June 22, 1997.

21. Scudder Kemper, "Baby Boom Generation Poll," Business Wire, February 10, 1998.

22. Steve Farkas and Jean Johnson, "Status Report: How Americans Plan for Retirement," *Compensation and Benefits Management,* Spring 1998.

23. Roper Starch Worldwide, *The Boomer Balancing Act.*

24. Smith and Clurman, *Rocking the Ages,* p. 28.

25. Ibid., p. 48.

26. Juliet B. Schor, *The Overspent American: Upscaling, Downshifting, and the New Consumer* (New York: Basic Books, 1998), p. 72.

27. Federal Reserve Board, Statistics: Releases and Historical Data, "Consumer Credit Outstanding," http://www.bog.frb.fed.us/ releases/. Note: These figures are not seasonally adjusted.

28. Dina Ingber Stein, "Going for Broke," *Success,* May 1, 1999.

29. John Wyatt, "What You'll Need to Survive . . . and Prosper," *Fortune*, August 19, 1996.

30. Scudder Kemper, "Baby Boom Generation Poll."

31. Those initially covered typically were employed in the transportation, banking, mining, utility, and manufacturing sectors. For more historical information on pensions see Employee Benefit Research Institute, "Facts from EBRI, History of Pension Plans," http://www.ebri.org/facts/0398afact. htm.

32. David Hochman, "Talkin' About My Generation," *Swing*, August 1998.

33. U.S. Department of Labor, Working Group Report, "Advisory Council on Employee Welfare and Pension Benefits Report of the Working Group on Retirement Plan Leakage: 'Are We Cashing Out Our Future?'" November 13, 1998, http://www2.dol.gov/dol/pwba/public/adcoun/leaknew1. htm.

34. Daniel J. Mitchell and Robert P. O'Quinn, "Australia's Privatized Retirement System: Lessons for the United States," *Heritage Foundation Reports*, December 8, 1997.

35. Ibid.

36. Piñera, *Empowering Workers: The Privatization of Social Security in Chile*.

37. Adam Carasso, et al., prepared by the Employee Benefit Research Institute for the Urban Institute, Project 06870, *Managing Mandatory Savings Plans: Implications of Foreign Experience* (Washington, DC: Urban Institute, November 1998).

38. "Not Old Against Young, but Rich Against Poor," *Economist*, January 11, 1997.

39. Carter, *The Virtues of Aging*, pp. 27–29.

40. U.S. Bureau of the Census, Current Population Reports, series P60–200, *Money Income in the United States: 1997 (With Separate Data on Valuation of Noncash Benefits)* (Washington, DC: GPO, 1998).

41. U.S. Bureau of the Census, *Poverty in the United States 1997*.

42. Peterson, "Will America Grow Up Before It Grows Old?" *Atlantic Monthly*.

43. Louis D. Enoff and Robert E. Moffit, "Social Security Privatization in Britain: Key Lessons for America's Reformers," *Heritage Foundation Reports*, August 6, 1997.

44. Ibid.

45. Carasso, et al., *Managing Mandatory Savings Plans*.

46. Linda Feldmann, "Social Security: Going Private?" *Christian Science Monitor*, April 7, 1998; and Alice Ann Love, "Most Do Not Want to Invest Their Own Social Security Taxes," Associated Press, April 3, 1998.

47. Lawrence Summers and Janet Yellen, "Saving the Surplus Will Protect Retirees," *Wall Street Journal*, February 18, 1999.

CHAPTER EIGHT

1. Smith and Clurman, *Rocking the Ages*, pp. 9, 36.
2. Tom Brokaw, *The Greatest Generation* (New York: Random House, 1998).
3. Smith and Clurman, *Rocking the Ages*, p. 23.
4. U.S. Bureau of the Census, Current Population Reports, Special Studies, P23-190, *65+ in the United States* (Washington, DC: GPO, 1996).
5. U.S. Bureau of the Census, Current Population Reports, March 1999 (Washington, DC: GPO, 1999). Subsequent figures on racial makeup are from the same source.
6. Smith and Clurman, *Rocking the Ages*, p. 43.
7. Ibid., p. 107.
8. Mark Jannot, "Screw the Young," *Playboy*, August 1995.
9. "Not Old Against Young, but Rich Against Poor," *Economist*, January 11, 1997.
10. Georges Minois, *History of Old Age* (Chicago: University of Chicago Press, 1989), p. 7.
11. Richard B. du Boff, "Thurow on Social Security: The 'Left' Strikes Again," *Monthly Review*, October 1996.
12. The Independent Sector, "America's Senior Volunteers," 1997 and "America's Volunteers," 1998 (Washington, DC: Independent Sector, 1997 and 1998).

Age Group	Volunteerism Rate
33–44	55%
45–54	55%
55–74	46%
75+	34%

SOURCE: INDEPENDENT SECTOR

13. Daniel Levinson, *The Seasons of a Man's Life* (New York: Knopf, 1978), p. 158.
14. Carl Jung, ed. and trans. by G. Adler and R. F. Hull, "The Stages of Life," *The Structure and Dynamics of the Psyche* (Princeton, NJ: Princeton University Press, 1969).
15. Erik H. Erikson, *The Life Cycle Completed* (New York: W.W. Norton, 1997).
16. Ibid., pp. 6–9.
17. Ibid., p. 112.

18. Ibid., pp. 4, 105–106.

19. President Jimmy Carter, conversation with the author, October 21, 1998, Atlanta, GA.

20. Timothy Spence, "Lawmakers, AARP Cite Heavy Opposition to Endorsement of Health Plans," States News Service, August 11, 1994.

21. Tom Otwell, AARP, conversation with the author, May 5, 1999, Washington, DC.

22. Thomas DiLorenzo, "Who Really Speaks for the Elderly?" *Consumer's Research*, September 1996.

23. Thomas McClusky and Jared B. Adams, National Taxpayers Union Foundation, "The Budgetary Impact of AARP's Legislative Agenda," April 28, 1999, http://www.ntu.org/aarp_intro.htm.

24. Habitat is in 60 countries, and it has 1,600 centers around the world. Former President Carter personally works on Habitat projects one week each year. http://www.habitat.org/.

INDEX

ABOUT THE AUTHOR

The bestselling author of books such as *Age Wave* and *Bodymind*, **Dr. Ken Dychtwald** is a psychologist, gerontologist, sought-after public speaker, frequent guest on national media, and the founding president of Age Wave, LLC, a leading business development firm. His strikingly accurate forecasts have been featured on television and radio programs nationwide, and in such publications as *The New York Times*, *The Wall Street Journal*, *The Financial Times*, *Inc.*, *Fortune*, *Time*, *Newsweek*, *Business Week*, and *USA Today*. Dr. Dychtwald, who has been honored with the American Society on Aging Award for outstanding national leadership in the field, is a Fellow of the World Economic Forum in Geneva. He is widely viewed as the foremost visionary and leading authority on the aging of America.

To contact Ken Dychtwald:
Ken Dychtwald
President
Age Wave, LLC
2000 Powell Street
11th Floor
Emeryville, CA 94608
www.agewave.com
Kdychtwald@agewave.com